NO ONE KNOWS THE SON

THERE IS ONLY SO FAR DOWN YOU
CAN GO BEFORE THE ONLY WAY IS UP

By James Cobb

With Stephen Cirfus

VANRIJS & CIRFUS, LLC

~

For information about special discounts for bulk purchases, please
contact Vanrijs & Cirfus Publishing Special Sales at business
www.vcoliving.com
The VANRIJS & CIRFUS Speakers Bureau can bring James H.
Cobb to your live event. For more information or to book an event,
contact the Vanrijs & Cirfus Speaker Bureau at speakers
www.vcoliving.com

Jacket design by David M. Joseph
Manufactured in United States of America
10 9 8 7 6 5 4 3 2 1
Cataloging-in publication data is on file with the
Library of Congress.

ISBN: 978-0-9990132-4-3
Cobb, James
A Son, His Father, and the Underground World of European
Cartels.
First Vanrijs & Cirfus edition.
1. Cobb, James. 2.--Family. 3. Artist United States Memoir. I. Title
PN 1971.7.J194C8 2014 070.94-jc80(b)
This book was based on true life story of James H. Cobb. Dates,
places, and the names of all parties involved have been changed.
Some events have been altered. Details in some anecdotes and
stories have been changed to protect the identities of the persons
involved.

ACKNOWLEDGMENTS

If it was not for the mercy of God and the people mentioned below, this book would not have been possible. I would like to thank Ray and Janet Cobb, my Mama and Daddy, for never giving up on me when I was in the wilderness: wayward and out of control. My son, Kyle Cobb, for loving me through the thousands of hours I've spent working on this book. Kyle, I am very proud of the way you've turned out, and I love you. Lindsey Brown for her firm ways. My mentor and coach, Dale Brown, for believing in me and for his friendship. My professor, Rev. Levert Kemp, for teaching me the Bible in a way I can understand. My web designer, David Joseph, for his friendship and hard work. My friend Bill McCracken. Winston Groom the author of *Forrest Gump* for his advice. The safety team and family at Cajun Constructors, LLC, for giving me the chance to better my life with a good job. The staff at Mobile Strickland Youth Center and the kids who sent letters after my talks and believe in me. Warden Cain at Angola State prison for giving me the chance to speak to inmates, and the love and friendship of the guys who wrote letters of encouragement at Angola. The Mobile Metro Jail and staff for letting me speak to inmates, and those who wrote letters conveying their stories of personal change after hearing mine.

This book is dedicated to my loving grandfather, Theo U. Mizell, for teaching me values of hard work and true sacrifice.

"Our prisons are packed. Our streets are filled with drugs. Who's winning the war on drugs? We've lost our minds."

—JOHN GRISHAM, AUTHOR

Volume 1

INNOCENCE

1

I was 13 years old in 1984.

IT'S STRANGE HOW SEEMINGLY inconsequential things at one point in your life connect to bigger things later on. That day in October, for instance, way back in 1971, when Mama brought me back from Charity Hospital in New Orleans. She was probably more concerned with how she and Daddy were going to feed one more kid than how she was going to tell me one day that they were actually my adoptive parents.

Either way, she had plenty to worry about. Despite this, Mama and Daddy couldn't stand to see a healthy baby boy enter the state system. My biological mom, Wendy Mizell, was in no position to care for me at the time, and seeing that her sister, Janet (who I'm assuming was the first one who came to mind, and the best one for the job), agreed to take me home with her to Alabama. Looking at what potentially could arise from this odd situation, I guess you could say I did OK.

Unfortunately, however, there was a drawback: I wasn't in on the details of this arrangement until much later. Regardless, I had a fine upbringing with Mama and Daddy. I had a sister, Lisa, and a brother, Jessie Ray, Jr. In the summers, there were great times on vacation with the family. Daddy took us down to the Dog River KOA in Alabama for fishing and to enjoy time away from the busy grocery store that he and Mama ran all day, every day.

Despite these good times, though, I must have given my folks some scares right from the beginning. When I was a newborn, Mama discussed my health with the attending physician over the telephone while I remained in the hospital. He had said to her that I might have some respiratory trouble later on in life, as I was born a little early and my lungs were not fully formed at birth. It seems, though, that my lungs somehow caught up and I was able to leave with Mama by the time she got there to pick me up. I don't know too much about the biology of the whole thing—or even if these things are connected in some way—but when I got to be about seven or eight, I realized that I couldn't read well and would get extremely frustrated. So frustrated that I would run outside and scare everybody half to death by holding my breath until I actually passed out. Hard to believe, isn't it? But that's the kind of stunt I'd pull, and I guess those lungs had something to do with it. And perhaps they also had something to do with the reading and scholastic problems with which I struggled. It's not easy to know if, or how, things are linked in these early formative years.

And it's a hard thing for a kid to be told publicly that he's an idiot. I'm not saying that the teachers at my school did that, or that they put up a sign or something, but they might as well have done so. Maybe you know, maybe you don't, what it feels like to go to a normal English class, and then for the next class, have to move down the hall into what they called a "learning disabled" class. I think the idea was that "learning disabled" didn't sound as bad as "mentally retarded," or "handicapped," or one of the other taboo words. Perhaps the school employees used those words, but the kids used stronger, more painful words, such as "dummy" and "retard" and many other names you might not believe third and fourth graders would even know.

The learning disabled classes were supposed to help us learn how to read. But they really served as kind of a waiting area for the next class. There were so many kids in the class, it seemed as if the teacher had given up on teaching before we even walked through the door. And who could blame her? When we arrived at her class, having been ridiculed and laughed at for being "slow", we were no picnic to be around. Let's just say we weren't exactly the Vienna Boys' Choir.

It's hard to remember exactly when I gave up trying to learn to read. I remember sitting in my English class, being allowed to draw to my heart's content, feeling good about that one aptitude I was pretty sure I had, but then would come the sick panic. A kind of steady, degrading humiliation only a child who's been through it can truly understand This feeling repeated, every day.

Unfortunately, this experience was heightened, as the teacher I had prior to attending the learning disabled classes was so wonderful. She encouraged me to draw—allowing me to do so in her class on the only condition that I'd leave her one of my pictures at the end of each day. It was such a great thing to feel my ability had value—and that a teacher wanted my pictures! Later, I believe those little daily votes of confidence would serve as a voice on the side of good, telling me to be smart and make the right choices.

I endured my tortured educational life for some years, but at least things at home were good, and I did my best to make my mama and daddy proud of me in ways that didn't have to do with school. That was all going to change, though.

One day in 1984, I felt the sky crash in on me.

It seemed that my Aunt Wendy, as I knew her, had been in and out of town forever. She lived in many places, did a lot of different kinds of work, but never seemed to settle. Sometimes, when she was around, she did stuff that was really not too cool. I'll never forget the time that we all had to stand in line for water after a hurricane came through. Well, she didn't want to stand in line. She was hot, tired, and wanted her water right away. I don't know if it ever occurred to her that the other folks wanted their water right away, too, but she wasn't thinking in terms of other folks.

She went straight out in front of everybody and faked a wild seizure of some sort. I was mortified as she laid there on the ground bucking up and down like a fish out of water. I knew she wasn't sick—she was just playing a trick. I wanted to run as far away as possible, but unable to, I had to stand there watching her performance as concerned citizens of Eight Mile, Alabama, raced to her rescue, fetching cold water, helping her to her car, and giving her everything she would have received in due course had she waited honestly with the rest of us. I just shook my head as she got into the car. "Man," I thought, "Ain't I lucky that ain't my mom!"

In fact, Wendy was actually a nice-looking lady with deep brown hair and a classic Latin, almost Italian, goddess look about her beautiful face. She was tall and, for the time I knew her, never carried an ounce of extra weight. As it turned out, she had come back to town, or somewhere nearby, and apparently she had something on her mind.

I didn't know what it was, but Mama and Daddy did, and so did Lisa and Jessie, Jr. That fateful day, I came home from school and was quickly herded into the living room where everybody was sitting. There was tension in the air, an urgency everybody seemed to feel. They had to tell me right there and then.

"Well, Son," my daddy said, "we'd like to tell you about something before you hear it from . . . somebody else." He paused, as if he was thinking about how to say what he had on his mind. Then it seemed he figured that there was no good way to say it, and just came out with it: "The fact is, you aren't actually our son, leastways not biological."

"But we love you just the same as if you were," Mama quickly added.

Wondering why only I was surprised. Lisa and Jessie, Jr., looked just as uncomfortable as Mama and Daddy. I caught on pretty quickly to that—I was the only one who hadn't known!

"What do you mean?" I said. My heart pounded in my ears and my breath came fast, as if it wanted to choke the life out of me. "Not your son, how can that be?"

"Well, what about them?" I said, pointing at Jessie, Jr., and Lisa who shifted around uneasily.

"No, honey, it's only you that's got different parents," Mama said.

I was stunned and didn't know how to react. If they weren't my parents—and I wasn't altogether convinced just yet that they weren't—then who was?

"Well . . . who are my real parents?" I asked.

My mama walked toward me, trying to put her arms around me, but I wouldn't have any of that. "You know your Aunt Wendy?" Mama began. "Well, she's—"

"Oh my God! Not her! Not Aunt Wendy!" I screamed. All I could see was that woman on the ground in the midst of her fake seizure, eyes bulging out and everybody looking at her. "Is this a joke or something?"

Nobody said anything. I was petrified. This sudden and completely out of left field revelation was true—they were serious. I didn't belong to them—I was Wendy's!

I walked over the red pine floors into the bathroom and pushed in the brass knob to lock the door behind me. I could hardly breathe. It was a panic I'd never known, a hundred times worse than having to go to the learning disabled classes. It was a paralyzing feeling.

The bathroom was muggy, as if someone had just taken

a hot shower, and the antique oval mirror over the sink was covered with condensation.

I could hear the brass knob rattling and Mama pleading through the unfinished yellow pine door, "Come on out, Jamie. It don't make no difference to me, the adoption. You're our son and we love you just the same as we love Jessie, Jr., and Lisa. I'm sorry we had to keep this from you for so long, but it was for your own good."

"My own good, Mama?" I shouted. "Oh come on! Just go away and leave me alone!" It felt like everything was coming at me like a freight train. "That's why y'all always treated me different. Like when Ruby's psycho ex-husband got outta jail and y'all sent me to stay with her instead of Jessie, even though he was fifteen and I was only twelve. Daddy never even tried to show me how to shoot a gun, and he was always taking Jessie, Jr., out, just them two on the boat . . ."

"We're your family, Jamie," Mama continued. "We've always been. That's never gonna change." It sounded like she was about to cry, but I didn't care.

"Families ain't supposed to lie to their kids. Everybody knew all about this but me. You have been lying to me every day of my life!"

Mama must have walked away about then, feeling terrible. I asked her later, "Mama, how come y'all didn't just tell me sooner?"

"You know, Jamie," she said, "we wanted to, but we didn't want you to be upset. Then we didn't have no choice."

It turned out that Wendy had announced that she was

planning to drop the bomb on me herself. As angry and hurt as I was, hearing it from Mama and Daddy, I know it would have been much worse coming from Aunt Wendy. But at that moment, I didn't like anybody around there very much, least of all myself.

A few days later, I was at my Aunt Ruby's house for some reason, barricading myself away from everything and everyone that had been part of the betrayal, right down to the living room furniture sitting in her house. From the front pocket of my jeans, I took out a poorly rolled joint that was given to me by a girl named Sunshine whom I'd walked home from school that day. She'd swiped it out of her hippie mom's stash for me after I'd told her how depressed I'd been feeling since I found out that my "family" wasn't really my family.

I took a deep drag, trying to hold the smoke in my lungs the way my buddy Jay had shown me. But those poor lungs were new to that hot stuff and I exhaled the whole thing, making a Cheech and Chong cloud around me the size of Nevada. I figured I'd better open the window. The stench of spent gasoline drifted in from the backyard, where Hubert Humphry, Aunt Ruby's ex-husband, hobbled around in nothing but his stained underwear, in a frenzy of activity, revving a chainsaw as big as he was, slicing straight through the trunks of Ruby's pear, chestnut, walnut, and fig trees like a hot knife through cold lard.

Everything beautiful gets destroyed in the end, it made me think. The trees were like my childhood, another trage-dy of time—wonderful to look back on for so long, but then suddenly toppled by a chainsaw-wielding maniac who was a bag of broiling hate with wrinkles covered in liver spots. Humphry had been released from Mobile's county jail in November of '85, and that's whom I had been sent to protect Aunt Ruby from on that balmy summer afternoon with nothing more than a Daisy pellet gun (the nearest thing to a firearm I had any experience shooting at the age of twelve).

But I was missing that childhood toy just then, and I was no longer twelve. I was a thirteen-year-old junior high student, getting stoned for the first time—in my Aunt Ruby's bathroom of all places.

Hunched over like an insane, seriously ailing gnome, Humphry turned in my direction for a second. With a hollow, toothless grin, he revved up his dirty orange chainsaw, which he maneuvered like a seasoned lumberjack, working on the last standing row of Ruby's fruit and nut trees stretching to the pine-wooded property boundary.

I flinched away from the aluminum-framed window and took another pull of hot smoke. It really burned my throat and lungs. I could feel it in my brain and in my toes, and somehow I just had to brush my teeth. I brushed too hard and my gums started to bleed. I rinsed away the sharp iron taste, and I was really feeling it then . . . a dream within a dream— my eyeballs vibrating inside my skull and my vision coming to me as scrolling still frames, my skin feeling like dust floating in the golden sun-bleached air.

I relit the joint and checked my eyes in the mirror. Sure enough, they were taking on that all too familiar red hue. My reflection seemed distorted by my new drug as I thought about my junior high school teacher, Coach Riley, and a warning he gave to me: "Wake up, boy. You need to learn your history, but all you wanna do is sleep all the time. That's OK, but one day you're gonna look in the mirror and not be too proud of what you see there."

He was right. I leaned in for a closer look and didn't like what I saw: Aunt Wendy, exhaling smoke from her nostrils the way she liked to do. "I hate you," I said.

It was then that the Molotov cocktail that Ruby's sadistic ex had fashioned from a Coca-Cola bottle sailed in through the open window. The bathroom quickly became a hotbox of shattered glass, smoke, and flames. I jumped up on the lid of the toilet to squeeze through the window, and then raced for Hubert Humphry's lime-green '67 Ford pickup parked at the road and still running, distinctive with its shiny chrome Cragar rims. The bald-headed gimp was right at my heels. He could move awfully fast for a man with one leg three inches shorter than the other—like the time they were playing ball at Grandma Cobb's place and Junior hit a pop fly into Ruby's yard. Old Humphry flew off the porch like a rabid dog and almost caught up with him before he got back to the hurricane fence.

I jammed that truck into gear, kicked the gas pedal to the floor mat, turned off on the first red dirt road to my left, and found myself barreling down Ganger Road with nothing around me but pinewoods, rolling hills, and crystal clear sandy bottom creeks. The guy was a freak, but I wasn't running from just him. I wanted to distance myself from my adoptive family. I wasn't seeing things quite right.

"All I want is to be left alone." In my mind, this was my mantra for what seemed like an eternity. I felt like shouting, *"I'd be better off if everyone just left me alone!"*

But in my heart, I knew this wasn't a true reflection of my feelings. It was simply a defense mechanism, like a mortally wounded animal in the wild, lashing out at everything in sight until it dies, frightened, cold, and alone.

As time passed, I grew more determined, obdurate—feelings that were fueled by my internal rage and weren't going to disappear of their own accord. I had no clue how to make them go away, or even if I wanted them to. It was not until the summer of '85, a few months before I would turn fourteen and almost a year after everything had come crashing down around me, that help was sought. I'd become such a recluse since leaving school that Jessie Ray and Janet thought I needed to see a psychiatrist. They found a fairly affordable one for me at Charter Hospital on Hillcrest Road in West Mobile. I failed the tests on purpose—I could have assembled the colorful-shaped puzzles with my eyes closed.

I said stuff like, "I cleaned my Paw Paw's Bonneville real good today, I sure did. And I waxed it, too. I made it look so shiny that he paid me five dollars."

The perceptive shrink saw right through that charade, and after playing along with me for the first few sessions, he finally told me that I'd make a "damn good lawyer," as I had a knack for leading folks wherever I wanted to take them.

"Be that as it may, Jamie, you're going to have to learn to tear down these mental walls you throw up to distance yourself from the people who have become your *real* family—your adopted mother and father. The way I see it, a person like you with an exceptionally sharp mind and so much potential, yet so much resentment holding you back . . ." He inhaled deeply and smiled, rubbed his salt and pepper beard and adjusted his square tinted glasses, searching for just the right words. "You need to accomplish something grand in your life, Jamie," he continued, "or you don't stand a chance in this world, plain and simple. Otherwise, the negative emotions that plague you will *become* you. But it doesn't have to be that way. You can fight back. Learn to cope with those burdensome feelings by letting people in. Not everyone is out to hurt you, son. You have no reason to resent Janet and Jessie Ray. They were only trying to protect you by keeping your adoption a secret.

"You're going to have to open up eventually—if not to me, then to someone who you know can understand what you've been through and how you'll feel about yourself when it's all said and done. You can't escape reality, Jamie. Your biological parents abandoned you. I'm sorry they did, but it's something that you just can't change now. However, if you can accept that you are who you are, and not who you came from . . . if you can make that real to you up here," he said, pointing with both index fingers to my temples, "then you'll have nothing ever to run from again. And aren't you tired of running?"

Doctor Chutie's words reverberated in my brain. *"You are who you are, and not who you came from"; "Your biological parents abandoned you.*"

My biological parents were Wendy and my biological father, whom I'd come to know was a foreign-born man called Jan van Rijn.

2

December 17, 1993
I was 22 years old.

"COME ON," SHE URGED, smoke billowing from her nostrils as she spoke. "I can sense your anxiety. And you *do* have every reason to be nervous, Jamie. Anyone in your position would be, twenty-two years old and getting an opportunity to speak with your real father for the first time in your life. A couple hits will help set your head straight and settle your nerves some."

I sat there in Aunt Wendy's trailer as she smoked a joint. She passed it over to me and I took a drag. Oh, that stuff made me cough. If I had ever bothered to think about what I was doing back then, I never would have smoked at all. It always made me hoarse and burned my eyes terribly.

"That's plenty enough for me," I said. I was there to be encouraged to have a conversation with my biological father. He was Dutch-born, and apparently very successful in his business. And for some reason, Aunt Wendy wanted me to have a relationship with him right then—when I was twenty-two years old.

I did not like being pressured into doing things. I didn't know what to do. Aunt Wendy kept on smoking. It didn't seem to bother her at all. She went into her bedroom and brought out a piece of artwork. It was a funny thing for her to have in that dusty old worn-out trailer in rural Fairview, Alabama.

"Jan mailed these to me while he was in that French prison," she said. "I know you can draw real well, too, and I figured you'd appreciate his talent."

They were mostly nature scenes on large postcards, native birds of France. One was an oil painting on a 16 × 20 canvas, an eerie portrait of a young kid. Apparently it was me looking very much like a Dutch boy wearing one of those bowl haircuts and wooden clogs on my feet. I guess my hair was a lot lighter when I was a little boy.

"He's pretty good, huh?" asked Aunt Wendy.

"He's all right," I chuckled. "It's out of focus or something. I don't ever remember looking quite that way . . . like a clown. He put too much blush in the cheeks. But it's better than I could do—for now."

"Well, I guess it's an impressionist sort of style he was using here. You know, painting something the way it makes you feel instead of exactly how it looks."

"I never understood that."

"He modeled it after a picture I sent him of you when you were only six years old," Aunt Wendy said.

"I like this one better," I told her, feeling the textured surface of an acrylic painting. It was a scene showing a father and son from behind, sitting with fishing poles on the edge of a canal near a wooden windmill. "This must be in Holland, huh?" I asked.

"He always dreamed of taking you fishing with him there. He's really a simple man once you get to know him. You can take those paintings home, baby. They were meant for you, anyway. Oh, and here's something Jan sent not too long ago, after we talked one night and I told him how you had your own car and everything. In Holland it's a pretty big deal to have a set of wheels at your age. Jan said a driver's license is hard to come by in that country."

"A bumper sticker?" I said a little bewildered. What would I want with that? It read "Sneek" and had a Dutch flag next to the word.

"That's the name of Jan's hometown in the Netherlands," Aunt Wendy said.

"Oh, OK."

"Food's done. You care for a plate?"

"Yeah, I'm feeling brave," I told her, laughing. "I think I could eat something, now that you got me all buzzed and everything."

"Is it any good?" she asked as we sat there with paper plates and plastic forks. "I do realize I'm not much of a cook anymore."

"It's fine," I said. "I appreciate it. Thanks."

"So, how's your girlfriend, Tanya, been doing lately?"

"She's fine. Actually, I haven't seen her in a couple weeks."

"How far along is she?"

"She's due next month," I said. "January 24 is what she told me."

"Wow, she must be about to pop."

"Yeah. I guess so."

As I sat eating, the buzz started to wear off, and the tension of being around Aunt Wendy returned. I never got over it and our relationship never went beyond an awkward distance, either one of us trying or knowing how to reach out. In her own way, I guess that's what she was trying to do—reach out.

In any case, if we were going to give my father a call, I'd rather be done with it. I kept looking at my watch. "I'm getting pretty tired, Aunt Wendy," I said. It was about quarter to eleven. "You think we could try calling my father? If not, I need to be heading home."

"OK, let's go give it a try," she said.

We had to go outside to a pay phone that was located on the wall of the laundry room near her trailer park. As I stood there waiting for her to get through, I looked through the chain-link fence around the park. Just beyond, I saw a nativity scene, beautifully lit. I somehow felt happy that it was still illuminated that late at night. I figured they just left the lights on all the time.

Aunt Wendy got through, but she had a hard time getting the number right, since she'd popped a couple of valium after dinner.

"How are you doing, Jan?" she asked. "This is Wendy. I

hope I didn't . . . huh? Oh sure, Jan, he's right here. We just got done eating dinner. OK." She handed me the receiver.

I took it, feeling about as awkward as you can feel without the other person standing right there with you, looking at you.

"Hello?"

"Hello, Son," Jan said. "I have been looking forward to hearing from you. Wendy told me she would be seeing you this night, so I woke up very early to wait for your call."

"Oh . . . all right," I said. "Y'all's time is different from ours, huh?" What was I supposed to say?

"Yes, it is. So, how is it with you, Son? Are, uh, things going good?"

"Yeah, I'm OK—I guess," I said. But I was thrown by his thick accent and had to pay close attention to understand what he was saying.

And of course I felt awkward, not knowing what I was supposed to say. The guy sounded nice enough, but it ruffled me how he kept calling me "Son." Until I was thirteen, I didn't even know he existed and I sure didn't feel like his son.

After a long pause, Jan asked, "What is it that you do, Son, for money?"

"Well, Sir, I got this real dead-end job," I said.

"Really? In what field?"

"I wash cars. It don't pay nothin'."

"Well, if the job is a dead-end, then why not find a better one?"

"I don't have any skills," I didn't mind saying. "I ain't even got my diploma. I dropped out of high school in the ninth grade. After I found out I was adopted, I had a pretty hard time concentrating on anything." I guess I thought I'd make my point good and early.

"Well, school is not for everyone," he said, sidestepping the issue. "I did not make it very far, either. But, believe me—you can do quite well on your own, if only you try."

"Yeah?" I said, getting a little cocky. "Well, I ain't doing all that well right now. I got a baby on the way and unless I can make some money real fast, I won't be around to see it born."

"Why not?"

"'Cause I got these past-due speeding tickets I got to pay. They'll lock me up if they don't get their money soon."

"Hmm . . . you are not in a good position," said Jan. "Jail is no place for a van Rijn."

"Could you come tell that to the sheriff's department?" I asked.

"Son, if you would not mind traveling to Europe, I can give you a job working on my boats in Spain. In a few short months you could make enough money to take care of everything that troubles you now."

I thought about it and the idea hit me with such relief, I think I laughed right then. The thought of going to some foreign country, getting away from all my troubles, and then making a little cash actually lifted my spirits. "Sounds like fun," I said. "Exactly what kinda work you talking about?"

"Different things," said Jan. "Washing the boats, and

maybe sometimes painting if they are in need."

"I got a little bit of experience sanding and painting. I worked in my adoptive brother Junior's cabinet shop part time for almost two years, so I might be able to handle that."

"Good . . . that is good to hear."

"But, come to think of it, I can't realistically afford a trip out there. I only pull in four dollars an hour washing cars . . .well, plus the 30 percent commission on every car I detail. I guess I don't make out so bad some days," I said, "but probably not good enough for any airline ticket."

"You will make much more with me," Jan told me, confidently. "I guarantee you. And don't worry about paying for the trip. I will fly to Alabama myself and buy you a plane ticket to come back with me. I will even take care of your speeding tickets while I am there so that you can leave the country with a clear name."

"C'mon," I said, not really believing him. "Why would you go through all that trouble for me?"

"Because you are my son! Listen, Jamie, I will be in your town very soon, maybe by the early part of this week. And if you are truly worried that you will be arrested for your tickets, why don't you go somewhere for a couple of days until I arrive? Jail is no fun, I know."

"Shoot, maybe I will," I said. This guy seemed to have a pretty good head on his shoulders. "I could use a vacation, anyway. I've been working my butt off."

"Yes, relax yourself, Son. You are much too young to be stressed out like this. I will see you in a few days. Goodbye,

Jamie," he said, and hung up.

"What'd he say?" Aunt Wendy wanted to know.

"He's coming here in a few days to take me back to Europe with him."

"Oh, baby, you must be so excited," she smiled.

"Well, I'm not expecting anything from a perfect stranger. If he comes, he comes. If not—then whatever," I said.

"He's good for his word, baby. You'll see," she said. "I'm so happy for you, Jamie. Let's go and smoke another one to celebrate. You can even crash here if you don't feel like driving way back to your house."

"No, I'm good," I said. "I'm heading out. I'm not religious or nothing, but something in my brain tells me it ain't right to be getting all high so close to Jesus' birthday."

That night I drove home to Eight Mile in a haze, excited about this guy's big promises, but cautious that it was just talk. You never know with people.

3

NEXT MORNING I HEADED to work, picking up Jay on the way. I hated the job of washing cars, "detailing" them I guess you'd call it, for my boss, Clyde Johnson. But at least I had learned the skill well from my mama's daddy, Theodore "Paw Paw" Mizell, who had shown me how to get them looking almost new. He'd tell me, "You don't do the job if you don't do it right." I took Paw Paw's advice to heart, put it to effective use, and I think Mr. Johnson appreciated it. Although the job was tough and the pay low, I did feel satisfaction in doing a good job on all the cars that passed through the business.

There was a problem, however, on this particular day: we never made it to work. Once I got to Jay's, Blaze was there, and I ended up sitting around while the two of them talked about "Boot Camp." If you screw up at a young age, they sometimes send you to Boot Camp rather than jail. It's supposed to straighten you out, scare you straight, or something. But as Blaze lit up a joint, I was pretty sure it hadn't worked with him.

"You wouldn't believe how hard they work you, Jamie," Jay said. "It's like the real thing. You really are in the army."

"If we were really in the army," Blaze said, "we wouldn't be sitting here getting high."

We all laughed. I was a bit nervous about not going to work and spoke up. "Look, I gotta get my paycheck today," I said. "Can we do this on the way?"

"You know he ain't gonna pass out no paychecks today," Blaze said. "If he does, he knows you won't be back next week."

"I never thought of that," Jay said. "You're sharp, Blaze." Jay was always saying stuff to make other people feel good. He'd been through a tough time and I admired that positive quality in him. "You're looking kinda rough this morning, man," he said to me. "You go out drinking last night?" Well, so much for his always trying to make other people feel good.

"No, not really," I said. "I went over to Wendy's for dinner. She's always smokin', gettin' high, you know. Wants me to join her."

"That's your mama, man."

"Ain't my mama," I reminded him. "She just give birth to me. You know my mama."

"Yeah, I know. Don't get all serious or nothin'."

"OK," I said. It was too early in the morning for that; all I wanted to do was get my head straightened out from the night before. It was as if my best friend was reading my mind.

"Why'd you go over there in the first place?" Jay asked.

I sighed, remembering the whole thing. Fortunately,

Blaze was preoccupied with some discussion on the phone about who got the best dope. I didn't feel like sharing all this with everyone. "She wanted me to call my real father in Spain," I said. "I guess suddenly he's decided he wants to be a part of my life."

"Man! Did you do it? What's the guy like?"

"Uh-huh, I sure did. And he was pretty nice, I guess. Offered me a job working with him over there . . . on his boats or something."

"His boats? What kind of boats he got?"

"I don't know," I said. I started wondering about what Jan had said, and what the job might actually entail. "He just said maybe I could help out on his boats. I guess I'll find out."

"Man, you're lucky," said Jay. "When I meet my daddy one day, I hope he's like that. You think this guy's for real?"

"I don't know," I said. "Said he was gonna come over here in a couple days and pay off my speeding tickets and take me back with him to his country."

"Spain, you mean?" he asked.

"I think he's Dutch," I said. "I don't really understand it all either—I guess things must be different over there in Europe."

"It sound like he got himself some money, whatever he does," said Jay.

"I guess. He done a little time, though."

Jay nodded.

I continued. "He give me some advice, too. He said I oughta maybe disappear till he come and pay off them tickets.

All the sudden I don't feel like going to that car wash. Maybe I should just drive outta town a few days."

"Outta town? Like where?"

"Shoot. There's so many different things racing through my brain right now, I'll probably drive down to Gulf Shores and do some thinking, try to sort things out."

"It's the dead of winter," said Jay. "What'cha gonna do at the beach? Ain't nobody gon' be there."

"Good. I can just sit back, relax, and watch them pretty blue waves roll in all day."

Jay gave me a look. He couldn't resist the chance to get away to the beach, dead of winter or not. "You know, man, that sounds real therapeutic," he said. "It's too nice out to be anywhere near that car wash."

"Come on with me, man," I said. "I ain't got much to spend, though. I never went in Friday to get my check."

"Me neither. I'm flat-ass broke. Hey, maybe Blaze wanna come along," Jay said. "I heard Blaze's been moving quarter pounds. I betcha' he'd have plenty to spend. Leastways he'll have something to smoke."

"All right, go ahead and ask 'im," I said. Jay could tell I wasn't excited about the idea, since I never cared too much for Blaze's company.

Sensing what I was thinking, Jay tried to persuade me. "Hey, come on, it's his mom that makes him act that way. She's always saying stuff, runnin' him down. Blaze's an OK person if you get to know him well enough."

"I'm sure he is. And oh—by the way—happy late birthday, Jay."

"Thanks."

"Just one year left of being a teenager, huh?"

"Yeah."

"I'm sorry I didn't get a chance to call yesterday. I was real busy with Wendy an' all. How'd it go for you?"

"Same ole' gyp. Grandma gave me one gift and wrote Happy Birthday *and* Merry Christmas on the card."

"Hey, at least you got something."

"That's true. It's a nice little CD player for my room. Now what I need's some CDs."

We laughed, but sadly, Jay might end up hocking the thing before he ever got any CDs to play on it. That's just the way things were.

"Hell, I ain't got a birthday present since me and Tanya was still together," I said.

"How's she doing, anyway?"

"She don't call me, I don't call her."

"You two still gonna try to work things out before the baby's born?"

"I don't know."

Before long, we were riding down Lott Road, en route to Highway 45. Blaze needed to return home before we left, and since I figured his reason was to pick up some cash, I didn't mind.

"I'll just wait till we get to Saraland before I gas up," I said. "I told Daddy that Mr. Johnson had us going in today. I don't wanna have to lie to him if he asks me something about it. You know, man, he's got them pale blue eyes that can see right through you. And once he figures I'm lying to him he starts trying to make me look like an idiot . . . especially if his friends are around."

"Talks to you like a little kid?" Jay sympathized.

"Yeah."

"My grandma's always doing me like that. It sucks, I know. But, shoot, I'm just glad she lets me stay there free of rent."

"Yeah, me too, with my old trailer," I said. This was true; Daddy never charged me to live there.

We took Shelton Beach Road to Highway 158 and then hung a left onto Highway 43 North. Once in Saraland we headed to Blaze Reed's place, on the corner of Cleveland and First Avenue. At the beginning of the pothole-ridden black-top driveway were two healthy cypresses that had grown up into points and resembled Christmas trees. The outspread, Spanish-moss-draped branches of live oaks in the front and side yards were intertwined and bathed Blaze's dull gray house in dark shadows. All the shutters were hanging off the windows and it had a screened-in front porch that was more holes than screen.

Parked in the side yard, just outside Blaze's bedroom window, was a '66 Chevrolet panel truck that Blaze's daddy used for his painting work before he was jailed. George Reed left it to Blaze, although it was mostly rust and didn't run.

As Blaze went inside, we could hear the caterwauling immediately.

"Your little friends better be taking you off to find a job, Blaze! You can't smoke dope in the men's shelter. I'm tellin' you, Son—the free ride is over. You got three days to start making the back payments you owe me for rent to live under *my* roof!"

"Ouch," said Jay. "See what I mean?"

I had to admit he had a point. Then came Blaze's voice just as loud, and sounding more like a younger boy than a nineteen-year-old. "I ain't paying rent to live in this dump, under your roof that leaks every time it rains. And why you always gotta scream at me in front of other people?"

That was the first time I ever thought of it from his perspective. The poor guy was really beaten down.

"I swear that's where he get that tic," Jay said.

"A tic?"

"Yeah, you know—nervous like, his eye muscles twitchin'."

"When did he pick that up?"

"He's had it for a month now. He says it's from his mom always going off on him, but I think it's also got a lot to do with him doing nothin' but sittin' around the house all day, smoking pot and talking to himself."

Blaze's hair was greasy and he wore round glasses, which made his face appear thin. He had a thin neck and an Adam's apple that stuck out too far—came to a point in the front and bobbed along to every syllable he spoke.

When he returned, he apologized for his mother and slumped into the backseat.

"Sorry about all that, fellas," he said, shaking his head.

"Since my dad got sent to Draper, all she ever does now is stay out drinking all night, every night after she leaves the Silver Dollar. And then she's ready to start yelling at me as soon as she gets home."

"What's Draper?" I asked.

"Alabama state prison," he said.

"What'd he do?"

"He stabbed one of them McIntosh Indians to death in the Silver Dollar with this old rusty buck knife he kept in his work truck," Blaze responded. "He walked in on my mom getting cozy with that guy behind the bar one night. My mom had been sleeping with him. I'd have done the same thing Dad did, too . . . if not worse."

We headed out to Interstate 10 with Pearl Jam's Eddie Vedder on the radio wailing about staying high and alive. The three of us caught an early morning buzz by cruising at 85 miles per hour between Polecat and Mobile Bay. The winter sun sent blinding white reflections off the choppy waters that surrounded us as we sped by.

"You know, Blaze, your tic goes away the minute you get high," remarked Jay.

"What tic?" asked Blaze.

"You know what tic. It goes away after you smoke, and I thought that was interesting."

"Whatever," said Blaze under his breath, turning his attention out the window. "Ain't got no tic. You got a tic."

From the front pocket of his corduroy pants, Jay pulled out an ink pen and a 2½" by 4½" memo pad, bound in black leather, a gift from his grandmother for graduating from Vigor High in Prichard. His first name and initials were emblazoned in gold script across the cover: Jay C. K.

He flipped up to a blank page and began scribbling in his own indecipherable way.

"What're you doing?" I asked.

"I don't know, man," replied Jay. "It's a nice day. I always get ideas on days like this, when I'm stoned in the morning and the sun's shining so bright."

"Ideas for what?"

"He likes to write poetry," Blaze cut in. "Read him one of your gay little poems, Jay."

"I like to keep a journal . . . that's all. I can't help if some of it rhymes. That's just the way it comes out on paper. It's completely incidental," he trailed off.

Blaze lunged forward from the backseat and snatched Jay's notepad from his hand, causing him to draw a thick black line to the bottom of the page.

". . . the USS *Alabama* looming to their right, a row of guns erect on its starboard deck, poised for battle and pointing eastward across the bay, like so many iron fingers compelling them to continue on their way," read Blaze mockingly.

"Give it here, you little prick," Jay said, becoming mad. He wrenched it back, making Blaze laugh harder. I guess it's true: misery loves company.

"That sounded good, man," I said. "Writing is a talent just the way drawing pictures is. It ain't nothin' to be embarrassed about."

"You don't read through another man's personal memoirs," Jay said, still mad, "not unless he gives you permission." He turned the Regal's stereo up too loud for the factory speakers, before putting his notes away. I had to lower the volume, but I knew Jay could be sensitive about his writing.

High as a kite, I missed the Loxley / Gulf Shores exit.

"Aw, we done passed it up," I said, several miles later. "Man, I ain't gonna lie, Blaze . . . that's some good-ass weed. I'm all in my own world."

"I'm tired of Gulf Shores," complained Jay. "Let's go someplace different. We should just drive until the road runs out, maybe cruise down to Miami or Key Largo. We're already almost in Florida."

"Shoot, I'm 'a turn around at the next exit," I said.

"Come on, man," Jay insisted. "It's a perfect day for a road trip. Hey, I know. How 'bout Cocoa Beach? It's on the Atlantic coast, right past Orlando. That's where my mama brung me when I turned four years old, a couple months before we left New Orleans and had to move in with Grandma in Saraland. Yeah, Cape Canaveral's right there, too." Here's the guy who tells me it's the dead of winter.

"Past Orlando? You talking about some serious mileage, man," I said.

"In a few days you'll be going way across the world to Spain. Are you really afraid to travel outside the boundaries of our little redneck paradise? And when's the last time we went on a for-real road trip, past Gulf Shores?"

"I hear you, man," I said. He had a point: it would be nice

to get away, as I could get tired of the place sometimes. "But we ain't got the money to be driving way across Florida, or at least I don't."

"So what?" he said. "What's money? Don't cost nothing but gas to drive. We have enough for that. We ain't gotta rent a room or anything. I'm just wanting to get away, like you said. If we run low on money, we'll just come up with a way to get more. We're clever enough to devise something if we have to."

"Yeah, OK," I said. "Sounds all right to me. Orlando ain't but a nine-hour drive, huh?"

"No further than eight hours from here, I guess," said Jay. "Seven if we keep speeding like we are. We gonna head that way?"

"We might. Let's see how far we can get on this tank of gas."

"Road trip sounds good to me," said Blaze. "All I got is another fifteen dollars, but I'll put it up for gas."

"I'll give you all I got, too," offered Jay. "With my five bucks you can fill your tank again. Well, hold on . . . that won't even get us halfway there. Never mind. Forget I said anything."

"Too late!" I said, laughing. "You done put me in a driving mood. Give me y'all's money. Like you said yourself, we'll figure a way to get more if we need. Hey, where's that roach?"

"It's in your ashtray."

We stopped in Tallahassee for fuel and junk food, and two hours later headed south at the junction to Interstate 75.

"I'm remembering a shortcut my mama used," said Jay, puffing on another of Blaze's joints. "Exit 414 to Providence . . . you follow that road east until it connects to Highway 100, which would eventually take us to 95 South, saving us the trouble of passing through Orlando."

"How old did you say you were last time you come this way?" I asked.

"Let's see. . .that was '78, and I had just turned four."

"You're high. I ain't listening to you," I said. "You gonna get us lost on all them back roads."

"Man, of the short time I spent with my mama, I can recall every single detail," said Jay, solemnly. "Trust me."

"All right, I'll trust you. I just hope your memory's still worth something, you being burnt like you are."

"I'm not burnt. That takes years and years of smoking every day. And weed only affects your short-term memory, anyway."

"When's the last day you went without getting high?" I asked.

"The last *whole* day?"

"Yeah, how long's it been? I bet you can't even remember."

Jay thought for a moment. "No. Sure can't."

"We gonna get lost."

We ended up in Cocoa Beach, not quite Miami, and a far cry from the Keys, but heck, it was Florida.

4

SOON, EVERYBODY WAS HUNGRY, and with me having a few bucks in my pocket, I was the one likely to be paying. That was OK with me, since it had taken us most of the day to get to that point. We stopped at McDonald's to get a ton of Big Macs and fries.

Blaze and Jay got a table while I waited for the food. Two girls were hanging around the checkout, and became interested when they saw me pay for the food.

"Y'all eat yet?" I asked. It looked like they maybe hadn't eaten for a few days.

"Nope," one of them said. She was heavyset, with long brown hair. The other one, smaller and blonder, stood staring at the fries heaped on my platter.

I'd heard about runaways, and where but McDonald's would young kids head who didn't know what to do next? "You can eat with us," I said, trying to think of a way to keep them from feeling embarrassed. "I think I messed this order up anyway." I asked the checkout guy for another couple of Big Mac meals and we walked over to join the guys.

"This is Blaze, and this is Jay," I said. "Ain't nothing but a bunch a' derelicts." I think I caught a smile on the face of the younger girl, "Sit down."

They didn't wait to be asked twice, and it was the first time I'd seen girls put away Big Macs faster than us guys. After a while, they said their names were Cheryl and Laticia, runaways from outside of Detroit. I guessed things at home were bad where they came from, too. I felt sorry for them, but also felt like the "big man," so I bought us all some more to eat.

"You know what would be great?" Jay said. We could get a fire going down on the beach, there—"

"Oh that's all we need," Blaze cut in. "The guys at Cape Canaveral will shoot us off the face of the earth."

"No, man." Jay was insistent. "Nowhere near them. I think it's allowed in some parts of the beach. Let's take a drive over and see."

By then it was getting late, and I was tired, so a rest at the beach sounded OK to me. Half an hour later, we piled out of the car with the girls and enough weed for us all. We headed out to make our beach bonfire, but just fifteen minutes after that, I was back at the car park having realized that you can't start a fire without kindling. I looked around the area, gathering up a couple of old newspapers and some trash, and was about to head back to the beach when a big black Lincoln Town Car came rolling up beside me. I glanced down to the beach: Jay and Blaze were lighting matches, trying to start a fire with a couple of pieces of driftwood.

A bald-headed man stepped out of the car and lit a cigarette. "What are those kids doing down there?" he asked.

"Oh nothing," I said, "we're just gonna have us a little fire, I guess."

"Fire?" he said, with a look of disapproval.

"Nothing big," I said. "Just thought it'd be nice on a cool day like today."

He nodded. "I guess it might. How come you're not down there with them?"

"I got elected to come and find some kindling." I showed him the newspapers and trash I'd picked up. "I guess this'll do it," I said.

"Sounds reasonable, but tell them to be careful. When you're that age, you never think anything can go wrong."

I looked up at him. He had just read my mind. I must have looked startled because he chuckled to himself.

"What's the matter, Son?" he asked.

"I was just thinking the same thing—I'm supposed to go and meet somebody off in Europe someplace, my biological father, actually, and I was just thinking, well, it'll be all right. What could go wrong?"

"Your father's European, is he?"

"Yep. Dutch."

"Oh, Dutch. Well, that should be a fine trip. The Dutch are a very knowledgeable people. He can probably give you a lot of pointers about history, agriculture, geographic land management, all kinds of things."

"Yes, Sir," I said, thinking it over. The idea of the trip was beginning to look good to me. "Thank you."

"Just try to pay attention and learn a lot—it could make a big difference in your life."

"I will," I said, smiling. "Thanks."

Looking back, this was a poignant moment, since I *did* take this stranger's advice and I learned a lot. Indeed, the experiences that would follow made a huge difference to my life. What I could not foresee, however, was that the lessons would be learned the hard way and takes me and my family through some incredibly tough and unhappy times.

The fire was OK, but by the time I'd returned to the beach crowd, it looked like *The Dating Game* goes tropical, and I felt like a fifth wheel. I grabbed a couple things and slept in the car. It was good—gave me time to think about things. The downside, however, was when everybody got up the next morning—or more like the next afternoon. The girls were gone, and of course, so was my wallet. They'd been eyeing me in the McDonald's all right, not as the *big* man, but more as their next mark.

Half an hour into our journey home via the back roads, we realized we were completely lost—with little money for gas.

5

Sunday, December 19, 1993

I BARELY HAD ENOUGH fuel left to get me to Daddy's convenience store, J&J Grocery, and unbelievably, that old engine died the minute I entered the lot. I rolled it to a stop beside the pumps and walked between a pair of Ford pickups parked near the front entrance—an old brown F-150 with a red Crimson Tide decal across the back glass and a newer F-150 carrying a camouflaged four-wheeler equipped with a gun rack.

My daddy, Jessie Ray Cobb, routinely opened his doors before dawn in the wintertime to accommodate the game hunters. I knew he'd credit me a couple of gallons from the pump, but I dreaded the lecture that was bound to come with it.

J&J Grocery was Daddy's first solo business venture after a two-year stint in a Pascagoula shipyard, where he did contract work for the navy. During this time, Daddy suffered a fall and seriously injured his back. He didn't sue the shipyard—he wasn't the type—but the corrective surgery left him with a limp in his right leg.

To make ends meet, Mama started a cashier job at a local supermarket. Daddy, while sitting at home recovering from his back surgery at the age of thirty-three, also had a mild heart attack. Immediately after the back surgery, Mama and Daddy took out a huge loan to build J&J Grocery so that they could make a living after Daddy's heart attack. It was always Mama's dream to have her own grocery store.

It was a rough road for Daddy and Mama getting their own store, but they had profited from it, especially in recent years. The place had become a hangout for the good ol' boys of rural Eight Mile. They'd start their days standing around the front counter with Daddy, sipping coffee, insulting each other's manhood *(janking,* people call it), and spreading the latest community dirt on who died, got killed, or went crazy and tried to kill themselves.

That's what I walked into, eyes bloodshot from lack of sleep.

"Son, what the hell are you doing up so early?" Jessie Ray demanded. Daddy wore faded blue jeans, a plain gray sweatshirt, and round eyeglasses. His ashy hair grew down the front of his face, so he kept it short rather like the ancient Roman senators. A white, neatly trimmed beard covered a resting facial expression that implied he was amused by most things, even when he was clearly agitated. "You been up all night getting drunk, haven't you, boy?"

Even in his black and yellow Timberland boots, Jessie

Ray stood only five foot seven, a head shorter than Henry Shanks—a grizzly, thick-necked fellow with a full chestnut beard. Henry's blue tartan flannel looked tight around his forearms as he leaned back against a cooler brimming with Blue Bell ice cream. Over his left shoulder hung a wooden plaque decorated with a bass fishing lure and a spent shotgun shell. *Hunters, fishermen, and other liars gather here,* it warned. Another one of the cronies that hung around the store, Ben Banks, stood beside him, silent but amused.

"Don't get your drawers in a knot, Ray," Henry started. "Young folks these days got no concept of day and night. They ain't gotta be in bed at 8:00 p.m. like us old geezers. It's their nature to go carousing and such until dawn, watching the sun come up and whatnot."

Jessie Ray laid his morning paper on the maple checkout counter and peered up at his burly companion. A smile tugged at both sides of his mouth where hard lines were becoming more defined with each passing year. "Henry," he said, "if I wanted your opinion, I'd call your wife and ask *her for* it. Now keep quiet when I'm talking to my son."

The other men chuckled at this well-placed blow below the belt. Henry eyed Jessie Ray contemptuously and sipped his coffee in silence.

"I ain't been drinking nothing, Daddy," I said.

"Come tomorrow you'll be running around with your dopehead friends from the car wash again. Don't give me that crap. You probably are lying to me, anyway," he said.

I sighed, but remained silent.

"You need to get that check from Mr. Johnson and go pay on your speeding tickets before they come arrest you. I ain't bailing you outta jail if they do. Don't call me."

"Ain't no one got their checks yet," I said. "Mr. Johnson's holding them till today."

"Now, why would he do a thing like that?" inquired Jessie Ray. "As long as you've worked there you've always been paid on Fridays."

"I can't figure why, either," I said nervously. "Probably because the holiday—I don't know, Daddy; he can be sort of funny about them kinda things." I made an effort to look at him in the eye and sound sincere. "I was wondering, Sir, if you could credit me a couple gallons for my car so I can make it to Saraland later. I'm running on fumes now. I don't believe I got enough to even get home. In fact, I'm sure I don't."

"I can sell you a couple gallons, Son. I can do that. Mr. Cochran from down the road come in here just a minute ago asking about you. He's up early this morning working in his shop and said his Cadillac could use a good washing. Why don't you go over there and see if he'll let you do it now? You can pay for your gas outta whatever he gives you."

"All right," I said. "I'll go over there."

"I'll set the pump for five dollars. You wash his car then come straight back here to pay me what you owe. Straight back, you hear? I'm not fooling around. If I don't get that money this morning, I won't think twice about taking back that shiny Regal of yours. Don't you forget whose name it's under."

"Yes, Sir."

6

December 20, 1993

I SLEPT THROUGHOUT MONDAY in the old trailer on Highland Road, and got up only for a couple hours after midnight to polish off a stack of miniature honey buns and a tall glass of chocolate milk. I dozed back off again, sitting in my recliner, the television on mute, never once giving a thought to my job at the carwash.

December 21, 1993

At 10:27 on Tuesday morning, a phone call startled me awake. It was Paw Paw Mizell. "Jamie?"

"Yeah, Paw Paw, it's me."

"Listen, I got bad news," he said. That got me awake.

"What happened?"

"There was a murder down here in Saraland. Some folks know that you and your buddies left town. That makes you all like mighty suspicious. You don't know nothing about it, do ya?"

"No, Sir, not at all. It was just me and Jay and Blaze. We took a road trip down to Florida's all."

"I believe you, Jamie. But you got to come down with me and see this fellow, the detective, so they can clear things up."

"I'll be right there."

Later as we sat talking to the detective, I counted my lucky stars that I had people in my family who stood for something. The detective listened to everything Paw Paw said, and Paw Paw told him everything I'd told him. It wasn't much fun, but I wasn't guilty that day. Later, I would know how it felt to be on the other side of the law.

"Thanks for taking care of this for me, Paw Paw," I said. "I'd have hated to have them track me down like some kind of a criminal."

"He knows you're a good kid, Jamie," Paw Paw said.

I watched him head for his house, pausing for a minute to check the status of some evergreens that didn't take too well to the cold weather. He ran his hand along the long branches and must have been satisfied.

"Thanks again," I called, as I drove off.

He turned and waved.

I was emotionally drained, but there was to be no time for resting; as soon as I got in, the phone rang again.

"Hi, love." It was Wendy, calling from her trailer park's payphone. "We need to go by the airport today to pick up your father. His flight is scheduled to land in Mobile at 4:05, so come and pick me up around 3:30. OK? Oh, and wear something nice, sweetheart."

"I ain't trying to impress nobody. And I ain't got gas enough to be driving all over creation," I said. "I'm serious, Wendy."

"I'll pay you for some gas, Jamie. Just get over here on time."

7

TEN MINUTES FROM the Mississippi state line, I eased my '84 Buick Regal off of Highway 98. It was a few days before Christmas, sunny out but still cold and breezy. The father I never knew would be arriving at the Mobile Municipal Airport later that afternoon. Driving past a Baptist church nestled in the shade of longleaf pines, I felt conflicted over meeting the man who abandoned me before I was even born.

Aunt Wendy, the woman who brought me into this world, lived in a secluded trailer park, alone. Hers was the third to last lot to the right, near the end of a quarter-mile blacktop driveway, past two speed bumps and after an abandoned trailer with every front window busted in. She sat waiting on her mildewed steps, bearing a cozy smile and drawing on the last of a Kool.

Out of habit, she reached for her pack again, but she shot me a thoughtful glance through my windshield before dropping the smokes back into her big white purse full of Goody's headache powder and prescription pain meds. She must have remembered how I would complain if she got into my pride and joy with a lighted cigarette. Personally, I spent way too many aimless afternoons cruising the hilly byways of South Alabama, smothering my maroon velvet seats with the dense tar of sticky pine. But the scent of marijuana didn't bother me at all. It was my drug of choice, because it helped me to forget.

Out in front of her dilapidated brown trailer, Aunt Wendy pulled me into an awkward hug. Normally about six feet tall, she stood the same height as me that day in her three-inch heels. We both had the same dark brown eyes that appeared black farther than a few steps away. My sandy brown locks covered most of my brow, and her damaged, dyed-black hair hung lifelessly down to the middle of her back. Her caked-on makeup looked unnatural on her skin, which was graying and papery from years of chemical abuse. She rarely went out in the sun.

I was used to seeing Aunt Wendy in a baggy jogging suit and sneakers. The skintight acid-washed jeans and red blouse she wore that day under a black trench coat indicated that she meant to make a good impression on my biological father. She hadn't been able to stop talking about Jan since the trip she'd taken to Europe a couple of years earlier.

I held open the passenger's side door of my Buick Regal for Aunt Wendy.

"Aren't you excited, baby?" she asked as sweetly as she could, her voice low and gravelly from thousands of menthol cigarettes.

"I guess," I shrugged, pushing the door shut while she buckled herself in. I didn't know how to feel about the meeting. Part of me realized how odd it was for my father to suddenly start caring that I was alive after twenty-two years of never doing a thing for me. At the same time, I'd been curious about him ever since I was thirteen when I first found out that he even existed.

"I wonder if he still thinks I'm beautiful," Aunt Wendy said to me, glaring at the rolling hills beside Snow Road as I sped south toward the airport. Her outdated clothes had the inside of my Buick smelling like mothballs and dollar store perfume.

Aunt Wendy couldn't help having low self-esteem after all the terrible things that had happened to her over the years.

"I'm sure he does," I told her. A hopeful smile lit up her face.

I fidgeted with the radio dial on my car's factory deck and found a station playing Christmas hymns. I didn't know what kind of music my biological mother liked. I didn't know much about her at all outside of the talk I'd always heard from my adoptive daddy, Jessie Ray Cobb—that she was a hopeless drug addict and a con artist.

She lowered the passenger's side sun visor to touch up her makeup. "He's making good money on those crew boats. It's a shame you get so seasick. There's medicine you can take for that."

"I know," I said.

"Your father, Jan, practically lives out on the sea," she said, doing what she could to hide the purple bags under her eyes. "Maybe you just haven't spent enough time on a boat yet."

"I'll be all right," I told her.

Aunt Wendy stowed her makeup kit and dug around in her purse for a moment. I could hear her prescription pill bottles rattling around in there. Besides her Goody's powder and Diet Coke, those meds were about the only things I'd ever seen that woman eat.

"What do you think of this, Jamie?" Aunt Wendy asked me. She passed me a heavy piece of tarnished jewelry. I turned the gaudy brass ring over in my free hand as I continued to steer my silver Buick southward. Pine-covered hills flattened into plains. Airfields crept onto the horizon, hazy in the last hour of soft winter sunlight.

Engraved into the ring was an image of Jesus standing behind the wheel of a ship. His face showed a calm, wise expression.

"Is he religious?" I asked her.

"Jan is a boat captain," she said. "He'll like it for that."

"Isn't that what he went to prison for . . . something with his boats?" I asked. "That's what Mama always said."

"No, no, no, no . . ." she said, shaking her head in a way that told me she was good and dosed up on her pain meds. "Janet doesn't know what she's talking about. Your father is *not* a criminal, he's a good man. Trust me, Jamie—it was those pirates that set him up, off the coast of France. It was those pirates," she echoed.

I hated when she would start talking out of her head like that.

8

AT THE M. C. Farmer Terminal of Mobile Municipal Airport, an escalator carried Aunt Wendy and me up to a collection of cast-iron tables and chairs. In front of a long plate glass window that offered a view of the airstrip, I sat staring at the blinding runway lights, thinking about my seventeen-year-old girlfriend, Tanya. I wondered what kind of parents we were going to make—two high school dropouts, and me on the verge of going to jail for over a thousand dollars' worth of unpaid speeding tickets.

They were the reason I didn't hesitate to accept my biological father's offer to work on his boats in Spain. All I'd ever done since quitting high school was stock groceries, sand cabinets, and detail cars. Aunt Wendy bragged that Jan van Rijn was a great businessman, and I figured he could teach me a good trade to help me provide a better life for Tanya and the baby we were going to have in a month's time.

I remembered the awkward phone conversation I'd had with my father a few days earlier. He sounded so sure of himself, promising me a way out of my financial bind.

Listening to the confidence ringing out in Jan's foreign voice, all I could think of was a watercolor painting that Aunt Wendy had brought back from her recent trip to the Netherlands. It was a depiction of Jan sitting in a cramped prison cell, his face mostly hidden by shadows. A gold loop adorned one ear and an unkempt beard hung down over a ragged, long-sleeve shirt that brought out his piercing eyes. They were the color of the deep blue sea.

"Jamie," Aunt Wendy said, "your brother, Donny, is here."

His blonde mustache stretching across his round face into a broad grin, Jan's oldest son bear-hugged me and chuckled as if we were really that close. "Are you excited, Little Brother?" he asked me.

I just laughed. "Still working on them crew boats, Donny?" I asked him.

"Just got back from Morgan City," he told me.

"What kind of work has Dad got lined up for you?" Donny asked me.

"Refinishing his boats," I said. "That's what he told me on the phone."

"Doesn't sound too hard," Donny said, patting my shoulder like I was below him. "Maybe one day the three of us could go sailing together. Dad would love that."

He was originally from Portland, Oregon, and still had a faint West Coast accent. Donny was stocky and kept his long blonde hair styled into a mullet, combed over into a pompadour in the front. He was stuck in the eighties with his ripped jeans and Guns N' Roses T-shirts. I knew he did well repairing crew boat engines for a deep-water drilling company, but he always wore those cheap, dollar store high tops. I'd seen him in the summertime sporting cutoff jean shorts, knee-high socks, and a pink fanny pack.

I'd met him about six years earlier when he'd first walked into my adoptive parents' country store. I was filling a plastic barrel with cubed ice and glass bottles of Coca-Cola when he introduced himself to me, looking basically the same as he did that day in the airport. His blonde mullet gave off a gamey odor from his three-day bus ride down from Oregon, where our biological father had planted his first seed, four years before Jan and Aunt Wendy first met in New Orleans.

Donny loaned me a car amplifier that I traded for an ounce of weed. He settled down around Mobile, living with Aunt Wendy off and on before finding steady work offshore and renting his own place in Saraland. He never did say why he decided to move away from Portland, but I had a feeling he'd gotten into some kind of trouble up there, doing something for Jan.

"You have a lot on your mind, Jamie?" Donny asked me in Mobile Airport.

"Kinda," I shrugged.

"He's a great guy," Donny assured me. "In your entire life, you'll never meet anyone else quite like him."

Donny pointed toward a crowd of arrivals migrating from Gate 1. Standing out from the rest were two blonde figures that looked like they spent a lot of time out in the sun. They both wore dark blue blazers over button-down shirts, tucked into Levi 501 jeans. All that remained of my father's prison beard was a stylish five o'clock shadow of golden stubble. His straw-colored hair had been meticulously styled. At the part, an inverted V of bronzed scalp came to a point at about the crown of his skull. I felt like I was looking into the future, at the hairline I would have in my middle age.

The guy walking with Jan had loops in both ears, like a pirate. This Dutchman was my age and my height, in his early twenties and standing at just over six feet tall. He had a wiry build and a bony face, as if his fair skin were pulled too tight over his forehead and cheekbones. His crew cut was bleached blonde, and he had a pencil-thin black mustache.

Both Dutchmen carried a black briefcase in one hand and a tanned-leather suitcase in the other.

Aunt Wendy forced a hug on Jan. "Hey, handsome," she whispered into his ear.

"Did you have a good flight, Dad?" Donny asked.

"Good from Holland, but rough from Atlanta," Jan said. He presented a briefcase to me, and the younger fellow did the same for Donny.

"Something we found in the airport, Jamie," Jan said to me. I saw that it contained fine silver and gold flatware.

"This is nice," I said, meeting his curious stare for the first time. His aqua blue eyes sparkled and had the depth of an intelligent and cunning person, saturated with a passion for life. He had a strong, undeniable presence about him.

We shook hands and he pulled me into a hug.

"My son," Jan said quietly, joyfully. My father smelled of

elegance, like designer cologne and brand-new clothes. For some reason, I felt like I'd already known him for many years.

That was when my timid nature kicked in. Crowds of people and strange new faces always made me self-conscious. I began to worry that I would say something to make Jan think less of me. I wasn't an educated man, and there were a lot of words I had trouble pronouncing. Jan and Donny started talking and I felt even more out of place. They had similar short, round faces and the same hue of straw-blonde hair.

Then I saw that Jan and I shared a constant harsh squint, a cautious and studious view of the world. My father didn't just look at people he was speaking with; he peered right into them.

"How rude of me," Jan said, turning away from Donny, who was talking his ear off. "I want you all to meet my nephew, Trans van Rijn," he said, introducing my Dutch cousin. "He has always dreamed of one day seeing America."

I shook Trans's hand and he studied me with his calm, light green eyes. He had a mischievous look about him, as if harboring secrets he would never tell.

"Why don't we all head back to my place?" Aunt Wendy suggested. "I have drinks, and the two of you can get settled in for the night," she said to Jan and Trans.

Donny jabbed his elbow playfully into Jan's side. "Staying with Miss Wendy, huh, Dad?" Donny teased with a cheesy wink, making everyone uncomfortable with his big grin and rotten tooth.

Jan hesitated a moment, sighed, and then offered Aunt

Wendy a forward nod. We began to walk as a group, past an airport bar and toward the escalators. Jan looked around every which way except at Aunt Wendy, who couldn't keep her once tired but now lively black eyes off him. I wondered what kind of arrangement had been made between my biological parents to get me there that day.

Aunt Wendy was only forty-three years old, but next to Jan she looked much older. Although he pushed fifty and his hairline was receding, the hair that remained was thick, vibrant, and naturally devoid of gray. The skin on his face was thick and weathered, yet his cheeks were plump and rosy. At six feet tall, with his broad shoulders, straight back, and chin held high, Jan exuded an air of confidence and dignity in the way he carried himself. He was the kind of guy that would be in charge of things, and I felt good knowing that I would be learning a trade from him.

My mama, Janet Cobb, was waiting for us outside of the airport. From a distance I spotted her gray Chevy Astro van with a personalized license plate on the front that read "Miss J." Standing by my Buick Regal, Mama had her hands balled up into fists at her sides, a sure sign she was ready to confront someone.

Mama had hazel eyes that could shift from a dull brown to a light gray that perfectly matched her thin, shoulder-length gray hair. The color of her eyes depended on her mood and what she happened to be dealing with at the time. They glowed with a fierce gold tint that evening in the Mobile airport parking lot, despite her dark winter clothing. Mama was usually a peaceful woman of few words, but she had a hint of Irish blood from her Maw Maw's side of the family that occasionally showed through.

"Wendy, I told you I didn't want Jamie getting involved with *him*," she said sharply to her younger sister, while shooting spiteful glances at Jan van Rijn. "After all the sacrifices me and Mama have made through the years, raising your kids while you were living out your Mafia Mistress fantasy in New Orleans—how could you defy me like this?"

"You're just jealous, Janet," Aunt Wendy started, "because you never had the guts to leave home when you were young, like I did. You let Daddy run your life just like he wanted to while I was out experiencing the real world."

"What the hell do you know about the *real* world?" Mama asked, getting in Aunt Wendy's face. "With your Valiums, and your Lortabs, and your Xanbars, and your dope—and Lord knows what else." Her eyes suddenly glistening with tears, Mama turned to Jan and said with all the passion she could muster at that moment, "You *bette*r not let anything happen to him. He's *my* son, too. Me and my husband, we raised him a good boy."

"Yes, yes," Jan nodded emphatically. "I understand, Mrs. Cobb. I want to thank you for all that you have done. I am eternally grateful and prepared to reimburse you for your kindness."

"We don't need any reimbursement," Mama told him. "You just see to it that Jamie doesn't get caught up in any foolishness over there in Europe. You know what I'm talking about?" Jan's guilty eyes showed that he did.

"I'm old enough to take care of myself, Mama," I said meekly.

"I can't make your decisions for you, Jamie," Mama said. She reached up and hugged my neck. "But remember, you can come home whenever you're ready."

I got choked up watching Mama drive off alone. I never felt like anything less than her baby boy, even after I found out I was adopted. All the good things she did for me through the years flashed through my mind. I remembered the divided tray she bought me when I was four; I was so spoiled that I wouldn't eat the food if it touched each other. Then there were all those afternoons we spent in her ceramics shop, where I escaped from the daily stress of being teased at school for being slow—for having a learning disability.

Mama didn't just raise me, she loved me. And she saved me from having to be brought up around the darkness of Aunt Wendy's addictions. Nevertheless, I was at a point in my life where I felt trapped in a cycle of rough living and barely getting by. With my biological father, I saw a way out.

9

WAY OUT IN the middle of nowhere, Aunt Wendy's trailer
park was spooky at night. We rolled past rusty truck frames on
cement blocks, an abandoned trailer that had all but burned
to the ground, and a group of sooty children that stopped
playing in the rubble to send hard stares at the roar of my
turbo mufflers. Jan drove with me from the airport, and from
behind the wheel of my Buick I sensed that Aunt Wendy's
neighborhood was making my father uncomfortable.

I heard the chorus of Whitesnake's "Here I Go Again"
as the polished aluminum Center Line wheels on Donny's
white Camaro Z/28 rolled to a stop near a yellowing patch
of weeds in Aunt Wendy's front lawn. Our Dutch cousin,
Trans, emerged from the tiny backseat of Donny's muscle car
and immediately lit a Marlboro red. Trans seemed mildly an-
noyed by the power ballads Donny had been blasting on his
Alpine stereo all the way from Mobile.

Trans crossed his arms over his chest and studied Aunt
Wendy's brown trailer with its matching shutters all about to
fall off.

"A house on wheels," my cousin observed, smirking faintly in the pale lamppost light.

"That's basically what it is," I said. "Y'all ain't got trailers in Europe, I bet."

"Do you share this house with Wendy?" he asked me with his strange Dutch accent. I imagined he thought my South Alabama drawl sounded funny too.

"My parents let me stay in a trailer where my grandma used to live," I explained, "back towards Mobile, in Eight Mile. It's not in great shape either, but beats the hell out of sleeping in the woods."

Trans smoked quietly for a while, and then said, "You called the woman at the airport 'Mama,' but Wendy is your mother, yes?"

"Yes. . . and no," I said. "That big woman you saw at the airport, she's the one took care of me since I was a little boy. Technically, she's my aunt, but I know her as my *real* mama. It confused me, too, for a long time."

Trans leaned back against the trunk of my Buick. He had a casual friendliness, and I was finding it easy to talk with him, even with his funny accent. "I think I understand what you mean," he said. He watched Aunt Wendy lead Jan into her old trailer, still sitting on its axles, floor insulation like layered sheets of molded cotton candy hanging almost to the cold red dirt in places.

"You care much more about the woman at the airport," my cousin said after they were inside. "You feel closer to her . . . in your heart."

"That's a nice way of putting it," I told him.

"Ah, I like your bumper sticker," Trans grinned.

"Sneek," I read. "Aunt Wendy gave me that. She said it was Jan's hometown, in the Netherlands."

"In Holland, we say *Snake,*" he corrected me—something I was used to, even in my own language.

Aunt Wendy's normally stuffy living room smelled of Lemon Pledge and Pine-Sol. There were no musty clothes piled on the furniture. Across a bar that was usually cluttered with food-encrusted dishes, I saw that the kitchen was spotless. The shag carpet was an even lighter color than I remembered, leading me to believe that Aunt Wendy had gone the extra mile to impress Jan by renting a carpet shampooer. My father kept looking around at the inside of Aunt Wendy's trailer, at the cheap paneling on the walls and at the low ceiling, warped and stained from rainwater that had leaked down from the damaged roof. I could tell he was used to more luxurious surroundings.

Looking as happy as I'd ever seen her, Aunt Wendy wound up a dollar store disposable camera and started snapping pictures of me and Jan. "My two handsome men," she said.

"Sit with me, Son," my father invited. "I have my own pictures."

Jan reached into an exterior pouch on a lightly packed suitcase and produced a photo album brimming with Polaroids.

"Is that all the luggage you came with?" I asked him.

"In my line of work, you learn to travel light," he said. "You always have to be ready to leave a place at a moment's notice."

Jan produced shots of a dark-haired, photogenic woman smiling sweetly sitting behind the wheel of a black Mercedes Benz. We came to a side view of the same dark-haired woman leaning against white cement railings on a semicircular balcony—hills, valleys, and the distant sea behind her.

"This is my maid, Abby," he said. "She is a Jewish woman . . . drove tanks for the Israeli army. And here is my girlfriend, Sandra."

"That a nude beach?" I asked.

Jan laughed. "Are you still eager to work for my company in Spain? I believe it would be a nice change of pace for you, Son," he said, looking around again with a sympathetic look.

"Yes, Sir," I told him. "As long as I will be making better money than I do washing cars."

"A hundred times better!" Jan chuckled. "A million times better, my son!"

"Here!" said Aunt Wendy, slamming a green bottle down on a wooden TV tray in front of Jan. Beer fizzed out everywhere. Over Jan's shoulder, Aunt Wendy had been looking at the pictures too, and they were making her jealous.

"I'll show you later, Son," Jan said, stowing the Polaroids before grabbing the Heineken. "This is not cold," he complained after a sip.

"I thought you Dutch guys liked warm beer," she said, getting more upset by the minute.

"The Heineken we have in Holland . . . tastes different," Trans said as politely as he could, nursing his own bottle. He peered down the longneck at the suds. "This is . . . somewhat watered down. We would call it *fink bräu.*"

"Maybe you'll like this better," Aunt Wendy said. She pulled the flea market Jesus ring out of her pocket and presented it to Jan.

He sighed as he tried it on, just humoring her. "It is too big for me, Wendy, but I will keep it as a souvenir," he said, jamming it in his coat pocket.

Jan didn't say much to Aunt Wendy after that. She developed a worried look in her dark eyes. Then she did something that made my father even more uncomfortable.

Aunt Wendy took a seat on the armrest right next to Jan and started stroking his hair affectionately. "Is everything OK, sweetie?" she asked. "Didn't you miss me?"

Jan immediately jumped to his feet.

That hurt Aunt Wendy's feelings too. Looking like she was about to cry, she retreated down a dark hallway to her back bedroom, nearly tearing off a moth-eaten wool comforter that had been tacked up in place of a door. I felt bad for her.

"Donny," Jan said after an awkward moment of silence, rubbing the heels of his palms into his eye sockets like he had a migraine headache. "Is there a place nearby where we can all go and have a cold beer?"

A few minutes later, Aunt Wendy caught up with us outside. She slammed the front door, rifling through her big white purse. *"You're not leaving me behind tonight . . . Jan!"* she called out, slurring her words. It was clear that she'd been popping Valiums all evening to try to calm her nerves around the love of her life.

Donny had contacted Aunt Wendy's youngest sister, Aunt Kay, and arranged for her to meet us at a bar in the town of Tillman's Corner, about halfway between Mobile and Aunt Wendy's place near the Mississippi border. Aunt Kay was the spitting image of the Mizell bloodline with her thin lips and high cheekbones. We weren't in that cinderblock, hole-in-the-wall lounge for five minutes before Aunt Kay snuck up on Jan ordering drinks. She hugged Jan's wide shoulders from behind.

"The years have been good to you, Jan," she said, her doll face beaming.

"Wow, you are all grown up," my father told her, clearly more excited to see Aunt Kay than Aunt Wendy. She was a slender, attractive lady in her mid-thirties. It was obvious that she took good care of herself. Jan admired her figure while she primped her shoulder-length strawberry blonde hair.

"Jamie, I would babysit for Wendy and Jan back when we all lived in New Orleans together," Aunt Kay reminisced with her strong southern accent while she and Jan smiled warmly at one another. "That seems like another lifetime."

"*The good old days,*" Aunt Wendy slurred, knocking back a second glass of the most expensive wine the country bar had in stock. "Remember our beautiful apartment, Jan? You loved me then . . ." she complained more quietly, to herself.

"Of course," he nodded. "And I remember bringing your

little sister to the movies with us every Saturday."

"You always bought us all just whatever we wanted," Aunt Kay gushed. "Oh, Jamie, he's so generous," she said, touching my forearm. "You'll see!"

Trans and I tried a game of pool, though we couldn't seem to agree on the rules, since he was from a different country. At this point, I began to study my father. He offered me a beer, but I turned it down. I wanted my head to be clear so that I could make a good assessment of this man with whom I was about to travel halfway across the world to Spain to work on his boats. As he flirted with my pretty aunt, Jan's attention drifted from Donny to me and back. Donny just didn't have the style of our father. I sensed that Jan saw him as a clown with his mullet haircut and his gaudy fashion sense.

After a while, Donny's wife, a big country gal with puffed-up brown hair, showed up with one of her girlfriends. The three of them started visiting the restroom in succession. They came out sniffing, running their hands over their noses, their eyes wide and glazed over, and all stuck in that 1980s pace of living.

While Trans and I were arguing at the pool table over how he wasn't calling his shots, all the working-class folks in that dim, backwoods lounge turned their heads at the sound of glass breaking near the bar. Aunt Wendy had spilled red wine on the stained concrete floor and then took a hard spill herself when she tried standing up to get some napkins. Her legs were like rubber from all the downers she'd been mixing to try to deal with Jan's disinterest in her.

I ran over to help.

"Let's get her to the car, James. She is making a fool of herself," Jan griped.

She babbled incoherently as we carried her outside and set her in the backseat of my Buick. Oblivious to where she was, she quickly passed out on the maroon velvet seat and started to snore. Seeing Aunt Wendy in that condition opened up a floodgate of confusing memories for me. Throughout my childhood, she would buy me expensive gifts for Christmas. One year, it was a red-and-white-striped Coca-Cola shirt that was a lot nicer than the ones she had picked out for my adoptive brother and sister. That was before I knew the truth about her being my birth mother.

In 1979, Hurricane Frederic blew Aunt Wendy's trailer clean out of Bayou La Batre, Alabama, and she moved in with us. I remembered standing with her and my adoptive daddy in a line for fresh water and government cheese. This was when Aunt Wendy faked her epileptic seizure to get us to the front of the line on that sweltering August afternoon.

After any disasters, Aunt Wendy always made her way back to New Orleans, and that's what she did after Hurricane Frederic left her homeless. The next summer, we all went to Aunt Nancy's house in Marrero, Louisiana, just south of New Orleans. Aunt Nancy was boiling blue point crabs when Aunt Wendy showed up, making a scene on the front lawn. "You can't see him right now," I heard Mama and Aunt Nancy telling their crazy younger sister, the black sheep of the family. They'd left the front door open a crack when they'd gone outside to deal with her. I was being nosy when Aunt Nancy's poodle, Pierre, ran outside. I chased after him and Aunt Wendy stumbled toward me. "Get back in the house, Jamie!" Mama said, picking me up in her strong arms, rushing me inside and away from Aunt Wendy, who started sobbing.

I remained listening at the front door. "You keep taking them pills, Wendy, they gonna have to pump your stomach again . . . send you back to the Home of Grace," Aunt Nancy told her, referring to the women's recovery shelter in Eight Mile. Aunt Wendy had tried killing herself so many times.

Those were the scenes rushing through my mind as I stood outside that hole-in-the-wall bar in Tillman's Corner, Alabama, with the man who'd brought me into the world, before he ran away to Europe from Aunt Wendy and me for twenty-two years.

"She used to not be this way. At one time, she was a gorgeous woman with legs up to here," said Jan, placing the back of his hand under his chin. "I remember when I first met her. I was working on a tugboat, and we were docked in Morgan City. A Cajun longshoreman I made friends with, he knew of a go-go bar not far from the port. Wendy was dancing there that night."

"Uh-huh," I said uncomfortably, scratching the back of my head. Jan's eyes were red from a lot of beer, and I didn't like where this story was going.

"She was the only dancer I had ever met who could balance a champagne glass on her breasts . . ."

I looked across Highway 90 at the Mobile Lumber Yard

and tried to change the subject. "Looks like it floods here in this hollow," I said. A late December breeze ruffled the pines all around us. It felt like Christmastime and I wondered what Mama and Daddy were doing back in Eight Mile, if they were wrapping presents that night for Junior and Lisa's kids.

Jan snapped out of his flashback and patted me on the shoulder.

"It is good to be here with you tonight, Jamie," he said.

"OK," I sighed, feeling like I could use a joint.

Donny's brown-headed wife and her female friend, a much thinner redneck girl wearing black spandex tights showing her nice figure, stumbled out of the bar as if they were a couple. They fell against the long hood of Donny's Camaro and exchanged a passionate French kiss.

Taking measured steps, Donny walked out after them and approached my silver Buick. His pompadour had lost its body and was now hanging down over his eyes. In his corny way, he pulled me and Jan into a group hug.

"I love you, Dad . . . I love you, too, Little Brother," he said to me, "but I have to go now. Call me before you fly out."

"Donny's getting lucky tonight," Jan beamed as my half-brother sped off, burning rubber on the blacktop parking lot. "Two women! Damn van Rijn, he is just like me!"

Trans strolled out of the building. With a grunt, he pitched an empty Heineken bottle against the nearest pine tree, laughing at how it shattered well enough for some poor redneck to cut his foot on. *"Fink bräu!"* he called out to me and Jan.

We had to carry Aunt Wendy into her trailer that night and Jan said something about leaving early in the morning before she came to. I was OK with that.

"I will sleep on the floor," Jan said after we settled the matter. "You can have the sofa, Jamie."

"I know the carpet looks clean now, but there's no telling what's crawling around in this hellhole," I said. "Judging from them pictures you showed me earlier, I'm sure you're used to nicer surroundings."

"I have been in worse places, Son," Jan said. "When you have only a cement bed to sleep on and a wooden bucket to go in for eight years of your life, you can get quite comfortable almost anywhere."

I had a hard time nodding off. I stood up several times throughout the night and paced around the dark living room. In a month, I was going to be a father. But I was so broke, and bringing someone into the world without having the means to provide the stable environment my adoptive parents had always worked so hard to give me made me want to cry.

"Before I got into trouble in France," Jan started, sitting up from his place on the carpeted floor, "I sent money to your mother so she could take care of you. I very much loved that woman at one time. I had every intention of returning, to take you two back to Europe with me. Wendy changed, however, and then I went back to prison. When I was released, I learned you had been adopted by her sister Janet and knew nothing of me. I thought it would be easier if I just let you live a normal life and be happy with your adopted family.

"Forgive me, Jamie. If you have ever felt that I did not care enough to be there for you as a father, I am very, very sorry. I only left America, in the first place, for *you and Wendy's safety*. I wish I could make you understand this, but there are some things I still cannot talk about."

"I'm worried about this baby I got coming with my . . . well, she's my ex-girlfriend now," I explained to him, still pacing around. "We're not even together. And I don't have a clue how this all is gonna work out. I don't want to be a bad father."

"You will not be," Jan assured me.

"I don't want my family looking down on me for what I can't provide," I continued.

"Jamie, I will help you to avoid the mistakes I made," Jan said, speaking to my troubled soul. "Money will not be a problem for you anymore. Trust me, my son . . . you are about to begin living the life you were always meant to lead."

With all my heart, I started to believe every word Jan van Rijn had to say to me from that point on. He was my father, after all. And he had me hooked.

10

Wednesday, December 22, 1993

JAN SHOOK ME AWAKE the next morning.

"Son, get dressed," he said hastily. "We've got things to do today."

We were up and out within a couple of minutes.

"Take us to the place where we can pay off your fines, your tickets for speeding," Jan said.

"I should probably warn you; there are two separate tickets I need to pay in Saraland, and it comes out to over five hundred dollars."

"Two tickets in one town? This Saraland, it must be a speed trap," said Jan.

"I do tend to have a lead foot sometimes. Both tickets were from last summer. I'd get off early from washing cars and get in a big hurry to pick up my ex-girlfriend."

"The same girl that is having your baby?" asked Jan.

"Same girl," I said. "We used to get along real good, but things changed after we found out she was pregnant. I don't know. Maybe it's my fault. Maybe I ain't been trying hard enough to get along with her. She *is* gonna be a part of my life now forever . . . even if we don't end up getting married."

"You are too young to be married, Son. Even I am too young for that," he chuckled. "And don't fret too much over your relationship with this girl. These types of things always work themselves out in time."

At the police station, Jan paid my fines in cash.

"Thanks a lot," I said. "I can't wait till I can pay you back."

"No problem," Jan said. "I am glad I could help. And here, take this, Son," he said, handing me a wad of hundred dollar bills.

"What?" I exclaimed. "This is like a thousand dollars."

"Put it in your pocket and use it to buy yourself some winter clothes for your trip to Holland. It may be colder than what you are accustomed to."

"Son, do you have a passport?" asked Jan, after we were a mile down Lott Road.

"No, Sir, I don't."

"We can go to New Orleans today and have one made for you," said Jan.

We hopped on the interstate and traveled two hours west. Jan navigated the city effortlessly; we got off on the Poydras Street exit and followed South Claiborne to Tulane Avenue.

"You seem to know your way around," I said.

"I spent a lot of time in this area when I was a young man," said Jan. "We are going to a hospital, the same place you were born."

We left the car in a pay-by-the-hour parking lot and made our way for the Charity Hospital on foot. While Jan spoke to a young med student in green scrubs, I studied the windows on the east side of the hospital that bled mildew stains onto massive beige blocks of which the outer walls were constructed. "He tells me birth records are no longer kept in the hospital," said Jan. "We have to go up to Perdido Street."

We walked over to the Louisiana state office building across from city hall. Trans lit a cigarette and sat on a granite ledge with me while Jan strolled toward the front entrance of the state office building. "This should not take *too* long," Jan said over his shoulder.

I noticed a group of young black and Asian kids in bright red and white sweatshirts roll down a grassy knoll dotted with live oak saplings. Their parents sat on park benches set up in a plaza near a tall bronze statue honoring someone of historical interest to the area, a wise-looking black man in a suit and tie with his right hand raised in a lecturing manner.

For thirty minutes, we observed the scene and enjoyed the serenity of a sunny winter day. The distant laughter of children and ruffling of the hedge at our backs were the only things that broke the silence when the cold wind blew our way.

Trans jammed another cigarette into his mouth, the fourth since they'd sat down. "Do you want one?" he offered.

"No, I don't smoke cigarettes," I said. "Thanks, though."

"I don't blame you. These things will probably kill me someday."

He sighed introspectively. "I smoke way too much, especially when there is nothing else to do."

We waited for a while without talking much. Then, from under a red-tiled terrace beyond a knoll with some old oak saplings, came a blast of live horn music, an off-key rendition of "When the Saints Go Marching In."

"So, do you work with Jan on his boats?" I asked.

"Hmm? Oh yes, I do," answered Trans, smiling mischievously.

"Y'all sand them down and repaint 'em and stuff?"

"No, we only drive the boats," said Trans, still smiling and referring to his uncle, "Oom" Jan (Dutch for uncle). "If one needed painting, Oom Jan would probably just purchase a new one."

"Oh. He did show me pictures of his house in Spain. It does look like he's pretty well off. I bet he's got a little money to throw around."

"Yes. Tons of it."

"So, y'all drive those boats around and what else?" I continued. "Go fishing?"

Trans drew deeply on his cigarette, squinting his perceptive emerald eyes, while French-inhaling thick bands of smoke from his mouth. He took another drag and puffed out a couple rings for good measure.

Trans perked up his thin blonde eyebrows and turned his attention away from me. Out of nowhere, Jan placed his hand on my shoulder, startling me to death. From his other hand dangled a blue and white sheet of crisp paper that had the

State of Louisiana Vital Records Registry stamp on the bottom, a mother pelican feeding a nest of her young with her blood.

"Look, Son," said Jan, pointing to the first line of type. "You were brought into the world as a van Rijn."

"What is this, my birth certificate?"

"Yes, and now we can get your passport made with your real name on it."

"James Harold Hendrik van Rijn? That must be Dutch, huh—Hendrik?"

"It comes from my father . . .your grandfather. His name was Hendrik van Rijn. Many of your cousins have the same middle name, after him."

After walking back to the car, we drove to the post office on Canal Street, where, after a partially fabricated family history, and a bit of coaxing from Jan, the clerk agreed to make up my passport based on my name at birth, and not what was on my driver's license. With four hours to kill before it would be ready, we strolled on up to the Hog Bar, owned by a friend of Jan's, sitting on the corner of Chartres and Bienville Streets in the French Quarter. We had some oysters on the half shell and a bunch of Heinekens before heading back to the post office to pick up my passport, and instead of heading home, we decided to stay the night in the Holiday Inn. I was starting to really enjoy myself.

11

THE NEXT DAY, we went back to Alabama to visit my adopted mother, Janet. On the way home, my Buick Regal backfired and began belching out thick gray smoke.

Jan looked over his left shoulder at Trans; they eyed each other anxiously. "Is your car OK?" asked Trans.

"I think after we visit your mother, we should get a rent-a-car," said Jan. "I *would* like to drive while I am here. It has been a very long time since I have been behind the wheel on an American road."

"Might be a good idea," I said. "My car ain't been the same since I took it to Florida the other day with my friend Jay."

I took them to J&J Grocery. "My adopted mama and daddy own this place," I said as we pulled up to the grocery store.

"They must have been robbed before," said Trans after he got out the car. "What makes you think that?" I asked.

"There are bars on the door and all the windows." Trans lit a cigarette and walked across the blacktop parking lot.

"Well, Prichard is just up the road from here and that's the ghetto. Better safe than sorry. Hey, that building next to the store is my adopted brother, Junior's, cabinet shop," I added. "I worked for Junior some when I was eighteen. I already had a job at the time, but the money I made with Junior is really how I afforded the car."

Trans took a drag on his cigarette and nodded his head while kicking at the sand and tiny white shells that made up the edge of the parking lot.

A cold gust rushed down from the overcast sky and rustled the high branches of a cluster of water oaks between the store and the cabinet shop. I looked at the gray clouds for a second and when I looked back down, there was a metallic blue station wagon parked against the dark yellow hitching post in front of the store. "Hey, Granny," I said.

"Hey, baby . . . run inside right quick and get me a paper from your daddy."

"Yes, Ma'am."

Jan was hugging Granny's neck when I came back outside and handed her a copy of the *Mobile Register*.

"Good to see you again, Jan," she said. "I gotta run by the post office now, but you and Jamie should come by the house if y'all get the time. I'll be there working on my dolls, same as always."

"OK, we'll try," Jan answered, smiling. We waved goodbye to her. "I have not seen Wendy's mother since I was picking cotton at the Parchman Prison in Mississippi," he said.

As I took Jan into the store, the jangling of the cowbell on the door announced our arrival. Daddy was feather-dusting a black and blue sign on a wall to the right of his front counter.

It read, *"Avenge Yourself. Live Long Enough to be a problem to your children."*

It felt weird introducing my daddy, Ray Cobb, to my birth father, Jan van Rijn, for the first time. I didn't want Daddy to think I didn't love him any less. I just wanted to get to know my father better and learn a new trade to support myself and my child on the way.

"Daddy," I said, "I want you to meet my biological father, Jan van Rijn. Jan, this is Jessie Ray Cobb."

Daddy took his hand with a good grip. "I know who he is, Jamie."

Two sets of bright blue eyes spoke a silent conversation.

"I've seen him in pictures, recognize the face. Nice to finally meet you, Jan," Daddy said.

"The pleasure is mine." Jan said.

"We just come from paying off my speeding tickets," I said, trying to sound casual. "Jan wanted my record to be clean before I went to Spain with him. He gave me a job working on his boats over there. We got my passport, too."

"Let's take a look," Daddy said.

I presented it to him, but when he saw my Dutch name, he seemed upset. "That's not your name," he said, looking at me and then at Jan.

"That was what was on my birth certificate," I said. "I guess they gotta go by that."

Jan nodded.

"Well, you're a grown man, Jamie," Daddy said. "You can do whatever you please. You don't need my approval."

"I know," I said, my shoulders sagging. "I just want to keep you and Mama informed, don't wanna pick up and go without telling y'all where I was gonna be."

"Your mama's some kind of upset with you right now for that very reason," Daddy said. "You know how she doesn't like to be kept in the dark about nothing. Why don't we go over and talk to her? We can let her in on exactly what's going on with you two."

Daddy left the store in the hands of his hired help and went through the rear exit to his pickup truck, a baby blue F-150 with a white top. We followed behind, heading a quarter-mile down Lott Road in the Regal and taking a right into a long blacktop driveway lined with big chunks of limestone; Daddy didn't like anybody driving on his grass.

The tan brick house had beige trim and a light brown shingled roof with black burglar bars on the doors and windows. An American flag hung off the front of the house, and below it a tiny pond that Daddy had dug himself and stocked with bream. A low hedge ran along the edges of the yard enclosed within a four-foot-high hurricane fence. There were two large rectangular flowerbeds at the front corners of the house, barren for the season.

When I got out of the car, I noticed that Daddy seemed disgusted at the sight of all that smoke pouring out the Regal. I guess I was a little hard on cars. Together, Jan, my Dutch cousin Trans, and I moved toward the back door. The sound of the squeaky hinges against the black iron burglar bars startled Mama. She was snoozing in her recliner. Daddy went in first, and we followed. My little nephew came running up to me with his sketch pad.

"Look, Uncle Jamie . . . look what I drew," he said, proudly holding his sketch pad above his head. "It's one of them camps next to Paw Paw's camp. I drew it from memory. What'cha think?"

"Wow, that's real good, Dusty . . . real good. I can tell how far your drawing has come since the last time I seen you. Just keep practicing and it'll keep getting better and better. It looks real good, though," I told him.

"Janet, we have company," Daddy said. "Jamie's father, Mr. van Rijn, wanted to have a talk with us about taking Jamie to Europe with him."

"Please, call me Jan," Jan insisted.

"Well, why don't the three of us all go sit at the kitchen table and talk some in the other room? You boys want a soda or something?" Mama said, pushing herself up from the recliner.

"I'm good," I said, and Trans shook his head.

"Is this the house you grew up in?" asked Trans as we sat on the leather couch. Dusty had relocated himself and his drawing to Mama's still-warm recliner.

"I was actually raised in another house down the way in Indian Hills, on Cheyenne Parkway," I replied. "My parents bought this a couple years back. It's a little bigger than the one we had before."

"This is much nicer than Wendy's home," said Trans as he ran his eyes up and down the polished knotty pine walls.

"Always Coca-Cola," sang an enormous green parrot perched in a five-foot brass cage in the corner of the living room.

"Look at this crazy bird," said Trans. He approached its cage and let out a friendly whistle. "Hello, pretty bird. What is your name?"

"Always Coca-Cola."

"Is that all it can say?" asked Trans with a laugh.

"Yeah, pretty much. Dusty there taught him that a long time ago," I said, "and he's kinda stuck on it."

"Whose little boy is that?" asked Trans.

"He's my sister's—my adopted sister, Lisa."

"Does she live here as well?"

"No. She took off with some dopehead to Pascagoula, Mississippi," I said quietly so Dusty couldn't hear, "and she left her three kids for my Mama and Daddy to raise."

"Oh," nodded Trans.

"Yeah, she ain't been the same since her and her second husband split up. He used to beat the hell outta her, and then she turned to drugs and really lost sight of her priorities."

"That is a shame," Trans sympathized.

The others were talking rather solemnly in the kitchen.

"So, what exactly is Jamie gonna be doing on your boats?" Mama asked Jan at the kitchen table. Then she said something else that I couldn't make out.

"Janet," said Daddy, "he's our company."

"I just want to know what our son's gonna be doing on the other side of the world—that's all," she said.

"Can I offer you a beer, Jan?" Daddy said. "I got Miller Lite if you drink that."

"Sure, I will have one," Jan said politely. "Mrs. Cobb, I am a different man than when I was much younger. I want to train Jamie to sail boats for my chartering company."

"I can tell you right now Jamie's not gonna go for that," she said. "He gets seasick just ridin' the streams in Jessie Ray's little aluminum boat."

"He ain't that bad off, Janet," my daddy said, chuckling. "I watched the boy ride a Jet Ski for hours down in Gulf Shores. You're just thinking of that one time. We all get spells of being seasick."

"I certainly have had mine," agreed Jan. "If the boats are not his thing, I have partial ownership of designer clothing outlets throughout Spain and France, in Paris and Barcelona, and I could find him a job in that. We import from every corner of the globe. It would be a good chance for him to experience what the world has to offer."

"You know he's got a kid on the way," Mama said. "Maybe I'm old-fashioned, but I don't believe in skipping out on priorities. Every child deserves to have his real father around."

"Jamie will be free to return whenever he wishes," said Jan. "I am not trying to keep him from his family. I want only to help him get onto his feet. I have been down and out before as well. Right now, he needs someone to motivate him and set his life in the right direction."

"We appreciate what you're doing for Jamie," said Daddy sincerely. "My wife is just overprotective. She's like this with

NO ONE KNOWS THE SON

all the kids."

"Yes, of course," said Jan. "A mother's natural instinct. I assure you, Mr. and Mrs. Cobb—I only want the best for my son. I would never place his life in any sort of danger."

"You can call me Ray," said Daddy. "Look, Jan, the last thing we want is to give you a hard time about Jamie."

Jan paused and assumed a humble tone. "I also came because I want to thank the both of you for raising my son to be a healthy and respectful man. He is very lucky there are people like you in this world."

Mama quickly interjected, "All right, but don't go and ruin all our hard work now. He is a good boy. But if he comes home an international fugitive, I'm sending him right back to you."

12

ON THURSDAY, DECEMBER 29, 1993, Mama, Daddy, my nephew, Dusty, and Tanya traveled to see me off at the airport. It was a little awkward, being such a big move to Europe. Tanya and I sat in back of the car. I hadn't seen much of her since she became pregnant. We'd been arguing over everything, it seemed. She was understandably upset about having to quit high school in her junior year. I don't think she felt ready to be a mother and I knew for a fact that I wasn't prepared for the responsibility of fatherhood. I had grown tired of hustling car detailing jobs and was spending most of my time getting high—trying to forget how complicated life was becoming.

"You know it's a little boy we're gonna be having," she said, passing a gentle hand over her bulging abdomen.

"That's good," I said.

"Yeah," she nodded.

"Yep, that baby's gonna be here before we know it," I said.

"Sure is."

"Yeah, sure is."

"I can't wait."

"Me neither." I assumed we both lied to save face—it seemed the right thing to say, since we didn't have a clue on how to raise a baby or what our future was together with little education and no money.

At the entrance to Gate 1 of the M. C. Farmer Terminal, I gave Tanya a hug and then Mama and Daddy, and then Dusty came jumping up for his. Before I knew it, it was time to board the plane." It was exciting, but a little scary too, since this was my first plane ride.

The plane climbed into the sky, and I was intrigued by the geometric shapes created by fields, roads, and property boundaries in the countryside seen from high above through a soft blue haze.

After a one-hour layover in Atlanta, we boarded a Delta flight bound for Amsterdam's Schiphol International Airport, where we landed early on New Year's Eve morning. Jan somehow tracked me down in the sprawling Dutch airport, near the luggage reclaim area. From Amsterdam, we headed north in a light green Volkswagen Jetta with a diesel engine. It was his get-around vehicle that he kept in Holland, he explained.

One of the first things I noticed about the Dutch countryside was that there wasn't a run-down house or unpainted fence anywhere to be seen. My father's people obviously took great pride in their nation's appearance, which I admired.

From the highway, I watched windmills turning like crazy as a storm blew in from the North Sea, dropping thick blankets of snow across cow pastures and on the orange-tiled roofs of rustic farmhouses that looked like they had been there for hundreds of years.

"The windmills pump water out of the ground and into the canals, to protect us from flooding," Jan explained. "Like New Orleans, much of our country lies below sea level, and we have had to reclaim much of our coastal regions from the North Sea."

I asked Jan to stop somewhere so I could call Mama and let her know that I had arrived safely. The cell phone he pulled out of his coat pocket was the first real one I'd ever seen. Mama had a car phone in her Chevy van, but it came with ten pounds of hardware. The device Jan flipped open and handed to me wasn't much bulkier than an iPhone.

Mama sounded drowsy. I realized that it was the middle of the night where she was, seven time zones away. She wished me a happy 1994, and I thought back to what she had said at the airport, about me coming home a different person.

Jan's hometown of Sneek was a two-hour drive from Amsterdam. It was a tidy village in a northern province of the country called Friesland. Though it didn't appear to have snowed there that day, I was surprised to see folks out walking and riding bikes against the bitterly cold gusts of wind.

Our first stop was a houseboat on the outskirts of Sneek where Trans lived with his unmarried parents and three siblings. That was where I had my first real taste of the guttural Dutch language. I sensed that it wasn't something I would be picking up on anytime soon. Trans and his siblings had been required to learn English in school, and they spoke the language fluently compared to their parents. Heck, their English was better than mine.

At first, I felt that I was an exhibit on display: Jan's long lost son that he rescued from the backwoods of Alabama. Trans's mother, an angel of a woman with dark red hair, eased my discomfort by sitting me down in the kitchen and serving me a bowl of tomato soup topped with grated Gouda cheese, some of the best food I've ever eaten. While enjoying my meal, I realized the unmistakable warmth that existed amongst everyone. It was obvious that they all spent a lot of time together and accepted one another for who they were. Although their language was foreign to me, I could tell that no hurtful gossip was passing between them, no character judgments being made. Sensing that everyone was sincerely grateful to be in the company of the people they loved most, I felt safe and welcomed.

Mindful of my jet lag, Jan showed me to a tiny bedroom after my meal.

After my nap, Jan couldn't wait to introduce me to his mama. *Oma* (Dutch for grandmother) lived in a freestanding home, which Jan explained was a big deal, with the high price of land in their country. The rest of Jan's siblings were there, as well as members from his stepfather's side of the family. Oma had remarried after Jan's daddy, Hendrik, passed away. I never heard much about my Dutch grandfather, except that he was a hotshot salesman. Jan boasted that his daddy could "sell the shoes right off a horse."

Oma served us tea and cheese, and then Jan led me into

the attic of her home to show me a chess set he had carved by hand while he was incarcerated in France. Sifting through a box of trinkets he'd sent Oma during his world travels, Jan told me how she'd beaten breast cancer several years earlier. I could tell that he had great respect for his mama and loved her very much.

13

WE TOOK FAMILY PICTURES in front of a red velvet curtain in Oma's living room, and afterwards I went off with Trans to the townhouse that he shared with his sister and her boyfriend. In his upstairs bedroom, Trans opened a drawer and passed me what looked like a bar of dark brown soap. "Moroccan hashish," he said after a minute. "It is like weed, but better."

"Is this legal here?" I asked my cousin, who shrugged nonchalantly.

He brought the bar of compacted marijuana resin downstairs. Trans knelt down in front of a marble coffee table and chopped a bit of his hashish up until it looked like a small pile of dark brown sugar. Then we passed a glass pipe between us, destroying our brain cells while listening to "Mr. Blue," a song by a popular Dutch artist who had lost his life to AIDS earlier that same year. Trans told me stories about growing up in Sneek and being a rebellious teenager. He and his friends would steal bicycles just to run them into the canals. Trans's daddy supported his family on a fisherman's wages and couldn't always afford to buy bicycles and other luxuries for his children.

My cousin's emerald eyes lit up as he described how things would change every time his Oom Jan came back to town. "He believes in the good life," Trans said. "Your father gave us a taste of how the other side lives: every night a different restaurant; shopping sprees; all the beer you could drink; and, of course, the use of his yachts. Oom Jan always has a new toy to show off."

Those were all material things, I wanted to say. I subconsciously passed my hand down over the fine black leather of my new jacket Jan had bought me and wondered if he was trying to buy my affection. *He can't make up for what he put me through, not with money,* a voice inside my head complained. But I was so stoned from the hashish that the flash of resentment was quickly drowned out by Trans's accented English.

"We all learned trades to keep busy while Oom Jan was serving his years in France," Trans continued.

"Why did he have to go to prison for so long?" I asked.

"It is complicated," Trans answered. "Maybe he will explain it to you one day. I can tell you that Oom Jan escaped from that prison for six months. In that time, he came to Holland and earned more money than he had made his entire life."

"Doing what?" I asked.

Trans shrugged, "I really do not know. He only gives me bits and pieces."

"Yeah, I know the feeling," I said.

"After all the trouble of breaking out, he turned himself in to the French government. Why a free and wealthy man would choose to return to prison . . . ?" my cousin trailed off, shrugging again. "Perhaps prison was suddenly a safe place to be."

We met back up with Jan that evening at the houseboat where Trans's parents lived. As midnight drew closer, fireworks could be heard throughout the community of floating homes. Trans's daddy, an old fisherman in a black stocking cap, took the opportunity to dig out a double-barrel shotgun and fire it into the sky. Everyone kind of froze where they stood and gasped at the thundering report.

Trans must have picked up on the unimpressed look on my face. He walked up and patted my shoulder, smiling broadly. "Everyone in America has a gun, yes? Well, Cousin, in Holland they are not as common," he explained.

"Hell, that's a good thing," I said. "I wish there were fewer guns in America, too. A couple of years ago, I had a sawed-off pointed at my head by some guys robbing the place I worked."

Close to midnight, I found myself standing in a big crowd made up of my newfound Dutch family. We were crammed inside a club near Sneek's downtown district, the Centrum. For hours, I'd been enjoying free drinks and special attention from strangers just for being Jan's son. I could feel love and happiness emanating from everyone around me. I should also mention that a short time earlier, I had swallowed a big purple pill that Trans had given me, which he said would knock out the jet lag I was still dealing with from my flight that morning.

Growing weak in the knees, even more so than the night Aunt Wendy slipped me a Valium, I listened to the crowd count off the last ten seconds of 1993 in their language.

"Vijf, vier, drie, twee, één," the crowd chanted.

Grinning like a joker, I was startled by what sounded like a motorcycle revving up inside the bar. The crowd parted for Jan, who made his way over to me and said, with a tear of joy in his eye, "Son, I have waited twenty years to have you at my side."

He threw his arm around me and shouted what must have been Dutch for "Happy New Year!" as his favorite song, "I'd Do Anything for Love," continued to play. For the first time in a long time, I felt that I was someplace I truly belonged: with my biological father, surrounded by droves of people who absolutely adored us.

14

THE MORNING OF JANUARY 1, 1994, I woke up on a steel cot in the tiny upstairs guestroom of Trans's townhouse in Sneek. I stood and bumped my head on a low, slanted ceiling. My brain was throbbing from a massive hangover. In a bathroom across the hall, I found my clothes from the night before folded and stacked neatly on the counter.

A hot shower refreshed my memory of our family's New Year celebration. We had ended up at a snack bar, a Dutch fast food restaurant run by Jan's only brother. I was feeling sick from too many beers, and Trans had given me a folded slip of paper containing a fine pink powder to swallow, a form of methamphetamine. Then, I'd listened to more of his outlandish stories, of robbing a cheese factory when he was a teenager, and of the reason why he wore gold loops on his ears. Apparently, my conniving first cousin considered himself a modern-day pirate.

"It is believed that piercing your ears improves your eyesight," I remembered him saying. "This makes it easier to spot enemy ships at a distance. And if your own ship goes down and your body washes ashore, whoever finds you there can use your gold to pay for a decent burial."

Trans was something else. He had introduced me to three new drugs all in a few hours, and their aftereffects had me on edge. As I was getting dressed, however, I glanced out a window at the auburn brick street below, and the beautiful view settled my nerves. It was a bright, sunny day in the village of Sneek, and the street was crowded with people of every walk of life, riding bicycles. I rolled the window open and an invigorating breeze whipped through the bathroom. A church bell chiming out the hour intermingled with the bells of passing cyclists gleefully exchanging greetings of *"Hoi!"* My problems in Alabama were a world away, and I felt that this was an opportunity for a fresh start.

15

THE NEXT MORNING, our flight touched down at Málaga International Airport. I had arrived with Jan and Trans.

The lines leading to the friendly Spanish customs officials were fast moving, and it wasn't long before we spotted Jan's maid, Abby, who arrived to pick us up in a black Mercedes Benz with dark yellow "Nederlands" plates. A stunning brunette in her late twenties, she had long silky hair and almond-shaped blue eyes.

It was sunny when we got on the highway. Jan handed me a cell phone as they approached the outer limits of the city.

"Hold on to it," said Jan. "You can use it to call your people in Alabama if you ever feel homesick."

"Oh . . . thanks."

"You are welcome, Son."

We traveled along the coast for a while until we reached a supermarket. It was interesting to watch the beautiful Spanish ladies, wearing plastic gloves, and handing out fresh fruit as the customers entered the grocery store. I was happy to hear Jan suggest that the rest of us go inside.

"I have to wait for a friend here," he said. "Go on in and shop and I'll be in to join you very soon."

Over a year later, I learned the real reason for this stop at the grocery store: he was waiting for a connection to drop him off a bag full of hot phones and night-vision goggles.

After shopping for groceries, we left for Jan's house, which was situated about six hundred feet above sea level on top of a hill at the end of a road in Málaga.

Abby idled around a shallow goldfish pond in the center of the courtyard, fed from one end by a stone cherub fountain. A passing cloud in the azure sky set off the vivid terracotta tiles atop the second story of Jan's villa, impressive in design and stature. The exterior walls of the structure were stucco and finished in a shade of pastel yellow—the color of brimstone—with a surrounding stone brick fence.

We followed the driveway to the left where it dipped under the first floor of the house to the entrance of a narrow shotgun garage. This allowed two cars to be parked bumper to bumper. Everyone grabbed their luggage from the trunk of the Mercedes, walked to the end of the garage, and into the door of the house.

A dark hallway with grayish marble floors lit by gold-plated wall fixtures brought us to a grand flight of stairs also of gray marble with occasional swirls of pearl white and the deepest black imaginable. Trans and Abby continued further down the curving subterranean hall and disappeared through a doorway on their right.

Jan and I climbed the stairwell that led into the living

room on the first level of the house. It was a spacious room with high ceilings, ivory-colored walls, and more Italian marble flooring in the form of a path that led us to two fat columns on either end of an archway. We passed beneath the archway and walked toward a pair of large windows facing the sea. In front of one window, at a round table to the far right-hand side of the living room, a man sat eating whole baked tomatoes from a wooden bowl.

The man had dark brown hair greased and combed straight back over his scalp, and I guessed he was around my age. He wore gold loops on both ears, a handlebar mustache, and said very little. Despite his economy with words, he seemed friendly and maintained a constant, genuine smile.

"Jamie, I would like you to meet Trans's younger sister's boyfriend, Zonder." said Jan. "Zonder, this is my son from America that I have told you so much about."

"P-pleased to m-meet you, Jamie," Zonder said, as he shook my hand.

"Come with me, Son," said Jan, leading me away. "I will show you where you will be sleeping."

We climbed another flight of stairs. The second story had ceilings as high as the living room, and at the top the stairs, an oval stained glass window that cast blue-, red-, and orange-tinted sunlight onto the white banisters. Like the other floors in the house, this one was laid with massive 22" × 22" slabs of exquisite Italian marble. No carpets or throw rugs anywhere—just cold, hard, polished stone. "Here is your bathroom," said Jan, gripping a brass knob to his right past the landing. "It is connected to your room only, but you have to share it with Trans," he said, thumbing over his shoulder at the single doorway on the other side of the hallway. I saw an open door on the east wing of the place, which had floors of a much lighter color than any of the others I'd seen. To my left, at the other end of the hallway, was the door to Jan's room. Trans stayed in the middle room between us, which had a view of the sea. Jan opened the arched mahogany door nearest the top of the stairwell to the right. As I stepped in, it took me a couple of seconds to adjust to the sudden brightness.

"And here is your room, Son," he said.

The room was not decorated. An easel stood in the middle of the floor with an acrylic painting of two blonde boys and a man who looked very much like Jan. "This you?" I asked.

"It is of me, with you and Donny," he said. "This is what I did with those years in prison, Son. I painted scenes that were in my imagination. Here, you, Donny, and I are all in the Caribbean, enjoying a wonderful time."

I could see from the beautiful image, and the look on his face, that he meant what he said. "Them prisons ain't too nice, huh?" I said.

"I never want to go back there again" was all he said before pointing out, "The view from your balcony is nice, and the bed is comfortable. Make yourself at home. I am a bit worn out from the flight. I believe I will spend a little while soaking in my Jacuzzi."

"All right," I laughed. "Do I have one of them in my bathroom, too?"

"No . . . only in mine. You are certainly welcome to use it on nights when I am not here. It is quite roomy; I am sure you could fit at least a couple of women in there with you. I have before," he smiled.

I took a shower and changed my clothes. Before long, I began to smell the distinct aroma of fresh-baked bread seeping under my mahogany door. I traced the scent down to the round table in front of the bay window in the living room. Just behind the dining area was the arched doorway to the kitchen through which Abby carried plates and silverware, arranging them around Jan, sipping on a glass of red wine.

He appeared to be deep in thought, rolling the stained end of a cork from a freshly opened bottle between his thick fingers. "Abby prepared a special lunch for us, Son. Roasted duck and a loaf of her special bread that she bakes so well," said Jan.

"I smelled it from way upstairs," I said. "It smells great." Beyond Jan, through a pair of French doors, I noticed a white stone terrace and swimming pool, within view from the balcony of my room.

"Have a seat, Jamie. The others will be down shortly, I am sure. Your bedroom, is it to your liking?" asked Jan.

"Are you kidding me? I've been living in a dumpy old trailer since I was eighteen with holes in the floors. I feel like I'm staying in a five-star hotel, or in some kind of high-class vacation resort."

"I am glad that you like my house." He closed his eyes, inhaling the scent of the wine. "I wanted to inform you, Son, that we still have more than a week before our first job. I know you are anxious to begin working, but I think you will find that life here on the coast can be quite enjoyable, even this time of the year when the water is cold and the beaches are mostly empty."

That night we celebrated my arrival. Jan took Trans, Zonder, and me to visit one of his business associates, a Jewish man named Alberto. His place resembled a fancy brothel. Decorated with red lights and carved out of the side of a mountain, it was the most unusual place I'd seen so far.

After we'd been there for a while, another of Jan's business associates, Christianne, showed up. He and Alberto had served time together with Jan in France. In fact, they were fresh out of the French prison when they received the "seed money," I guess you'd call it, for their current business. When they were released, they stole a Mercedes in Paris that happened to have the handy sum of $100,000 worth of French Francs in its trunk. Alberto moved to Morocco and learned the language, hoping to get a connection with the royal family. In the meantime, Christianne set up the boats and locations in Spain, while waiting for my father to get out of the French prison to do their first job.

16

Later that first week in January 1994

ONE AFTERNOON, WHILE I was in the kitchen with Abby, showing her how we fry chicken in Alabama, Jan asked me to join him on the balcony.

"So, Son, are you ready to work?"

"Am I ever," I said.

"Good. Well let me tell you a little bit about the job."

I braced myself. By this time, I knew it would be unlikely that I'd be sanding and painting boats. And of course I'd heard some of the rumblings about illegal activities from the start.

"So what will I have to do?" I asked.

"You're going to have to carry some packages about 40 meters' distance," he began. "They're very heavy, and it's important that they be carried very, very quickly. You will unload them on the beach and put them into their transport car, a Range Rover."

I sat waiting for him to tell me the rest, until it occurred to me that there wasn't any "rest." "Is that it?" I asked.

"That's about it," he said. I could tell he was amused. "It shouldn't take any longer than twenty minutes. And you will be working with Zonder. He will show you what to do."

"Well that sounds pretty easy," I said. "I guess you just sort of start me out slowly."

"It is important work, Jamie. I will pay you very well for it. In fact, you'll be getting more in that twenty minutes than you would make in a whole year at your American job."

I could see him watching me tensely. I guess he thought I might be getting ready to back out of the deal. A flood of thoughts rushed through my head, until finally I asked, "It ain't gonna be no dead bodies we're carrying is it?"

That must have struck a chord, as he just burst out laughing. "No, Son," he said, taking a breath, "no dead bodies."

Within a week, Abby had returned to Israel.

I was briefed a little more about the actual job, and on the appointed day, the four of us—Zonder, Trans, Jan, and I—took a ride by car out to Gibraltar to meet Christianne at Sheppard's Marina.

"You understand what you are to do?" Jan asked me quietly.

"Yeah, I think I got it."

"All right then, Son, do a good job. There will be a good payoff for you."

Soon after, Jan and Christianne headed out in an all-black thirty-meter Zodiac, fired with a pair of Yamaha 225 outboard motors. It was quite a sight to see.

"OK, let's go," said Trans. "Let's go and catch the view from the top of the Rock of Gibraltar."

Trans drove Zonder and me halfway up the fourteen-hundred-foot-high limestone formation known as the Rock. We parked the car near a lookout point, and I was in complete awe of the view. Standing on English soil, I could see the Spanish coast over my shoulder and the outline of the Rif mountains in Africa across the strait. The stretch of water separating Europe and Africa was dotted with super-tankers and bathed in late-afternoon sunlight, the unique richness of which has never been matched in my memory. *This is a long way from home and Big Creek Lake, I thought.*

We used viewfinders to observe a small fleet of suspicious-looking boats zip around the southern tip of the Rock below. It was nearly dark by then and I noticed that none of the vessels were using lights of any kind. Jan's Zodiac boat was the only one speeding toward the Moroccan coast with only its wake visible.

We drove back home to my father's villa to wait on the call for the shipment to come in, when I saw an unusual sight—a bunch of guys on the beach looked like they were playing catch with boxes from a beach craft.

"What the heck is that?" I asked Trans.

"Oh, those guys!" he laughed. "Look how excited they are! They're catching cigarettes that haven't been taxed to sell privately. See them running? Can you imagine using all that effort for what that sale might bring in, if you're lucky?" He laughed again.

"I guess it depends on how many are in there and how much they go for," I said. "I bet you could pull in a few hundred bucks easy on something like that."

Trans shook his head. "I bet you could."

I believed I should be making at least that much on my first job. I'd been in Spain for some time and I hadn't earned a dime. I wasn't banking on a year's salary at the car wash, but I expected to earn about $400, or maybe even $500.

Back at the villa, we waited for Jan's call, which could come at any time. We stayed up all night as instructed, amusing ourselves by playing with the night-vision goggles. In any case, it was good to practice with the gear, since we knew we might need to use it one day.

Just before daybreak, Trans received the beeps he was waiting for on the two-way radio.

"Did you hear?" Trans yelled at Zonder, emerging from the garage. "Let's move then." We jumped into the rented white Opel.

The dark streets winding through the foothills rarely saw much traffic, but they were especially deserted at that time in the early morning. At the coastal road, Trans followed Zonder eastward and after a mile he pointed inland and said to me, "This white building coming up to our left, it is a police station. All night they are out patrolling, but at a quarter to six every morning they return to the station to change shifts. The new shift does not usually leave until 6:15 or 6:20. This is the timeframe we have to work with."

"OK," I said.

Trans pulled onto the shoulder of a large roundabout, while Zonder continued driving for another block before turning into the front parking lot of a beach hotel situated next to a casino. Two vehicles idled by as we remained parked on the shoulder, but this didn't seem to bother Trans. The second vehicle was an old beat-up Toyota van—dark maroon with an ugly front grill. Its brake lights flashed briefly upon passing the Opel, before making a left turn a hundred yards further along and driving out of sight.

"Do you have any final questions, Cousin?" Trans asked.

"Uh, I don't think so. All I gotta do is go down on the beach and tell y'all when I spot the Zodiac, right?"

"Yes, that is it. And keep an eye out for headlights. Let us know if you see anyone on the shore except for Zonder."

"Gotcha."

"Go quickly now before other cars pass."

My jogging pants were quite baggy and the front pockets big enough to accommodate my radio and compact binoculars, though I had to cram them in and pull the drawstring tight around my waist to move comfortably. I headed along the guardrails and jogged to the end of the roundabout to arrive at the top of a brick stairway a few yards beyond. I took the steps slowly and carefully, one at a time—not wanting to fall and damage my father's equipment, which I figured had to be worth a small fortune. Hanging over the foot of the stairway was a thorn bush. I held my hands out and reared my head back to avoid getting my face scratched.

The incessant crashing of waves was the only sound as

I walked further into the pitch darkness, away from the red lights of the casino. Sporadically peering over my shoulder, I used my binoculars to locate the center of the cove where the waterline came to a point, as if the sea were saying to me, *Right here. This is where you need to be.*

Just beyond the spot, against the cliff side, was a beach bar, a chiringuito, that was elevated off the sand. The bottom limits of its tile roof (which I assumed was terracotta-colored, although everything appeared green to me through the filter of the binoculars), were lined with tall windows on all sides. I wondered if the owners of the little bar had any notion of the activities that occurred in their backyard. I stooped down and began to scan the sea from east to west—from the surf to the horizon in every direction, intently searching the turbulent waves for the Zodiac.

After twenty minutes, my legs started to ache and I developed a crick in my neck, so I took a break.

Then, from the radio in my front pocket I heard in English, *"They are getting very close. He can see the lights on the casino."* In addition to the bright-red-glowing vertical rows of letters spelling out "CASINO MAR," the top of the casino housed a lightning rod with a blood-violet pulse on the end. On a night as clear and dark as this, it could be seen from miles away on the open water.

Cutting through great rolling waves in the distance, the Zodiac bobbed into view, sitting low in the black water and moving fast on a tailwind.

"I can see 'em, I can see 'em," I excitedly communicated

to Trans.

A surge of adrenaline began to circulate through my body. My heart raced and my pupils dilated, causing my vision to become extraordinarily clear. Blips of low chatter like grunts cut occasionally through the steady hum of static and feedback on my two-way radio. I heard a droning noise in the distance, gradually growing louder, emanating from the chiringuito to my left. For several seconds I fought an urge to run to the brick stairs and back up the cliff. I checked out the shoreline and exhaled with relief when I saw what I thought must surely be Zonder's Range Rover approaching with its headlights off.

"That's what that night vision's for in that truck," I whispered to myself.

Zonder parked the Range Rover near to the water, facing the cliff side, and I hopped up to meet him. I tossed my radio and binoculars on the passenger seat when Zonder said politely, "Help me with this, J-Jamie," while tugging at a massive roll of chicken wire within the vehicle.

We unrolled it as a means to prevent the vehicle sinking into the sand. Zonder backed the Range Rover up and straightened out the tires until all four of them sat completely on the wire. Coming closer over the roar of the waves, I heard motors churning through the water. Zonder stared through the dark surf, his eyes squinting, then immediately stripped down to his wet suit and yanked two tanks of gasoline from the Range Rover. "Get the other two and follow me!" he said, like a battle cry.

I hastily pulled off my jogging suit and grabbed the remaining metal containers. An instant later, a powerful wave broke against my legs. Inside my rubber shoes, my feet rapidly grew numb in the icy salt water that splashed up and stung my eyes. Jan killed the motors and I watched him kick them up on the back of the Zodiac.

Though it was very dark, my eyesight had adjusted well and I could see that Jan and Christianne wore headsets and infrared goggles with long metal eyepieces pushed up high on their brows.

Waist deep in water, we handed the tanks of fuel to Jan. Christianne jumped into the water and pulled the Zodiac closer to shore by its thick docking rope.

Jan began dumping out coarse, brown burlap sacks—like the "croaker sacks" that Mama and Daddy would bring home full of oysters when I was a kid. They'd been stacked wall to wall in the vessel like bulky stone blocks, but now they were quickly disappearing under the black surface of the water.

"Get the packages out, Son!" Jan commanded. *"Get the packages out!"*

I lunged into the Zodiac, straining my lower back to reach the ones at the bottom, as I frantically hauled sack after sack clear of the walls of the vessel.

Zonder began dragging them ashore two at a time, and after the entire load was off, I followed suit.

Each burlap sack was wrapped in a pair of hemp ropes that intersected at ninety-degree angles dead center on top. Here, the end of one of the ropes held the croaker sack closed like a twist tie on a trash bag.

The sacks were cumbersome and I fell repeatedly while trying move fast under orders from Jan. I tripped over my own feet and inhaled painful gulps of the freezing water when it slapped my face. Mercifully, the chicken wire prevented my feet from sinking deeper into the wet sand as I toted the cargo to the Range Rover.

By my second trip into the waves, Jan and Christianne were out of sight, Zonder having shoved the Zodiac off into deeper water.

After my fourth trip (I didn't think I had the energy for a fifth), my hands were chapped and starting to bleed from the makeshift rope handles.

Zonder did a quick hand count of the burlap sacks spread across the sand. "There are still a c-couple missing," he said. "They must be s-somewhere on the b-bottom. We have to f-find them quick."

We splashed back out into the shore break near where the drop had been made and stumbled into the last two. They were now even heavier, since water had seeped in through the fibers.

Zonder immediately began loading up the Range Rover.

Having regained my senses, I estimated that each burlap sack had weighed at least eighty pounds and each trip inland required me to drag the equivalent of my own weight. It took all of my willpower and energy to keep pace with Zonder, who labored like a workhorse. With the tail end of the vehicle now suspended only eight inches off the sand, I was sure

Zonder would bog down.

Taking advantage of the initial support of the chicken wire, Zonder shifted into four-wheel drive and pushed the pedal to the floor. The Range Rover sunk a little but the burst of power got him safely away from the water and onto hard-packed sand. He stopped and raced back to help me roll up the chicken wire.

"Run up f-fast now and m-meet Trans," instructed Zonder after we'd jammed it in place atop the cargo.

I set off on a dead sprint, my legs carrying me quickly to the foot of the stairs where the thorn bushes scratched my face, but with the adrenaline pumping, I didn't feel a thing. I stopped for breath at the top on the salmon-colored sidewalk where the white Opel crept up to me, ready to head for Jan's villa.

"Fifteen minutes past six," Trans said as I climbed in. "Right on time. How did things go down there?"

"Good, I guess. For a minute we thought we lost some of them bags in the water, but we found 'em all, I'm pretty sure."

"Let us hope that you did."

Trans slowed to a crawl and steered to the far right, letting the Range Rover move ahead, its gears straining and creating a racket. We tailed it closely as the first traces of dawn crept up on the horizon, turning the bottom limits a plum violet that gave way to a hard navy blue, blotting out the stars in the moonless sky.

Halfway to Jan's house, we came to a steep leg on the road, and I was thinking how much I hated that part of the track back up the mountain—something I'd experienced on my cycling trips along the coast. After this point, every sizable bump and pothole Zonder tried to avoid sent the tail end of the Range Rover crashing down against the road, a shower of sparks accompanying each occurrence, raining behind the vehicle like the wake of a gigantic bottle rocket.

"Damn, man," I exclaimed, "that stuff weighs a ton."

"Yes . . . if all the packages are there. I hope the truck does not stop on him. We would have to leave it behind," said Trans.

"Hey, I know we're almost to the house now, but what would Zonder have done if a cop tried pulling him over with everything that he's hauling?"

"I would ram this car into the police truck to give Zonder a chance to get away on foot."

"Hmph. That's a hell of a plan. And what about us?"

"What *about us?"* Trans reached into the glove compartment to retrieve a sipping-size bottle of Jack Daniel's. He took a long pull and then passed it to me.

"Officer, I have been drinking all day and I did not see you stopped there in the road. Please do not arrest me. I have never done anything like this in my entire life. I am only a simple Dutch boy from the country, on a holiday here in Spain with my Uncle Jan."

"All right, they might buy that."

"This is a rental car. It is not stolen, and we would not be in any serious trouble. I paid the extra pesetas for the insurance, and it was rented under my name."

"That's good to know."

From the second I stepped out of the Opel in the garage, I could smell the strain that had been put on the Range Rover, the heavy scent of burnt oil evaporating off a hot engine. It reminded me of my first Buick Regal, which would leak two quarts a week. Zonder hopped out blubbering in Dutch and waving his arms around in a complaining manner.

"What's the matter?" I asked.

"Zonder is very stressed out because he did not think he would make it all the way up here," said Trans. "He believes we will need more than one truck for the next time."

"The next time?"

Trans and Zonder discussed the situation, while I just hung around feeling spaced out.

"There is a bathroom back there where you can change your clothes after Zonder gets out," said Trans, startling me. "And in the closet by the shower there is a pair of shorts you could wear to go to your room upstairs. Just leave your wetsuit and shoes in the bathtub; the maid will take care of them when she returns tomorrow."

"She will, huh? That's real nice."

"You are bleeding," noticed Trans, staring at my hands hanging at my sides.

"Man, all that crap was heavy, and them ropes was all there was to grab 'em with," I said, wiping my palms on the front of my jogging pants, as I'd been doing since we left the beach.

A ringing came from Trans's jacket. He pulled out his cell

phone and held a very brief conversation in Dutch. The person on the other end was screaming; I figured it was Jan hollering over the noise of the outboard motors.

Trans finished the call and looked at me. "We need to head to Gibraltar so we can be there to pick up your father up when he arrives," he said, "but first . . ." He walked toward a hacksaw hanging beside a rubber-handled axe and removed it from the wall.

Trans opened the Range Rover and pulled down one of the bulky burlap sacks that had been stacked two high. He tried working out the knot in the rope but soon grew impatient and sawed through it to access the gray tape-wrapped bricks inside. He laid a few of them on the tailgate, and I could see they had little uniformity. Some were rectangular and equivalent in size to about two fresh bars of soap; others were shaped more like flying saucers.

Trans hopped up on the tailgate, laid his knee upon the largest brick and sawed it through the middle.

"Nobody will miss this little bit," he said, showing me the black hashish on the inside. "We just have to be sure this bag goes with Big Man's share." That was the nickname of Popeye McLean. "Jan will sell him half of this load."

"Why they call that guy Big Man? Is he some kind of mafia boss or something?"

"I don't know," shrugged Trans. "Who is the judge of these sorts of things? All I know about McLean is that he drives a Rolls Royce, and he has a lot of people working under him."

Inside the villa, Trans removed the video recorder and rows of VHS tapes from the entertainment center, making space to hide the hash he had just stolen. "I will slice it up later," he said when he was done. "We really need to get to Gibraltar now. Someone should stay behind to watch the house. Do you mind, Cousin? We will only be gone a few hours."

"A few hours? Naw, I don't mind."

"You will be OK, yes?" Trans asked. "You look a little pale."

"Uh-huh," I said. "Yeah, sure. I'm fine. Y'all go on ahead, man. I'll see y'all in a while. I'll probably take me a hot shower, then kick my feet up and watch some TV. My back's a little sore from all that heavy lifting."

"There will be more to come," warned Trans. "There are cotton balls and peroxide in the medicine cabinet of the upstairs bathroom. You should clean your hands so that they do not become infected."

Zonder came in, fresh from a shower.

"It is time to go, Zonder," said Trans. "Jamie is going to stay behind and guard the load."

A few minutes after they left, I started wondering how safe it was for me to be there alone with two thousand pounds of high-quality hash. People had been killed for much less. My heart started pounding, as I imagined all kinds of villains lurking about the villa with machine guns. I made the rounds, slamming down the black iron bars over the downstairs windows and doors.

Once I'd finished locking down the house and I had

calmed down, a combination of fear and a sense of foolishness swept through me. I wondered if what I had just done—helping to move a ton of hashish from Africa to Europe—was a sin that could ever be forgiven.

17

I FELL ASLEEP LONG enough to be startled awake by helicopters flying overhead. Why were they here? To haul me into some foreign jail? To the same French prison Jan had spoken about?

After a while, Jan arrived back with the others.

"Man, what was all that air traffic overhead?" I asked. "Did somebody tip them off?"

Jan looked at Trans. "You need to relax, Son," he said. "Helicopters are always flying overhead—this is a resort area. They are almost as common as automobiles!"

I decided I must get a grip. I had smuggled some hash, but as far as I could tell, nobody knew anything and everything had gone as planned.

Hard work helped to focus my mind away from any doubts. Jan told us to take half of the hash out of the Range Rover and store it in the spare bedroom downstairs. Next, we headed out to the supermarket that we'd visited on my arrival. Zonder drove the Range Rover with me, Jan, and Trans following in the Opel.

Zonder parked the Range Rover near the supermarket and, after we pulled up next to him, the four of us walked up a nearby side street to a café.

"We'd like a table outside," Jan said.

It was a pleasant enough day, so we sat down and had a nice brunch. Before long, Jan received a call. I couldn't hear everything that was said, but I could tell the guy had an English accent.

Shortly, a white Range Rover pulled up beside us.

"Excuse me. I have some business to take care of. I will join you later, all right?" Jan said.

As soon as he left, Trans looked at me. "So, do you know who that was?" he asked.

"Sounded like an English guy," I said.

"That was Popeye McLean. He's the boss of the English, I guess you'd call it. He buys Jan's share of the Moroccan stuff, takes it straight to Great Britain."

"Pretty handy guy to have around," I said.

Trans didn't find that funny. I was playing everything down—the only way I could handle all of the rapid changes happening in my life. Since we'd done the job, I'd worked out that I was receiving roughly the equivalent of $40,000 for my twenty minutes of work—$2,000 a minute! I guess this radical turnaround in lifestyle and income was taking its toll on me. Of course, I had no idea just how much of a toll until years later when I looked back. At the time, I seemed to simultaneously embrace and reject the notion of receiving so much money for apparently little effort.

Before long, Jan returned. "Listen, Jamie, would you like to make an extra $10,000?" he asked.

"Ten thousand dollars?" I replied nervously. I had visions of having to carry another huge load of packages that night. I didn't feel ready for it.

Jan must have read my mind—he chuckled quietly and said, "Nothing strenuous. We simply need someone to drive the empty Range Rover back home."

My reservations must have been clear, "Ain't that a stolen vehicle?" I asked.

"Yes, it is stolen, but its papers are straight. And it has nothing in it—all of the packages have been removed."

I pondered on the prospect for a moment and figured, *Heck everything went right the first time, so why not go for the gold?* "Sure," I said. "Just drive it on home?"

"Yes," Jan replied. "Trans and Zonder and I will follow you in the Opel."

When I got into the Range Rover, it wasn't sagging as low to the ground, but it was still loaded with something. They looked like huge duffel bags. Nevertheless, I figured, *OK, didn't know about that, but I guess I'll handle it.*

The ride was easy; I picked the Range Rover up as planned and drove it back to Jan's villa. When I pulled into the driveway, Alberto and Christianne were seated nearby in a maroon Toyota van. One of the duffel bags went straight to them. It was jam packed with English pounds.

We loaded their share of the Moroccan hash into the Toyota and they drove off. I was glad not to be in that van, as

I'd had enough adrenaline for one day.

"Why don't we step inside a minute," Jan said as the van traveled out of sight. "I'd like to pay you for your hard work."

I just stood there overwhelmed, accepting £30,000 sterling, the equivalent of $50,000 for all my "hard work." As soon as Jan turned his attention to something else, I went upstairs and stashed the pile under my mattress.

We took it easy that night, and slept late next morning. But Trans and Zonder were up early. They were ready to hit the stores.

"Jamie, you will love Main Street in Gibraltar. And now you can afford some nice things. Let's head out and hit the gold shops."

"Let Jamie decide for himself what he wants to do with his money," Jan said. "But if I were you, Jamie, I would invest in at least a little gold. You never know when you might need it."

"Makes sense to me," I said. "Besides, I don't have any other plans for today."

Zonder and Trans laughed. I didn't get it, but I joined in anyway. "OK, when do we go?"

We spent a good deal of time in Gibraltar. There were some decent shops in the area, and if like me, you had money for the first time in your life, you were inclined to buy whatever you wanted. There was a yellow, red, and white gold chain with a dog tag that caught my eye.

"Could you inscribe that with James van H. H. Rijn?" I asked.

"Sure," the shopkeeper answered, and went ahead and did it on the spot.

I bought another gold chain, and then treated myself to a nice watch. Paw Paw Mizell had always owned a nice one, and I thought that was as good a time as any to treat myself. I bought a fine gold Cartier.

We moved on to another place, where I picked out a wedding band and diamond ring for Tanya. I still had no idea what I was going to do about that situation, but in my heart I felt that buying the gift was the right thing, and it made me feel good. It also made me feel good to get some things for my mama and daddy. I bought Mama an emerald ring and Daddy a gold Krugerrand coin.

I went home that night feeling less guilty about how I'd earned all of that loot. In hindsight, I guess that's what you sometimes do when you're feeling guilty—you try to buy it off with presents and what you think are possessions of value. All I knew was that, at that moment, I didn't feel quite as bad about the way I made my living.

18

January 24, 1994

A FEW NIGHTS LATER, Jan invited his girlfriend, Sandra, for
a night out, along with his friend Leo, and Leo's wife, Inga,
who happened to be Sandra's sister. We spent the early morning hours in an all-night dance club on the beach that had
an enormous tropical fish aquarium embedded in the ceiling.
Just before we left, I stepped outside to answer a call Mama
made to my pirated cell phone. She informed me that Tanya
had gone into labor and was having some complications.

As Jan drove us up to his villa, Mama called again. "Everything turned out just fine, Jamie," she told me. "She had a
little boy, as healthy as can be. He was born with your hands,
so Tanya gave him your name: James Kyle Cobb."

The joy I experienced at that moment overpowered all the
empty feelings that had been plaguing me. I wanted to up and
leave right then, but I'd been irresponsible and selfish with
the money I had earned on the first job.

One more job, I told myself. *Just one more job, then I can go
home where I belong.*

That night, on the mattress concealing what remained of my dirty money, I tossed and turned as a number of unsettling thoughts raced through my mind.

I have a little boy back home now, and I'm here in Europe smuggling drugs. Am I following in my father's footsteps? Is this how my own son is going to come to know me: as a drug runner? What kind of an impact will all of this have on his life?

I considered the unusual sequence of events that led up to my acceptance of my father's offer to travel to Europe with him.

What other choice did I have? I asked myself. *Was this my fate?*

19

IT SEEMS THAT often in life, you find a little bit of something turning sour before the rest is affected. It's like opening the refrigerator door and seeing a bit of blue on that cheddar cheese, and you know you don't have much time before it all goes bad. Well, I guess when you're experienced, or older, or just plain smart, you pay attention to that little bit of something, adjust your sails, and tack away in another direction. But sometimes, you do things for reasons you don't understand, and, in my case, I decided to ignore what I sensed, and hoped the little things I noticed were insignificant bumps in the road. They'd go away in time.

But that's not what happened.

One day in late January, the regular suspects, me, Jan, Trans, and Zonder, went to the Fuengirola Marina to see Jan's "cigarette boat," which is a name for an extremely powerful lightweight cruiser. The only reason such a boat was ever made was for the purpose of smuggling, but who could prove it? Jan's boat, the *Fine Wine III* was a sleek vessel, a typical cigarette boat, very classy, very beautiful.

"It's a fine-looking boat, Jan," I said.

Zonder and Trans thought that was funny. Half the time, I wasn't sure what they were laughing about, but I figured, *Hey, that's just foreigners for you—you don't speak their language, you're gonna get that.*

"Thank you, Son," Jan said. "It is one of the fastest vessels for its size and weight that can be found."

"Did you give it that name?" I asked.

"Yes," Jan said. "Although it is technically the property of Alberto, I was the one who christened it."

"Oh, so it ain't yours?"

"No, it is mine, but I like to put some of my possessions in other people's names," he said. "It keeps things simple for me, and it makes them happy."

"Sounds reasonable to me," I said

Generally, the weather was sunny and warm in the area, and this particular day was no exception: fine and sunny. We drove home enjoying the day with some good conversation and laughs as usual. When we arrived at the house, I noticed Sandra's silver Saab parked outside.

"Hey, looks like your girlfriend's come for a visit," I said to Jan.

He turned to Zonder and Trans and spoke to them in Dutch. *Oh, great,* I thought, *more secrets.* Nevertheless, I sat quietly, not making anything of it. After all, lunch had been nice and I was still the new kid on the block.

As soon as Jan and I got out of the car, Trans and Zonder took off out of the driveway. As we walked toward the house, Jan said, "Sandra and Ingrid are inside with Leo, I think."

"Oh yeah? I didn't know you were meeting them today."

Inside, Leo sat on his own having a beer and watching the ocean. I walked by and said my hellos, but not wishing to intrude, went on upstairs to take a nap. As soon as I got up there, Jan caught up with me, called me aside, and asked me to spend my time downstairs instead.

"Sandra and Ingrid have been here all day cleaning the house," he said. "I just want to have a word with them to show my appreciation. You should join us."

"OK, Jan, sure," I said.

Downstairs, I sat with Leo. He sensed I was a little confused. He was an older fellow, probably close to three times the age of his wife and I knew he had heart trouble. It was a good thing she was the one doing the cleaning upstairs.

"It's a beautiful view from the villa, isn't it?" he said.

"Yes, Sir, it is. Can I get you another beer?"

"No, no, Jamie. Have a seat. You look a little . . . confused."

"Well, I guess I am a little. Jan said he had to show his appreciation . . ." As I said the words, the meaning behind them struck me. Leo could see I was just getting the idea.

"It's all right with me, Jamie," he said warmly. "I'm an old man, my heart can't take a lot of excitement, and Ingrid is so young. She needs things sometimes I can't give her. So . . . Jan, he helps with this."

"He's helping out, is he?" I said. *What a crock,* I thought.

"Yes."

"All three of them's upstairs?" I asked, just to confirm in my mind what he was saying.

He shrugged and raised his eyebrows.

At this point, the marble-smooth impression I had of my biological father began to crumble. What would Mama and Daddy think of this man if they had any idea how he spent his free time? And Aunt Wendy—she was starting to look increasingly like the good parent. In some ways, I figured I deserved it. You go out and deal in large quantities of heavy-duty drugs from Africa, make yourself a pile of money doing so, and you start seeing the world without rose-tinted glasses. But none of this logic mattered.

20

WHEN THE SECOND JOB came along, Trans rode with Jan and Christianne. They took the *Fine Wine III* from Fuengirola's marina, while Zonder and I stayed behind to wait for the load. Alberto was assigned to watch duty this time.

It was dark by the time we passed a section of beach just outside of La Línea. It was here I had seen the civil police force, known as the *Guardia Civil*, chase barefoot kids on the beach who were catching packs of cigarettes from smugglers.

But tonight was different.

It was scary, as the Guardia Civil had dispatched a helicopter with a distinctive long drive shaft that moved rapidly toward the sheer limestone cliffs on the east side of the Rock. The cliffs were also lit from beneath by massive flood lamps. In the distance we could see the chopper lower its altitude, running a huge spotlight over the water.

"What're they looking for?" I asked.

"Suspicious-looking vessels," Zonder said. "If they see a Zodiac full of cigarettes or whatever else, they will shoot rubber bullets at whoever is on board."

"What about Jan?"

"There are so many cigarette boats around here, they tend to blend in pretty well. But the Guardia Civil still conducts random searches on those, too. If the ones in the h-h-helicopters come across a cigarette boat that looks more suspicious than the rest, they will send a patrol boat to intercept it and see what they have aboard, which usually turns out to be nothing but a bunch of cigarettes."

"Yeah," I said. "By the way, has Jan always been rich?" I asked.

"No, he had nothing," said Zonder.

"Well what exactly did he have to go to prison for in France?" I asked. "Stuff like we're doing now?"

"No," he replied. "Jan rented one of his sailing boats in Holland to a Frenchman for a week, and the man got caught trying to smuggle heroin into his country from Africa using Jan's boat."

"Jan wasn't even on the boat?"

"No, he was in Sneek," said Zonder.

"But he knew what that French guy was gonna use his boat for, huh?"

"He doesn't say much about that part of his life. I heard many stories when I was a child. They say he escaped the prison in France after two years, came back to Holland for six months, made more money than he had made his entire life, but then lost it all and ended up turning himself in to the French authorities."

"I wonder what he did in those six months."

"Yeah, me too."

At 5:35 the next morning, with heavy cloud cover making the night seem much darker, and while Zonder and I sat in a hotel car park waiting for the "packages," we spotted a pair of headlights coming toward us from the beach. We waited in a customized Montero with no backseat and newly outfitted with airbags to keep the rear end from banging on the road. When I first saw the vehicle, I wondered what kind of convincing lie we would be able to conjure up if apprehended.

Zonder panicked when the Land Rover bounced up off the hard-packed sand and launched itself through the seaside entrance of the hotel's concrete parking lot. "It is th-the p-p-police," he stuttered. "They will s-see how we are dr-dressed and all the g-gas t-tanks and we will g-go to j-jail tonight."

"Relax, man," I said, trying to be cool. "They ain't even gonna notice anyone is in here. Just sit back and keep still."

The interior of the Montero lit up when a powerful spotlight mounted on the driver's side of the dark blue Land Rover was trained on us. I was completely startled, my heart in my throat. The headlights on the Land Rover began to flicker automatically, much like the unmarked narcotics vehicles I'd seen around Mobile when they were about to bust somebody.

"Cut off your radio, man," I said, freaking out. "Turn it off and stick it under your seat. Hurry!"

A Guardia Civil officer slowly stepped out of his truck and—in a flash of genius—Zonder wrapped his thick arms around my head, startling the living crap out of me, and pulled our faces in close, nose-to-nose. "Here, pr-pretend you k-kiss me," he whispered.

Hell, all I could think of was that cold cement slab Jan slept on for eight years, and I kissed that giant Dutchman with everything I had.

The officer cautiously approached the driver's side window and shone a flashlight in through the dark tint. After visually confirming that Zonder and I were both men—and wincing at the way the big one rolled his head side to side while the little one rubbed his arms up and down over the length of the big one's broad back—the mustached officer shook his head and walked away.

Talk about the survival instinct. I think we took it to new limits that night.

Zonder spotted the cigarette boat, the *Fine Wine III*, anchored a good distance out. He and I splashed through the cold, black surf to meet Jan, who had motored closer to the beach in a twelve-foot Zodiac capable of venturing into much shallower water. With great heaving motions, he tumbled heavy burlap sacks over the walls of the vessel.

"Good work, men . . . keep it up," said Jan as we worked to take the heavy packages from him. With a running momentum, we tossed them along a line between us to where the smallest waves crashed into foam on the saturated sand.

"That is it for me, but Christianne has the rest in his Zodiac," said Jan, as he jumped down to push himself into deeper water and sputtered away. Christianne immediately motored up to where Jan had been and began unloading another fifteen hundred pounds off his Zodiac.

"Man, that all just barely fit," I said, catching my breath. My palms were stiff within the damp black leather of my gloves, but they at least they didn't bleed this time.

Like the Range Rover, the Montero struggled when the road became steeper halfway to Jan's villa. That first time, I remembered Zonder in near despair, pounding the steering wheel and cursing every time it stalled and threatened to slip out of gear.

This time, however, things went smoothly and the next morning we loaded half of it back into the Montero and drove it up the coast to a parking lot near a McDonald's. We left the Montero, as we'd done before, and waited in the Opel some distance away.

After a while, we observed a middle-aged English guy approach, who got into the Montero and left, just as naturally as if the van belonged to him.

We left to get some lunch at the Chevy Bar not too far away, and Jan received a phone call. I could hear the same English voice I'd heard on the previous job and assumed it was McLean, but he sounded louder this time. When Jan hung up, he wore a twisted expression on his face.

"Trans," he said, "McLean is claiming that he was shorted a couple of packages—maybe two or three."

"You think that guy took off with some of them before he delivered to McLean?"

"That is the only explanation," Jan said, shaking his head.

"I thought McLean had better judgment. I am sure there will be trouble for that fellow. How could he think he'd get away with it?"

It was a sobering moment. I wondered if that English guy we had seen for the first time picking up the Montero would turn up dead. How idiotic, though. Maybe a few ounces here and there wouldn't go amiss—but two or three whole bundles? What a nut, I thought. Yeah, maybe McLean did need a few lessons in judgment. Even I could see that hiring this guy was a mistake.

But our day was far from over. When we got back home, we had to stack the rest of the load into the Range Rover to take over to Alberto's place in Marbella. Trans and I were to lead in the Opel, followed by Christianne, driving the truck full of packed croaker sacks. Christianne was to stay a kilometer behind so that if we encountered a checkpoint, one of us could call and let him know. Jan and Zonder would trail him, to warn him of anybody approaching from the rear.

Luckily, a few blocks beyond the roundabout, a big Guardia Civil officer stood in the middle directing traffic, much of which appeared to be going to and from the direction of the marina. I happened to notice another pair of officers in distinctive military-style uniforms, green with short-brimmed, Fidel Castro–style hats. They were on the side of the road next to their Land Rovers, holding German shepherds on leashes. That wasn't particularly heartwarming.

It could be that the officer directing traffic took note of Trans's facial expression when he yelled at me to get on the phone and tell Christianne to turn off of the coastal road, but whatever the reason, the officer took it upon himself to order us to the shoulder under a palm tree while waving the other cars on.

I managed to reach Christianne just before the cop came up to the door. "Hey, man, you need to get off this road!" I told Christianne. "We're coming up on a checkpoint and they're making us pull over."

Unfortunately, being French with limited English, Christianne didn't have a clue what I'd just told him. "*Je ne comprends pas.* Can you say in Español?"

"I don't know no Español, man!"

By this time, one of the narcotics officers was knocking on my window with his nightstick, so I hung up. "*Salte del carro.* Out of the car," the cop said, through the glass.

While the Guardia Civil ran their canines through the Opel, I happened to notice the Range Rover a few cars back and watched Christianne's blue eyes bulge out of his head when he finally got the picture.

The stop seemed pretty routine, and the officers were satisfied as soon as their dogs were done sniffing around the backseat and in the trunk of the Opel. My heart was jumping as the Range Rover was waved on through the checkpoint. We got back on the road just behind Jan and Zonder.

Before long, we made it to Alberto's house. Christianne pulled into the garage. Inside, there were many boxes of money from all over Europe, plus an Enduro dirt bike.

I guess everybody was about ready for a break. Alberto

invited us all in for something to eat, and his maid cooked a Moroccan variety of semolina called couscous. Christianne's French fiancée invited over some girlfriends, and the atmosphere turned celebratory.

"Jan," Alberto said, "I think I'm ready to make a change in my life."

My father took that in his stride, "I think I know what you're going to say."

"Yes," Alberto continued, "it's been only a short time since I was picked up in Morocco with the stolen vehicle, and now this today—I'm too old for all this excitement."

I sat there listening, wondering if Jan was gonna pull a *Godfather* on him. But he just laughed and nodded.

"It's getting harder for me, too," Jan said.

Alberto looked a little relieved. "Yeah, well, I think I'd like to concentrate a little more on Scoop Paris Fashions," he said, referring to their joint venture in the designer clothing business.

I could see it. Nobody wants to go to jail. I'd been close enough that time in the car with Zonder—our homosexual masquerade.

We drove on home, and that night I was paid £40,000, approximately $80,000.

The money was getting better, but I wasn't.

21

February 8, 1994

SINCE IT WAS JAN'S birthday, we celebrated the following night by going out to a fine French restaurant. I was looking forward to it, but I had a foreboding sense of apprehension. A heavy, dark feeling.

There was reason for that feeling. Earlier that day, Zonder had taken me aside, looking serious. Despite his apparent mood, I joked around as usual.

"You're not gonna kiss me again, are ya?" I said.

But this time he didn't laugh. He said, "Listen, Jamie, I have t-t-to talk to you about something."

"Well what is it?" I asked.

"Do you remember when Mc-c-c-Lean called Oom Jan and said he didn't get the right amount?"

"Sure," I said. "I was sitting right there. What about it?"

"I got to thinking maybe they were still in the water. It was so hard that day, with the Guardia and all, and I didn't do the package count like I did before."

"Oh crap, Zonder. You mean that guy mighta been right? We mighta shorted him?"

"We *did*."

"*What!*"

"We did short him. I told Trans what I was thinking, and we snuck back there to see, and they are still there, Jamie. They were waterlogged in the shallow water. We left them and got out of there as quick as we could."

"Oh my God."

"But since it has already been . . . taken care of, don't say anything, OK? Just leave it alone. I just thought you should know."

"Yeah, well, OK, I guess. Thanks."

That was a bombshell. I was a little paranoid at first, but the feeling soon turned to heavy guilt. The English fellow was blamed for what I had done. What happened to him and did he get killed for it?

I wasn't exactly in a party mood.

As we got ready to go out, I heard a snippet of a telephone conversation that Jan was having with McLean.

"Ten packages; 360 kilos—give or take a little . . . Yes, it is less than the last time. Why? Because the Moroccans asked for a bigger portion, that is why. Do you want it or not, McLean? I could easily . . . OK, then . . . uh-huh . . . that will work."

"Not enough weight, says the Englishman," Jan said, as he hung up the phone. "If he wants more weight, he needs to get out there and sail the damn boat himself."

He paced a little and shook his head.

"I am tired of being taken for granted."

"I don't blame you, Jan. It is hard work. Those guys don't even get their hands dirty," I said.

"I was never afraid of work, but you're right. They don't know the meaning of it," said Jan.

"Hey man, it's your birthday party. Let's go on out and enjoy it!"

We arrived at the restaurant, which was elegant and posh. But we didn't have time to be seated before a middle-aged guy came up to Jan and yanked him around by the shoulder. Everyone was shocked. Zonder and Trans moved to intercept before I even knew what was going on. I turned around to see them getting in the guy's face.

That's when I recognized him. It was the English guy who'd come to pick up the Montero full of hash, but he didn't look quite the same as he had on that day. His face was swollen and he had a cut under one of his eyes. But the most noticeable thing about him was the anger—you could almost see steam coming out his ears. *Well, at least he wasn't dead,* I thought.

"You brought me a lot of trouble," he said, getting in Jan's face.

We all started for the guy, but Jan said, "No. I'll meet you inside. Go on ahead in."

"Are you sure?" Zonder said, rearing to fight.

"Yes, go ahead in," Jan repeated.

Reluctantly, we obeyed, and left them to it.

My thoughts returned to the conversation I'd had earlier with Zonder. Neither one of those guys had any idea what had actually happened. And there they were, each of them thinking the other was the guilty party. I felt like a traitor, a thief, and a fool at the same time. And yet I didn't say a word.

We got to the table and everybody ordered drinks. After a while, Jan came in. He was sweating, his shirt was torn at the collar, and he seemed to be pulling himself back together, both physically and mentally. It sure was a birthday to remember for him.

Sandra was all over Jan, trying to soothe him. He ordered a drink and, after a while, things calmed down. He made a few phone calls and received a few, but they didn't seem to be much about his birthday celebration.

After dinner, he motioned to us, "Listen, Trans, Zonder, and Jamie—why don't you all enjoy the comforts of the *Forsikker t*onight?" My father was talking about his fifty-one-foot sailing yacht, which was moored at Puerto Benalmádena marina, next to Elizabeth Taylor's yacht. "You could spend a little time at Club 92."

Zonder liked that idea. Club 92 was nothing more than the local whorehouse for wealthy clients, I guess. But if Zonder had a weakness, it was for women—any kind of women. So we went along to the club, dropped a little acid, and picked up some Brazilian girls.

"Is this where you live?" one of them asked Zonder, as we escorted them to the sailboat.

"Only when we feel like it," Zonder said. He must have

still been tripping, because that was kind of out of character for him—he'd never normally reveal where he was living.

We all had drinks and sat around listening to music. Things from my point of view were getting less intriguing, and I was now starting to miss home badly. It was good to get away and see how other folks do things, and of course nice to make some real money, but the whole picture was skewed from how I'd been brought up. After just a few months, things were beginning to feel genuinely alien to me.

Zonder and Trans were all over those girls, but I just felt like sitting and talking with them. One of them wanted to know about America, so we just sat and talked about America for a while.

After we returned next morning, I caught some of the local news on television. It was in Spanish, but I got the gist of it. It seemed there had been a massive explosion a little way up the coast from us and they showed footage of the destruction. A home was pretty much done for, and all that remained was a burnt structure and a big hole. The TV announcer was saying *"Inglaterra, un hombre Inglaterra."* Despite my sketchy Spanish, I knew the word *Inglaterra*—an English person. And the English person had been found *"matado."* Killed. It wasn't Popeye McLean; it was the guy who'd worked for him. Did Jan do it? I didn't know. Maybe Jan told McLean that the guy had become "expendable" or whatever. But the doom I'd felt the day before was back, and back hard.

Jan came in and noticed I was watching the TV news report and immediately snapped off the TV. "It's not good to watch TV all day," he said. "You got to get out and see Spain!"

"I just got in, Jan. I'm beat."

"I'm tired, too, Son. I think the next job we do will be our last one for a while."

"I'll probably go home, then, after the next one. It's only been a little over a month now that I've been here, but it seems like a lifetime since I've been home."

Jan put his hand on my shoulder. "No matter where you go and what you do, Son, you will always come to miss the place where you grew up. I understand how you feel."

Trans came in, and Jan sprang into life.

"Trans! Just the fellow I wanted to see. Go and take Jamie shopping today. He's got too much time on his hands, and he needs to use it more wisely."

So that's how that story ended. The English guy died, and we all went shopping.

22

Late February 1994

AT 3:34 ONE SUNDAY morning in late February, Zonder relayed a call from Jan. "Your f-father will not m-make it in tonight. They hit some roughage at sea. One of the m-motors lost its prop."

"What's he gonna do?" I asked.

"He says he will idle around unt-t-til tuhh . . . tomorrow night. But, if he has to, he will throw the entire load overboard."

"Wait—so, he can't make it in time with that busted prop?" I asked.

"Not before d-dawn," said Zonder. "He wants me to go t-talk to the Moroccans in the m-morning"

"The ones that live here in Spain?" I asked.

"Yeah."

"Good luck," I said. I didn't envy the poor guy doing that job.

"You are c-coming with me," said Zonder.

"Why have I gotta go?"

"You can t-talk with them in English. My Dutch is clear b-but, I have trouble m-m-making some of the English sounds."

"Zonder, you tellin' me you don't stutter one bit when you're speaking that Dutch?"

"I am not stupid, Jamie. I can speak my own language well."

"You sure never stutter when ordering me around for those jobs."

Jan had instructed us to scope out alternate landing spots on the beach. Even I knew you couldn't do the same thing more than a couple of times and not expect to get caught. We had noticed an increased Guardia presence out there since we'd done the second job, so this time we found an alternate place and mapped it out roughly, so everybody understood where it was.

He also told us that we should be prepared to take the entire load—roughly double the size of the first two jobs—to Sandra's apartment in Benalmádena. So on this job, things were different from the outset. In my eyes, this new development only made it a whole lot shakier. And now we had to go and talk to some Moroccans. I figured I could take it if Harrison Ford could take it. Actually, I was terrified—we'd be working with a completely different culture.

But we had to do what we had to do.

The Moroccans lived in a suburb of houses encircled by sandstone and cement walls in the foothills of Arroyo de la

Miel. They were of Arab descent, and to my surprise, they were very polite and hospitable to us.

"Now, to what do we owe this pleasure?" asked the older of the two Moroccan brothers, whose short hair was starting to show traces of gray. The beards of both brothers were neatly trimmed and they had sharp features. Both were dressed casually in slacks, collared shirts, and tennis shoes.

"My father, he's not gonna be able to make it in tonight," I said. "He hit some roughage out at sea and one of his engines lost its prop."

"Oh."

"Yeah, he said he was gonna float around and try to make it in tonight, but that he'd throw it all overboard if he had to."

"That is entirely understandable," said the older Moroccan. "We would not want to put your father in harm's way to protect something so easily replaced. His skills as a sailor have become a valuable asset to us. When you speak to Jan again, assure him that we support whatever he decides to do in this situation."

"OK, I'll do that," I said, cutting into the conversation; I was hoping to leave as soon as I could.

Back in the car, Zonder told me how he understood the arrangement. "Jan has done m-many jobs for the Moroccans. Remember, they get a piece of every job we do," Zonder explained, as we sped toward the coastal highway in Jan's Lamborghini Diablo SE. "They trust him v-very m-m-much."

Meanwhile, I guess old Jan and Trans and Christianne got well sunburned after spending the entire Sunday standing on the deck of the *Fine Wine III* with rods and reels, fishing.

In fact, Jan and Trans were accomplished fishermen, having been raised in the countryside near the North Sea and the waters that surround Sneek. Indeed, they caught fish all day, but they were strictly catch and release—there was enough weight in the boat as it was.

At 3:15 Monday morning, Jan phoned Sandra to let her know that he was going to be able to make it. She contacted Zonder, and we headed out.

When we arrived, we hadn't been in the parking lot for five minutes before I noticed an undercover cop. He seemed to be paying particular attention to the area of the beach where we'd made our first two hauls. I was glad we'd arrived early.

"Hey Zonder," I said. "I guess you better contact him and let him know to meet us at Carihuela Beach instead. They got this place totally covered."

The plan was that Jan, Trans, and Christianne would go to our new spot and we instructed Sandra and Ingrid to keep watch some distance away. With me and Zonder in one Montero, and Leo in another, we waited for the giant load to arrive.

"There they are," I said. The *Fine Wine III* had anchored, was silent for a bit, and then Jan, Trans, and Christianne lowered a pair of twelve-foot Zodiacs into the water. Trans strapped on his bulky night-vision goggles, carefully stepped aboard one of the smaller vessels, and waited for the others to pass him the heavy burlap sacks.

On the sands of Carihuela, the high-pitched whine of

an outboard motor cutting through the stillness of the night sent me and Zonder charging into the surf to meet Trans. He cut the engine and we got hold of the first six hundred kilos of the load, or about thirteen hundred pounds. We helped Trans turn his Zodiac around, with Christianne shoving off from the *Fine Wine III* for the next run the moment he heard Trans's motor fire up.

Christianne's run went without a hitch and Trans's second haul fitted easily into Zonder's two-toned Montero. Once loaded, we quickly rolled up the chicken wire and jammed it in on top of the cargo.

Sandra led the way to her apartment complex's subterranean parking garage and told us to park in some clear spots near the fire escape stairway.

"Nobody ever uses these stairs," she said, her voice echoing against the low concrete ceilings. "We always take the elevator instead."

The girls lending a hand, we managed seven packages on the first trip, with me, Zonder, and Trans trudging up the steep stairway with a burlap sack over each shoulder.

It took a little less than an hour but, with the constant threat of being seen and the physical strain of carrying the equivalent a twelve-year-old on each shoulder, it felt like an eternity. The haul filled Sandra's ten-by-twelve-foot guest bedroom more than halfway to the eight-foot ceiling. I stood completely exhausted, looking at the sight.

"Four *thousand* pounds," I puffed.

Jan and Trans were already at the villa when Zonder and

I arrived. "How'd y'all make it here from Gibraltar so fast?" I asked.

"We didn't go back to Gibraltar. I took the *Fine Wine* into Benalmádena marina and made plans to have it dry-docked for repairs," Jan said.

"Y'all lost a propeller?"

"Yes."

"How'd it happen?"

"Something very large surfaced near the back end of the boat. We all believe it must have been a whale."

"They got whales in the Mediterranean?" I asked.

"In the strait there are pilot and killer whales," replied Jan. "But this one was *big*. It may have been a sperm whale."

Later that day, after we'd taken a short rest, we went to have lunch at a pizzeria in Benalmádena. Jan was enjoying a fragrant coffee and brandy. Zonder, Trans, and Leo had gone back to Jan's house with a load of hash to vacuum-pack. This is how we'd portion it out and measure its weight.

"Son, do you know why I wanted you to take the load to Sandra's apartment?"

"So Alberto wouldn't know where it was going?"

"Yes . . . Alberto and the Moroccans. Christianne and I are ending our partnership with Alberto. I will give Alberto £75,000 for the wear and tear I have put on the *Fine Wine*. Yesterday, I saw a much nicer cigarette boat for sale in Sheppard's Marina. I am taking a break after this job and Christianne has agreed to help me oversee the diamond fields in Sierra Leone, where I plan to grow tulips with a prince I met in prison in France. Then, I will ship the raw diamonds in the pots of the flowers back to Holland and sell them on the black market."

He complacently sipped his spiked coffee, and after a silent moment, said in quiet tones, "It is very important, Son, for you not to mention the events of last night when the Moroccans show up here soon."

"OK."

"Because they believe those tons are sitting on the bottom of the sea."

"They think you threw it all overboard?" I said.

"Yes."

"Why they think that?"

"Because that is what I told them," said Jan, smugly.

"Oh."

"Wait until you see how much you will be getting paid," Jan said, smiling. "I don't have to give half to Alberto and the Moroccans, so everyone will be making a lot more than usual for what we are moving."

"Wow, you really pulled the wool over their eyes. You think they suspect anything?"

"I am not the least bit worried. You will see how they are in a minute. Once you get into this circle, you just have to show them what you are capable of. They know my work now, and they would go to great lengths to stay on good terms with me."

While we waited outside the café in front of the yacht club, some kind of sheik arrived, in full sheik garb, with a group of guards around him and a briefcase handcuffed to his wrist. Like a scene out of a movie. The whole parade jumped into a Bentley with gold door handles and drove away. No one seemed fazed; I guess you saw a lot of that kind of thing in Benalmádena.

Eventually, and with a less dramatic arrival than the sheik, the Moroccan brothers showed up. Jan escorted them to a section of the marina behind a chain-link fence that had a view of the coastal highway and the neon-lit London Pub. Utilizing a massive crane, several men had just lowered the *Fine Wine III* onto an iron apparatus rather like a boat trailer without wheels. The missing prop as well as additional damage to the tail end was easily visible.

"How did it happen?" asked the younger of the two Moroccan brothers.

"I think it was a whale trying to surface. We are lucky it did not hit us in the center of the hull. We would have been in big trouble then."

"We will buy you a whole new boat, Jan. Just please keep doing these jobs for us," pleaded the older brother. "There is no one we know who is such an expert sailor as you."

"I am not interested in any more work," said Jan, sternly. "I will be taking a break for now. The summer will be here soon, and you know that I do not work in the summer."

"OK, then before the end of this year we will buy you a new boat and you will work for us again," insisted the older Moroccan.

"I will think about it," Jan said.

We spent the next few days vacuum-packing the hash, and every so often, Christianne would show up in some newly outfitted car with special hiding places for the stuff. To make the most of this last job, I guessed Jan would send it up north where it would fetch a higher price.

There was so much of that stuff, it seemed like we'd have it forever. But things were winding down. We took a portion of it to some Italians, and then the last of it went to Mr. McLean.

One night, Jan and I met up with Christianne, his French girlfriends, Trans, Zonder, Sandra, and Inga at a French restaurant. The only person missing was Leo, who stayed home as he wasn't feeling well. It was a nice dinner, and afterwards, Jan, Sandra, Inga, and I prepared to drive back to Jan's house. "Today is payday," Jan said, as we got in. The car was filled with bags of money.

Trans drove behind us, and on arrival at the house, the two of them began to count the huge sum of money we had traveled with.

Even though I was aware of the potential rewards in this business, it was overwhelming seeing all of that money laying around. It seemed unreal standing there with bags of drug money in front of me.

"So what do you think you're worth, Jamie?" Trans asked.

I was in no frame of mind to make that kind of a decision. "I don't know, Trans. What's the going rate for smuggling?"

Everybody chuckled, and Jan said, "Let him make up his own mind. He's a van Rijn! The love of money is in his blood!"

That might do something to you when you read that—cringe at the very least, maybe. Well, I knew it wasn't quite correct, but in the spirit of the moment, I didn't say anything, and enjoyed the intoxicating feeling of being around so much paper power.

That night, I took away as my pay £80,000 and 30,000 French francs.

23

"LET'S DO SOME ERRANDS, today, Son," Jan said a few days later. "You've made some money, but you can't carry it all around in your wallet."

"No, I guess I can't," I said. "But it's all foreign—what do you do with that?"

"I'll show you," he said. "In my business, I've met some people in the banking industry who can help us."

"I'd appreciate that, Jan," I said.

In Gibraltar, Jan introduced me to a friend of his who worked at Barclays Bank near Sheppard's Marina. This man spoke good English, and was of Indian descent.

"It is always nice to meet one of Jan's friends," he said. "Are you enjoying this country?"

"I like it just fine," I said.

"Actually, Jamie is heading back to the States soon, and that is why we have come," Jan explained. He would like to have his cash in a more easily transferable form. Can you help us with that?"

"Oh, yes, of course, Jan," he said, smiling.

Up to this point, I wasn't sure why I had brought *all* of my loot, but then I got the picture. "So you are going to give me a money order, something like that?" I asked.

"If your father approves, I will convert your currency to bank drafts, which is suitable for transfer without so much paperwork."

That was exactly what Jan had in mind, and so this fellow set about organizing a healthy number of $10,000 bank drafts for me. I'd become a little complacent, I guess you'd call it, about money by then: *$10,000 bank drafts*—hey, good, whatever! Looking back now, though, just one of those bank drafts would come in *very* handy. Earned legally, of course.

Jan sat patiently while his trusty friend converted the money into thousand-guilder notes to smuggle into Holland.

After returning to the villa with the bank drafts, I stood outside with Jan in the courtyard, watching the fish, koi carp, swimming around at the bottom of the water fountain. The skies had a golden tint as the sun set, making for an idyllic view over the distant mountains, as a Spanish shepherd guided a herd of sheep using a tall staff.

"Son, I need for you to find someone when you return to Untied States who no one will trust or believe. This person will help us with a *big job*, moving two tons of South American snow to Denmark," said Jan, staring into the distance. "I have a plan for us to do this in the winter months next year. This way, if he talks, no one will ever believe him."

The first person who came to mind was Blaze. I said, "Sure I know someone," and smiled.

As we looked out at the shepherd and his sheep, melting into the landscape with the fading light, my father said, "Son, you will betray me one day and write a book about all that you have seen and done here." I stood silent, somewhat perplexed, and thinking that this man really did not know me. I was unable to spell, read, or even fill out a job application form, so writing a book was not something I could foresee in my lifetime.

My immediate priorities were more simple: I was just grateful to have had the opportunity to learn a new trade and make some real money.

24

IT'S STRANGE HOW the trip over to Spain was so different from my return home. I was in the dark on the way over to see Europe, wide-eyed, and naive perhaps. That's not to say I was particularly *enlightened* once I was in Spain; that word doesn't give the right impression. Of course, I'd had my eyes opened, but maybe to the wrong things. Certainly, I was excited, tense, and a little nervous on the way over, and I was all those things on the way back, but for completely different reasons.

My gifts were packed and ready to give, and I was sitting on the plane dressed up like some kind of gangster. I wore my thick gold-rope chain and new clothes that said "Notice me!" I had it in my mind that I was a big man. I had clothes, jewelry, and money to burn on whatever I damn well pleased. I'd walked on marble floors and looked out the windows of mansions overlooking the Mediterranean Sea; this was the new Jamie.

I landed and took a taxi directly to my first stop: J&J Grocery.

Unfortunately, my big entrance was ruined since neither Daddy nor Mama was there, only Aunt Kay.

"Well how are you, Jamie? Come on over here! It's so good to see you," she said. "Was the flight OK?"

"It was fine," I said. "You here by yourself?"

"Yes, but your Daddy told me to call when you got here," she said. "And listen, you know your house has no electric, no water, right?"

"Yeah," I said. "Daddy told me he turned them off since I was gone."

"Right. Well, I don't know if you know this, but your mama's got a bunch of houseguests that are going to be there for a while. Why don't you sleep over at the house with me once you get settled and see everybody? You're just as welcome as you can be."

"Thanks, Aunt Kay," I said. "If that's how it is at the house, I'd love it. That would be just great."

She called Daddy, who said he was on his way.

Daddy came pulling up in his new truck, a full-sized pick-up. "Hey Daddy!" I said as I went to get in the truck.

"Good Lord, Son, what are you all snazzed up for?" Daddy wasn't big on dressing up, but I sensed there might be a little more to his comment. Nevertheless, I just went along with it. "Your mama's got dinner cooking," he said.

At the house, things were just as busy as Aunt Kay had said. Kids and kid paraphernalia everywhere you looked.

"Good to see you, Son! Boy, you look mighty fancy in those clothes and all," said Mama, eyeballing my gold chain.

I was beginning to wonder if I should have worn it. What in the world was I thinking? In some ways, it was as if I'd never been gone. I couldn't tell anybody at home what I'd been through or experienced, so I was just Good Ol' Jamie to them. On that night, it is a shame I didn't appreciate the value of that.

The TV was on, tuned in to the news, and I happened to glance at it when a shot of an eighteen-wheeler appeared on the screen. The on-screen reporter was talking. "As the eighteen-wheeler was pulled over for inspection, State Troopers found out quite the surprise. They discovered what they estimate to be ten million dollars in cocaine. Investigators say it is likely to trigger the RICO statute, which carries heavy penalties and lengthy jail time . . ."

Boy, I didn't need to see that. Just the sight of it made me paranoid. Was it a message, or perhaps a warning, to me personally? As time went by, I think maybe is way, and not just to me—also to other folks about to make wrong choices and turn away from good. If I had sat and concentrated on that story, and what was about to happen to those guys, the direction of my life might have been completely different. I would never have embarked on a journey that would take me down some dark roads with some dangerous people.

But I *didn't* concentrate on that news report.

At that point in my life, it was somebody else who was doing that, somebody who was stupid enough to get caught, or who didn't have a smart enough team, or good enough equipment. Somebody else, not me.

It was around then that I handed out my presents: Daddy, the Krugerrand coin, and Mama, her emerald ring.

"It's real nice, Son," Daddy said. But he didn't have quite the excitement I'd pictured, and Mama was pleased with the gift I gave her, but she, too, seemed reserved.

"Oh Jamie, ain't that nice . . . thank you!"

I'm not sure what response I expected, but I had the definite feeling that discussions had taken place before my arrival about how to handle anything new or different that I did, like for instance, giving five- and ten-thousand-dollar gifts. To me, it seemed like they were expecting something along those lines, but it was hard to pin down. Whatever it was, I didn't get the feeling that I'd impressed them much. And that was my disappointment.

"It's from Gibraltar," I said.

"And it's just beautiful. Thank you."

"Yes, thank you, Son. It was real nice of you to remember your mama and daddy."

Hmm. Remember them? Did they have any idea? No, I guess they didn't. "Sure," I said smiling. But I felt almost as if I'd done something wrong. Back then, it was hard for me to fathom it out.

"After dinner, we can go see your new baby boy," Mama said. "He's beautiful, Jamie. You're gonna love him."

"Well, I'm looking forward to that," I said.

When we arrived at Tanya's parents' house, I started to get butterflies. Not about Tanya so much as about seeing the little baby. When she came to the door holding him, you could have knocked me over with a feather.

"Hi, Jamie," she said.

I was speechless for a minute, looking from her to the baby.

Then she looked at me, "So this is him," she continued. "What do you think?"

"Come on inside, y'all," said Tanya's mother, who came to greet us from inside. "Don't stand in the doorway. Hi, Janet."

"Hi, Mrs. Young. He's getting bigger already," said Janet.

"Yeah, he eats good. How are you, Jamie?"

"Real good."

"Can I hold him?" I asked. "I won't drop him."

"Course you can," Tanya said. She was very kind, almost flirtatious, if you can be flirtatious with a baby in your arms.

"Look at those hands," Mama said. "He's got a lot of Jamie in him, hasn't he?"

"He sure has," said Mrs. Young.

It was an experience I'd never known, and even today it makes my heart jump when I think of it. Just putting my hands on a living, breathing human being that came from me. The feeling was both heart-wrenching and amazing. I just wanted to sit and stare at him and watch his every move. But after a while, I guess Tanya had her fill of my fixation on Kyle.

"So what are you up to tonight?" she asked.

"Oh, not too much," I said. "I just got in. I will be staying with Aunt Kay."

"Come on in my room. I'll show you some of the baby clothes I got with what you sent me."

In her room, I gave her the diamond ring and the wedding band. I didn't propose because I really didn't know if I should; I didn't know what the future held for us. Had she changed at all? I knew I had, but I wasn't sure I had changed in the way a father should.

"So what are you doing tomorrow?"

"Well, I'm going shopping for a vehicle," I said.

"How 'bout I come along? Help you find something?"

"I guess so," I said. I didn't particularly want her to come along—things had just become more complicated for me with the arrival of the baby. But in the end, I figured it wouldn't be a bad idea.

As we all left for the evening, Mr. Young stopped me. "Listen Jamie, I sure appreciate your generosity with Tanya, and taking care of little Kyle financially. But what do you think is going to come of this relationship with my daughter? Do you plan on marrying her?"

I wanted badly to say, "Yes, Sir, I do," just to make him happy, to make everything all right. But deep down, I knew *that* would be a lie. I still had a lot of thinking to do, and a lot of decisions to make. Finally, I said, "I really don't know, Sir."

He nodded, rather sadly, but I guess he understood.

The next day, I went out looking at vehicles with Tanya. It was a nice day, and I felt on top of the world. We stopped off at the Chevy dealership my daddy used, and it didn't take me long to decide on a Silverado. The truck was priced at fifteen grand, but I went ahead and dumped in another ten grand on options, including a top-of-the-range Alpine stereo system, auto start, remote-controlled windows, those kind of expensive extras.

When I arrived home from Spain, I had 140 grand—35 of it was gone by the beginning of the second day. And I wasn't finished yet.

I picked up Tanya and met up with Daddy at Crabtree's Mobile Homes, where I put $7,000 down on a trailer. With all of my spending, things should have run smoothly from that point, but then the arguing started.

"So this is where we gonna live after we get married?" Tanya asked as she hugged me and looked around inside the brand-new unit.

"I don't know," I said, "but it's where we gonna live now."

"Well, you live here, and then I'll move in once we're married."

"What do you mean? I thought we were going to live together with Kyle, the three of us, right here."

"I know. But you don't expect me to move in with you without getting married, do you?"

I could see her point, but she was throwing me a curveball. We hadn't talked about any of this before—as far as I knew, we were moving in together with the baby, period. "Look, Tanya, do you want us all to live together or what?"

"*Live* together! You mean like a tramp? So you can run all over town and not worry about a thing, because, hell, you're not married, what's the difference? And, I can stay home and take care of the baby? I don't think so!"

"All right, all right, let's take this outside," I said, walking toward the truck. But she kept coming at me.

"Are you walking away? Already? You're barely home and already there you go, running away from the first thing that comes up!"

Once we got in the truck, I gave her an earful. "Listen, Tanya, if you don't like it this way, fine. I'm not going and making any crazy decisions with a woman who don't know how to be faithful to one guy—how do I know what you're going to do? Getting married don't change people. You could go right on making the rounds—"

Boy, she didn't like that one.

"Making the rounds?" she said. "Who the hell's talking about making the rounds? I'd have to have roller skates to keep up with the bedrooms you come out of!"

In the end, I dropped her off back home, and the whole plan was off. "Grow up, Jamie!" she shouted, as she slammed the front door on the way into her parents' house. She must have started huffing and puffing the second she walked in, because her daddy immediately came outside. He said we "needed to talk" at a neutral location, so I agreed to meet up the following day with him and Mrs. Young at the Hardee's on Highway 90.

I had a ton of respect for Tanya's daddy, and I like to think that he saw something good in me as well. Like Paw Paw, he believed in hard work and putting his best effort into everything he did. A quiet man with a strong character, he had always gone out of his way to make me feel part of his family, even when his daughter and I weren't getting along.

But sitting in his driveway that afternoon, my pockets stuffed with dirty money, I could tell by the tone of his voice that he sensed a change in me.

At Hardee's restaurant in Theodore, it was not easy telling Tanya's parents that I had no intentions of marrying their daughter. I was not surprised when her Daddy asked me to stay away from Tanya so that she could get on with her life.

"I want to be able to see my son," I argued.

"If you provide for him, financially, you have every right to visit him," her Daddy said.

"I've given Tanya a lot of money already," I said. "I'm gonna keep giving her as much as she needs to buy things for him."

"That's all good and well, Jamie," he sighed. "Thing is, it takes more than money to raise a child. No question, Kyle will need a father in his life. I just hope you're the man for the job."

25

FROM THE MOMENT DONNY caught sight of how things had changed for me, as I sat there in a nice restaurant, well dressed and with money in my pocket, I could tell he was in. Jan had asked me to set up the meeting with Donny to inform him of what was going on and how things worked. Specifically, he wanted me to tell him how easy it was to make good money.

Unlike me, Donny had a ton of nautical experience and worked offshore regularly. He did well with the company he was working for, but you can only go so far in a situation like that. There's something about a family business that offers a guy a little more. And I couldn't think of a more lucrative family business than Jan's.

"Why don't we take a walk?" I said. "I think Jan likes the idea of your help especially, Donny, because you know boats and you're OK out there on them seas. Not me, boy. I like to die sometimes."

Donny chuckled, "Have you ever taken Dramamine?"

"Don't do nothing for me," I said. "The water just ain't for me. As much as I like it, *it* don't like me."

"Well, so he told you to clue me in, then?"

"Yeah, we're supposed to talk pretty soon, and maybe you can go and visit Jan there in Holland, or Spain. The business is pretty lucrative."

"Well, it sounds it. You look like you done all right for yourself."

"Yeah, I can't complain." I said. The truth, however, was not as ideal as it appeared. I was hoping that Jan's *big job* would come off soon—things were getting pretty tight, and money sure can fly when you're an idiot.

We enjoyed a great meal that day—on me, of course—and made plans for Donny to travel to Holland later that month.

Without work, it seemed that all there was for me to do was sit around and wait for the next job. What is that expression—*Idle hands are the devil's workshop? They sure got that right.* And when you add a little money to the mix, things can get ugly real fast.

One of my worst moves was to reacquaint myself with my childhood friend Blaze. I probably would have been hanging around with Jay again, had his grandmother not decided "enough was enough" and enrolled him in a reform school. I felt bad for him at the time, but looking back, that was a blessing. Of course, Blaze and I figured we had it made. Lots of time on our hands, good drugs, and Jamie's money to play with.

"Let's head out to Creola," Blaze said one day. "I got a buddy named LSD you ought to meet."

His friend seemed OK, and we partied it up a little. While I was in Creola, I stopped at a service station to pick up some beer, and by chance, happened to meet a nice-looking young lady.

"I haven't seen you before," she said at the checkout counter. "Are you from around here?"

"No, I'm from up Eight Mile," I said, gathering up my stuff, as we both exited the store. "Well that's me over there," I said pointing to my brand-new truck.

Her eyebrows went up. "Nice truck!" Melissa said. As we walked over to it, she saw Blaze in the passenger seat. "Oh, hi, Blaze," she said, somewhat unenthusiastically.

"Hey, Melissa," he said.

"Y'all know each other?" I asked, as I put the stuff in my truck.

"Just through my ex-boyfriend," she said. "Well, I'll be seeing ya."

"OK, and . . ." I was a little out of practice, "how will I contact you?"

She smiled and wrote her number on a piece of paper from her purse and handed it to me, and then she turned away without another word to Blaze.

"She's a tough broad," he said as I got in. "LSD and her used to get high together a lot, but she didn't like this and she didn't like that, and—"

"He's her ex-boyfriend?" I asked. "Talk about coincidences."

"Yeah. Ain't it."

I should have taken my cue from Melissa's way of regarding Blaze. But I wasn't too sharp at that point; it didn't occur to me to give it much thought, and I don't think old Blaze even noticed.

"How about you take me to where she lives," I said. "There could be something in it for you, a few bucks."

"You don't have to ask me twice," he said.

Melissa had arrived home a short while ahead of us, but I could tell that, aside from being a little startled, she was glad to see me. "So what brings you by so soon?" she asked. "Did you lose something?"

I just smiled and before I knew it, we'd arranged a date for the following week. "Can't wait," she said as we left. Neither could I.

Back in Eight Mile, I received a phone call.

"Hi, Jamie," Tanya said. "OK if I come by there tonight? My folks'll drop us off."

"Us?"

"Me and our baby, silly!" she said. I could hear in her voice that she wanted to get back together.

"Well, come on over," I said. "I think we should talk about this."

That night, she arrived with our son. We sat and talked for a long while, trying not to raise our voices in front of the baby. But there really was no way.

"Listen," she said. "I get where you're coming from. OK, so we wait a while before we get married. That's OK with me."

"But, Tanya, you're already seeing that other guy. It

don't seem—"

"No!" she laughed. "You mean Eric? No, he and I are just friends. You didn't give me any time to explain that night."

"Ok. But see, it's been a long time, you know? We don't seem to be able to stick to each other, one on one, without letting a whole bunch of other people in on things . . ."

"Look, Jamie, you messed around as much as I did. You can't deny that. I think we both sewed our wild oats. Now it's time to settle in with our son."

I paced a little, trying to find the right words. "Look, Tanya. I met somebody. I think I might be fallin' for her."

"Oh great," she said. "Just a little too late, huh?"

"Tanya—"

"No, it's OK, Jamie. Look, my parents are probably not home, and Kyle's all settled in. Why don't I get them to come pick me up in the morning?"

"I guess that'll be OK. I'll just sleep over there, next to my son."

And that's how it was. I didn't waste any time, and it wasn't long before Melissa was with me most of the time. Indeed, Tanya didn't waste any time either—she and the guy, Eric, I saw her with that night were expecting a baby by the beginning of the following year.

I had little contact with Zonder during that period, or Trans and Jan. By August, Donny took off for Sneekweek (an inland sailing event) to see Jan, but I was unable to go, since things were getting pretty fuzzy for me by then. And with Melissa and I spending whole nights doing ecstasy or smoking pot, "fuzzy" was the right word for it. Then, we'd sleep all day long. I got Zonder to send me six hundred ecstasy tablets, which I was thinking of selling, but we were so immersed in it by then that between me, Melissa, Blaze—and his two cousins, Robby Wayne and Billy Joe, who had started coming around—we didn't have any left to sell.

Sometimes, Melissa and I would drive down to Gulf Shores and stay the night in some nice hotel. But by that time, all I could think of besides getting high, was the *big job* that Jan had mentioned.

"This is nice, Jamie," Melissa said, as we peered out of the window overlooking the beach one night in Gulf Shores. "We should go out there tonight."

"I don't know about that," I said. "I think we'd be more comfortable inside—safer, too."

"You wanna order something to eat?"

"If you're hungry, go ahead. I think I'm good."

But money was running through my fingers just like sand when you scoop out the kitty litter box. And I had virtually the same amount left that you have on that scooper when you're done. My life was moving in a downward spiral, and I had no idea. I thought all I had to do was call Jan and he'd fix me up.

Things weren't going exactly swimmingly around J&J Grocery either. Every night, there were dark dealings right there in the parking lot, with folks coming down to Eight Mile from the nearby town of Prichard. My Mama would be on the phone every time she saw anything suspicious.

"Hello, Police? I've got another drug deal to report, right in front of my eyes . . . Yes, I'm looking at it right now . . . What do I want? I want you to come over here and arrest these people!"

But nobody came. There was a detective on the force in Prichard where these guys came from, named Amos Smiley. He was one smart detective, though not what you would call reputable by any means. There were a couple of gangs in Prichard, the Prichard Boyz and the Black Disciples. Both of these gangs used to buy their crack from a group down in Miami who called themselves—you guessed it—the Miami Boyz. Real original. Good old Amos Smiley would find out when one of the shipments was sent to the Prichard Boyz, then go and bust them, confiscate the crack, and send it back down to Miami—I guess you'd say "return the merchandise," where he'd rake in a nice profit. He was stashing his income somewhere down there in Miami—looking to retire in style. But there was a less glamorous future in store for Amos Smiley . . . something I'll come to later on.

One night, I went over to see Daddy at the J&J, and out on Outlaw Road there were cop cars everywhere, lights spinning like the county fair. I don't know why they didn't stop me, but I drove by slowly and happened to look over at a Cadillac Coupe de Ville. I learned later that it was a drug deal gone bad. Yellow crime tape was being strung up all around and it was a sight that, even in my demented mental state, would stay with me forever. In the front of the Cadillac, this poor guy's brains were blown out, with little bits of him all across the posh white leather seats.

Soon after, I received the call for the *big job* and was told to fly to Denmark. In my possession, I had my ticket, $600 to pay Zonder for those six hundred ecstasy tabs, and just $1,000 remaining. I was ready to work!

26

I ARRIVED IN COPENHAGEN on time, expecting to see some-body familiar to pick me up. Nobody seemed to be there to meet me and, since I was very tired, I figured I'd just sit around and wait for a while—after all, traffic could be bad in European countries, so they might have been delayed. After a long wait, I decided to call Zonder in Sneek.

"Look, Jamie, I'll explain it to you when I see you, but just fly into Amsterdam. I'll pick you up," he said.

With my wallet growing lighter by the minute, I bought a ticket to Amsterdam.

"There was a problem with the boat," Zonder said as we left the airport. "Oom Jan was supposed to use the crane on board, but at the last minute, it didn't work, or it wasn't strong enough or something. So they had to fix it, and in the mean-time, the whole thing was called off. Why don't you come on back with me to my aunt's house and wait for a while?"

"He's got a crane on the boat?" I asked. "What's that for?"

"The crane picks up the packages," he explained. "They are dropped by a low-flying aircraft. And then the crane raises them into the boat. You were to collect them here, but unfortunately, there's nothing to collect."

My heart sank. I was totally broke. What on earth would I do and what was Melissa going to think? Things were not going my way, but I stayed positive, believing they'd come back around soon.

"Listen, Zonder, here's the six hundred I owe you for them ecstasy tabs."

"Oh, good. Did you make good money on that?"

I didn't know what to say. There were only a few of them left, and I doubted I'd be selling those. "I hope to," I said. "But I'm a little low now, so I sure hope that job comes through soon."

"At my aunt's house, we are remodeling," he said. "You could help us out with that."

That was like a rock hitting my stomach. Here I was thinking I'd be taking home another hundred or couple of hundred grand, but I was being offered the opportunity to do some odd jobs at someone's house.

I couldn't quite figure it out at the time, but I sensed that Zonder regarded me differently, and after I'd been there for a few days, I felt like the true outsider I really was. Although everyone was kind and took great care of me, somehow I was no longer part of the inner circle.

"I don't know, Melissa," I said, one night on the phone. "I just got here a few days ago."

"Jamie, it's been a week," she said. "If there's no work for you, why don't you come home?"

"Hey, I miss you, too," I said. "I really do. I feel like I should stick around for a little while, though. It'd be a whole lot better if I come home with a little paycheck, don't you think?"

She laughed and we went on to talk about other things. She said her mama was getting antsy about our relationship, and it was causing her some trouble. I knew then it was time for me to get serious about earning some money. But here was my problem: my perception of work and the amount I could earn had changed. I had never been afraid of good hard work, and I knew I would do it again, but I also knew how easy it had been to acquire that first $200,000. I wasn't thinking about how fast those large sums evaporated out of my hands, and I was sure I could earn it again. I reasoned that Jan couldn't have foreseen the problems with the boat, and things would come around again . . . it just wasn't time yet.

But a week later, it still wasn't time, so I went home to Melissa using my remaining money. I arrived at Mobile airport broke and confused. I could no longer afford the luxury of trying to be the big man.

"Listen, Melissa," I said, "I'm glad you came to pick me up in the Silverado, but I'm going to have to trade this thing in, at least for now. I got no money, baby, and so I got no choice."

She'd always wanted a car like that, and I felt bad having to strip it away from her, but she was OK with it—it was all only a temporary measure after all.

We drove to a car dealership not far from the airport to make an exchange.

"This is a very, very good car," said the Pakistani dealer, showing us an alternative car. "You will get very good mileage, and you will save money," he smiled.

We drove away in a VW Rabbit, with $5,000 in cash.

At least by that point, I realized that money doesn't last forever, and so I started looking for a regular job. Around five years before, at eighteen years old, I'd spent the summer working down in Patterson, Louisiana, on the Gulf Coast at an oilfield called Galaxy Marina. My buddy Blaze and I headed out that way, figuring we could make enough in a few months to coast along for a while. When we arrived, we started filling out some application forms when Blaze saw a poster pinned to the wall of the reception area.

"Look at that," he said. It was a nice rendering of Uncle Sam, and in bold lettering: *CASH REWARD! We pay cash money for information leading to the arrest and conviction of drug smugglers. Call Now!* It included a telephone number encouraging willing informants to get in touch.

"Hey, that's not a bad idea!" he continued. "We sure know our share of drug dealers, huh, Jamie?"

I felt uneasy but laughed it off and kept working on my application.

When we returned to the counter, however, the receptionist informed us of a mandatory drug test—to be taken that day. That clearly wasn't going to work, so we grabbed our applications and made a hasty exit.

"I don't know what I'm gonna do, Blaze," I said. "Seems like everything's just falling apart."

"Oh, you'll get something, Jamie. You got any of them tabs left?"

And so it went on.

The Rabbit was doing OK for me, just as the Pakistani guy said it would. I was scraping the bottom of the barrel to get the gas money for it, but at least the car seemed like it would be a worthy investment in the end.

As far as earning money was concerned, it was on to plan B.

"I don't know, Jamie," said Jessie Ray, Jr. "It's been a while, and I need people I can really count on. You . . . I don't know." Junior built cabinets, and when he was not doing that, he worked for Prichard Fire-Rescue Department as a fireman. So, with his hands full, there was an opportunity for me to help out with the cabinet business.

"Listen, I know I've been a little off lately," I said. "I guess this whole thing with Jan threw me. But I know I need to work now, just like I always did. I was always a good worker before, and I can be one now."

"Do you remember any of what I taught you?"

"I sure do. I think I can use the sanding machines still. And I'll do whatever you want. Heck, I'll sweep up—anything."

"All right, I guess we can try," he said. "But I got serious customers, so I need serious help, you got it?"

"I sure do. I'll be reliable and take things very serious from here on in. Thanks, Junior."

At last I had secured a decent job. I also maintained the car wash job with Mr. Clyde Johnson—he knew Blaze and I weren't serious about a long-term profession, but we were good at what we did, and he seemed happy to have us there. I think.

By then, it was around March 1995, and Melissa, Blaze, and his two cousins were frequently doing some kind of drugs. Invariably, they'd stay up late, and consequently, I'd show up late for work.

"So, this is what you call serious and reliable?" Jessie Ray, Jr., demanded, one morning. "I'm serious, and this business is reliable, so if you don't start showing up on time, you'll be right out of a job. You can count on me for that."

I went home feeling rattled. I hadn't heard from Jan or anybody over in Holland for a long time. I wondered what the problem was. It never occurred to me that you had to be on your best behavior to ingratiate yourself with a drug-dealing father. And I was a little upset by the reprimand I had received from Junior, especially seeing as he was my brother. Clyde Johnson never bothered about us being late or not showing up, but the work with him was sporadic anyway. With Jessie Ray, Jr., however, it was my duty to show up on time every day. And I was letting him down.

All I could think of was, *When am I gonna get that call? This is taking forever!* Jan was so fired up to come see me that Christmas of '93, and now I don't receive a single call. It was like I never existed. This was how I perceived it, but I had no understanding of the realities and motives behind Jan and his operation over in Holland.

To add to the mess, Melissa, who by then was living with me in the trailer, decided Blaze was a creep.

"What do you mean?" I said. "He's all right. No better, no worse than me."

"I don't know," she said. "He looks at me funny sometimes, and I don't like it at all when he comes by and you're not here."

"He comes by when I'm not here?"

"A couple times. I think he was thinking I wouldn't be here either, Jamie. I think he was looking for some stash or something. I don't know. But he really gives me the creeps."

Well that got me. I knew he had broken into a few other people's houses and stolen from them. I'd also heard from a buddy that he had been shorting people for drugs and pulling all kinds of stunts to support his habit. But I didn't realize he was betraying me as well.

"Are you sure about that, Melissa?" I asked.

"Jamie, one time I was in the bedroom and I seen him looking through that cabinet over there, where you keep your cash."

"Why didn't you tell me then!" I almost shouted.

"Because he said he just wanted a Styrofoam cup," she said. "He was thirsty and didn't want to take your last beer, so he was gonna get some water. That's what he told me. But after a while, I kind of figured he was looking for something else and didn't know I was here to catch him."

That was it for me. It wasn't long before I had a talk with Blaze and explained to him that my girlfriend was uncomfortable around him, and I'd like him to keep himself away from our place. He said he understood.

"That's all right, Jamie," he said. "She's probably worried she'll be tempted to switch over to me."

I didn't like the way he laughed when he said that, but I let it slide and didn't see him for a while.

One morning around the end of March, on a day that I had actually shown up on time for work, I was doing my best to get a set of doors smoothed out, and a car arrived looking like that of an undercover cop. I immediately assumed somebody must be in trouble with the law.

One guy stepped out wearing biker clothes and looking like Jesus, while his partner, an old hippy-looking guy, had a long beard.

"James Cobb?" said Jesus, flashing his badge. U.S. Customs, it said.

"Yes, Sir?" I said, having no idea what was going on.

"Could you come with us, Son? We need to ask you a few questions."

Jessie Ray, Jr., wasn't around and I had nothing to write with to leave a note. They could see I was flustered and the older guy said, "You want to call your boss?"

"No, that's all right," I said.

As we drove off, I thought it wouldn't hurt to ask a few questions. "Where are we headed—down to the courthouse?"

"No, we gotta go to Louisiana, Mr. Cobb. Homer, to be exact."

As we drove along the highway, Jesus explained a few things. "So, your buddy, goes by the name of Blaze I understand? He told us you might want to speak to us. He thought you might be able to help us out with some pretty major drug players."

"Oh," I said, nodding. Blaze. The guy who'd just helped me spend upwards of $50,000 on booze and dope. I guess when the money ran out, so did the "buddy."

They went on to say that they knew a fair amount about Jan van Rijn and that I might know a good deal more, and of course, that they'd like me to enlighten them.

"I'm sorry, I really don't think you've got it right." I said. "Yes, he's my biological father, and I did spend some time out there with him in Europe. But he's not into anything illegal. He's got a real successful designer clothing business."

"Blaze tells us you helped with the smuggling operation," Jesus continued. "He said you made a ton of cash doing it."

"Well, I don't know what to say to you," I said. "My father's generous and successful. But I will tell you this. My girlfriend caught your man, Blaze, trying to swipe stuff out of our home. After that I told him he better not come back around. And I can see why he'd make stuff up like this."

They brushed my reply off and began talking about a drug kingpin by the name of Barry Seals. Apparently, he had made a fortune in illegal drug trafficking but had not been so discerning in his choice of friends. At his first vulnerable moment, he was blown away by his cohorts when they suspected he had ratted on them.

I was thinking, *So what?* Did they believe such stories were going to make me turn in my father? *Were they nuts?* But then I thought of how Blaze must have told the story from his point of view. He probably said, "Yeah, ol' Jamie went all the way over to Denmark on his last dime, and that son of a bitch didn't even bother to show up. Gave him some sucker's line about problems with the deal, and Jamie came back here broke and real pissed off." So maybe these Customs guys thought I wanted revenge on the guy and blew him away? They didn't know me from Adam.

"That poor fellow," I said, when Jesus finished the story.

I ended up having to spend the night in Homer, in a Holiday Inn. They sat there, chatting with each other, while I read the hotel Bible.

At the time I thought I was smart, eavesdropping on the conversation without their knowledge.

"Yeah, looks like they got him good this time," said Southern Beard.

"Who's that?" the Jesus look-alike asked.

"You know, that fellow right here in Homer? Listen to this. He was getting that dope right there on that Texas border. Them Mexicans don't know what it's worth. That guy bought it for $150, maybe $200 a pound down there, and stuck it in the hull of that big bass boat of his."

"No kidding! Brought it back here over the border?"

"Yep. Fifty, sixty, seventy-five pounds a trip. You know

they're getting $500 for it now. So he made himself a nice little nest egg there for a while."

They both had a good laugh. "Except I don't know if there's gonna be anything left in that nest, now!" And they laughed some more.

At the time, I thought, *What a couple of idiots.* Don't they realize I can figure out the exact same trick?

Of course they did. And chances are, they were looking for me to involve Jan in the little plan, not realizing that Jan was into huge deals, "tons" as Trans used to proudly proclaim. Even $350 times a thousand wouldn't make Jan blink an eyelid. And it wasn't pot he was into—it was hashish, a much more valuable commodity.

I inwardly sighed with relief when they said we were going back home. Being close to everything those guys represented—especially jail time—was not at all comfortable. I couldn't know what they knew, and being that Blaze was not a reliable witness, they might have had doubts themselves.

I'm guessing they put a tail on me for a while, but seeing little activity or conversation between me and Jan, they probably backed off and started fishing for somebody else—for a while, anyway. And I was just happy to know I was going back to a steady job and a happy home.

Not.

When I got back, Junior had some words for me. "Now listen, Jamie. I hate to do this, but I warned you. You show up late all the time, dicking around and wasting time, and now you go and get yourself picked up by the cops. I am running a reputable business here. I can't be associated with that kind of stuff. And especially when there's problems with the law. I'm going to have to let you go."

Well, that did it. I went on home with my last paycheck, which wasn't much, and started smoking weed with Melissa and some friends and partying for days on end. I guess a couple of the guys got pretty loud, because my Aunt Ruby, whose house was adjacent to the trailer home, had had just about enough. She called my folks, and they came right over.

And there I was with Melissa, stoned out of my mind, while a couple of our friends made speedy exits.

"What on earth is going on here?" Mama said.

"We're just hanging out," I began. "I don't have to work today so . . ."

"Oh we know all about your work schedule with Junior," Daddy said. "What your mama wants to know is what is that foul odor in the air? Are you burning spinach or something?"

I knew he knew what it was and I wasn't getting out of it. "Daddy, Mama, I'm real sorry about this. It's just I been really depressing since I lost my job—"

It's funny how you think things are going to work out when you're caught up in feeding your habits. When you're in that state, it's hard to believe that anybody can see through you. I was sure they'd understand, but I was wrong, and the hammer came down.

"Young Lady," my mother said to Melissa. "Do your parents know you're here?"

"Well, yeah—" she began, but that was as far as she got.

"Well call her up and tell her to come get you and all your things. You're not going to be here a minute longer."

"Hey—" and I started what I thought would be an eloquent speech about how I was old enough to decide who would be allowed in my home and who would not, and that Melissa was a bright part of my life that I needed to help me and share my life with, but all my plans were summarily cut short.

"You get your stuff, too, Son," my father said. "You're also moving out."

"Moving out?" I said. "What do you mean? This is my house!"

"Not anymore it isn't," he said. "You put this thing in my name, you've missed four payments that I've had to make up, and it's sitting on my land. It's no longer your home and I suggest you take with you what you can carry and get on out."

Things deteriorated further after that, and I left with what I could fit into my VW Rabbit, while Melissa's mother arrived and took her off, crying.

One good piece of luck I had was that Blaze decided to try to rip off his cousin Billy Joe, and as a consequence, Billy Joe wanted nothing to do with him. I hoped Billy Joe would remember how much pot I'd supplied him with over the months, and sure enough, when I called, I got a green light for a change.

"Hey, buddy, I just lost my house," I said. "Mind if I crash there a while?"

"Come on over," he said. "Me and Uncle Beavis got some

room on the couch for ya."

So, at least I wasn't homeless, and I headed over to Billy Joe's, who lived with his Uncle Beavis. But I was still in a fog and not sure what I was doing, getting slowly strangled by my own addictions.

Volume 2

CRIMINALITY

27

Summer of 1995

HANGING AROUND BEAVIS'S PLACE—a ramshackle affair that wasn't going to win any *Good Housekeeping* awards—was not going to last too long. Nevertheless, I did make some new acquaintances, including one guy by the name of Garrett, who came by for weed and pills, which he bought off Beavis's son, Robby Wayne. I thought he was cool. I'd known a few black guys in my time, but Garrett had my sense of humor, such as it was in my degenerated state. Looking back, just about everybody around that time seemed to have my sense of humor—a result, perhaps, of the crowd I was with. But I liked Garrett and we used to hang around together. I guess we both liked some of the same drugs, too.

I had spent a good couple of weeks brooding about having been kicked out of my trailer with nowhere to live, with Daddy knowing that I had no money. I thought it was heartless and just plain cruel. Now, of course, I realize he and Mama were probably thinking that I would straighten out if they gave me a taste of tough love. What they didn't understand was that I was on a one-way street in a downward direction, and I had no intention of stopping until I reached my destination.

"He really kicked you out your own house?" Garrett said. He couldn't believe it either.

"Right there in front of Melissa, too. Made me look like a damn fool. And I put thousands of dollars into that place, too!"

Not long after that conversation, we hatched a plan whereby we would get even with Daddy for what he'd done to me. It was my idea to bust into Mama and Daddy's house while they were working at the grocery store and lift the safe Daddy kept there. I knew it would have the Krugerrand I gave him from Gibraltar, a stack of cash, and an old gun Daddy owned.

The irony of this plan didn't hit me at the time—I was such a "big man" when I came home from Spain with my gifts, jewelry, and floating on money. But not only had I lost it all, I was now reaching back to grab what I'd given away—in theft, no less. These are the things you don't think about when you're in that state—how to get money any way you can.

Despite our misguided and bizarre plan, we did just that. We broke in while they were away, as far as I knew without anyone seeing, took the safe, and stole everything that was in it after prying it open. I threw the gun in the Mobile River. I thank God every day that guns were never my thing. The only guns we'd been exposed to as kids were for hunting, and even then, we more often went fishing. So, mercifully, the gun was out of the picture. That could have made things a whole lot worse on that one-way downhill road.

In the state I was in, I don't remember exactly what we used the money for, but I guess drugs were the main thing, and whatever we had left to eat. It didn't paint a pretty picture with Melissa. When I was kicked out of the trailer, she had taken off to Iowa, which had only deepened my feelings of depression and guilt.

"You think things are gonna get better, Jamie? You gonna work for your biological father again, ever?"

"Oh I'm sure I will," I said. "He's just got to get things straightened out, and I'll be back over there in no time."

That was the stuff talking and I'd be lying if I said I could remember all of what I said and did during those times. But I do remember that there was a dark shadow of desperation hanging over me, over all of us, but me especially, as I had known a better life. Beavis and his boys had always roughed it, living a meager life paycheck to paycheck, until Beavis had convinced the authorities that he was insane and began to draw a monthly disability check. That brought in enough money for them to sustain their impoverished existence and enough drugs to keep them all safely out of touch with reality. And there I was, in the midst of it, having come from a stable family with roots and a deep love and respect for me.

But all I could think about was getting back to Spain and living the good life, making all that money and then *really* impressing folks—I'd show them!

One day, I received a call from Daddy telling me to go

and see him over at the grocery store. He'd sold my trailer and wanted to settle up. "Well, thank God," I said to Billy Joe. "This is what I've been waiting for! I put over twenty grand in that trailer. This ought to fix me up pretty good."

"Here's your money," Daddy said when I got to the store. "There's fifteen hundred."

"So, fifteen hundred here," I said, "and what, you got a check for the *rest* or something?"

"Rest? Ain't no *rest*. This is it."

"Fifteen hundred! Fifteen *hundred!*"

"Yeah, fifteen hundred, and you watch your tone or you won't get that."

It hit me like a bomb. I just about lost my breath out of disappointment, pain, and rage. "I put thousands into that trailer! I put $7,000 down for chrissakes!"

"Watch your language!" Daddy yelled. "Yes, you put money in it, but you took it out, too, didn't you?"

For a second, I thought he was going to raise the subject of the missing safe, but that was just my paranoia.

"How many months did you miss that note—six, seven? I had to make up all of that for you. And there's no appreciation on them trailers. I was lucky to get rid of the thing, all that pot smokin' smell and alcohol and Lord knows what all else. No, Sir. You consider yourself lucky!"

I flew out of the store, my heart in my throat. I could not see straight, and for once it had nothing to do with all the junk in my system. It was one thing to be cheated by a con man—it was a whole different story to stand there, listening to your daddy justify taking your money.

And there's another irony—I was destroyed by Daddy's taking what I felt was mine, but how did *he* feel when he found out I was the one who broke into his house and stole his safe? That part comes later.

"I can't believe it, Jamie. I'm so sorry to hear it," Melissa said on the phone, when I told her about it.

"Yeah. But I gotta get out of this hole that I'm living in. I'm going to go looking soon as I can."

"Where you moving to?" she asked.

"Not too far. I'm keeping my job with Mr. Johnson, washing cars and all. But I just gotta get outta *here.*"

I found myself a trailer down on Howell's Ferry Road. It wasn't exactly Disneyland, but it was cleaner and better than the squalor I'd just come from. Garrett came by to visit, and Melissa was glad I was away from the other guys.

I tried to stay sober enough to get to work when I was supposed to be on duty and do a good job when I was there. Fortunately, Mr. Johnson kept me around at the car wash, pothead that I was.

One day, while I was working, along came another suspicious looking vehicle. The U.S. Customs agents are at it again, I figured. There was no point in being evasive, so I walked over and asked them what they wanted.

"We'd like to speak to you a little more," said Southern Beard. "That is, if you don't mind."

"No Sir, I don't mind," I said. "Let me just tell my boss."

I suspected they'd gone back to Blaze for more information, and probably found my current whereabouts from him. This was confirmed when they started their questioning.

"Where we going?" I asked, as I got in the car.

"Just on down to Mobile," said the one that looked like Jesus. "Federal court building."

"Oh that's a real nice one," I said, just to show them I wasn't nervous.

Once we got there, I was seated in a more formal situation than the last time and told to answer the questions as best as I could.

"Have you ever heard of ecstasy, Mr. Cobb?"

"Yes, Sir."

"You know what it costs?"

"Costs?"

"Sure, do you know how much, say, one pill costs?"

I almost burst out laughing to hear it mentioned in such a formal way. "No, Sir," I said, truthfully. I knew it cost $2,000 for fifteen hundred pills wholesale, but I had little idea of the price for a single pill.

"Well, I'd say around twenty-five dollars apiece," another fellow answered.

"Yes, Sir," I said. At this point I was sure they'd gone back to Blaze. Only Blaze and Melissa knew I'd brought ecstasy into the country. And Melissa wasn't on their radar yet.

We went around in circles for a while—they interrogated me, while I frustrated them with "I don't know, Sir." Eventually they got around to asking about Jan.

"Do you know Jan van Rijn?"

"Yes, Sir."

"How do you know this man?"

"He's my biological father."

"Have you ever worked for him?"

"Yes, Sir."

"Doing what?"

"Taking care of his house, washing his car; once I washed his boat."

"Did you smuggle drugs into this country for him?"

"No, Sir."

"Do you like your biological father?"

"He's all right."

"You wouldn't want to get him into any trouble would you?"

"I don't want to get anybody into any trouble," I said.

"Do you fear him?"

"He didn't scare me none when I met him."

This charade was frustrating them no end, and I thought I was being clever.

"We're giving you this chance, Son," said Southern Beard. "Before long, you won't have an opportunity to talk to us. I'll be too late. Now, do you want to reconsider any of your answers?"

"I got nothing to reconsider, Sir," I answered.

One of the fellows sitting in the corner, a black guy with a northern accent said, "I wouldn't let that kid go. He looks like a rabbit to me."

"I reckon you're right, Jackson," said the Jesus look-alike.

"But we ain't got nothin' on 'im, yet."

When they had finished the questioning, they took me back to my job of washing cars. I might have been playing it cool, but their last comment rattled me. *They didn't have anything on me—yet.*

I realized that they might be closing in. The drugs I was using, a real paranoia cocktail, were making me so jittery that I worried all the time. In my mind I believed that if I could just get some money, I'd be able to put things right.

The first safe theft had gone smoothly, so we started cooking up a plan to steal the safe in Mr. Johnson's house. He had a son who used to brag about how much money his daddy had in there, and so that seemed the logical place to aim for. The plan was to go to the house and wait for Mr. Johnson to leave for work, and Garrett to enter through the back door as Billy Joe and I watched from the woods. With the feds already watching me, the rationale behind committing another crime was clearly dubious, but in my state of mind, rational thinking wasn't top of the agenda.

Nevertheless, Garrett, Billy Joe, and I pulled it off, quick and clean. Inside the safe was $80,000—an excellent payoff.

But in our small town, we knew it was only a matter of time—somebody was sure to latch on to who did it.

One night, while the three of us were over at Beavis's house, watching *60 Minutes* on TV, we learned how you could obtain a high-quality fake ID in California.

"You know, that ain't a bad idea," I said. "I think I'll get me one of them, and spend some time away, till this thing blows over."

"I'm with you," Garrett said. "Things is getting pretty hot around here."

Billy Joe preferred to leave to be with his immediate family, who lived down in Stone County, Mississippi. "They don't know me for nobody down there," he said. "I'm not flying out somewhere I don't know where in the world I am."

"I hear you," Garrett said. "If it weren't for my man Jamie here, I wouldn't be running off neither. But seein how he's an experienced world traveler . . ." Everybody laughed. Nervously.

As planned, we went out to California and it turned out that *60 Minutes* was the perfect textbook on how to get those fake IDs. A cab driver who seemed to know how things operated in the area was happy to make some money from us "loco gringos," so he took us on down to Tijuana, where we got our fake IDs with very little effort. He also told us about some "opportunities" in what he called the "sales profession."

"You should go a la Acapulco," he said. "Dey make beeeg money in Acapulco. The powder, ju know, the leetle powder?"

I didn't know if I was up to more work just yet, but I knew I had money to burn, so off I went to sunny Acapulco with Garrett. I also arranged for Melissa to fly in from Iowa in what turned out to be a pleasant reunion.

"I missed you so much, Jamie," she said. "I'm so glad you're doing better, now."

"I missed you, too. You didn't think I was gonna leave you there alone, did you?"

She laughed. "I sure hoped not. I'm just glad things are getting better."

"They sure are!" I said, giving her a hug. "I'm back on top."

And we acted like a couple of superstars, spending money like a couple of fools. Garrett was having fun too, hanging around a club called Extravaganza. They posted pictures of O. J. Simpson on the walls, and Michael Jackson, suggesting they were regulars there. There was powder cocaine flying all over the place and I indulged in the stuff for the first time. It was a nasty shock to the system—if I was thin before, I was flat-out scrawny, red-eyed, and puffy-faced on that stuff. It was a nasty drug.

But that's not all we did; there was plenty of substances of every kind to go around. If you wanted it, it was there for you. We killed brain cells and shorted-out synapses for years to come. I thought I was having a good time and that things would go on that way forever. At least that was what I wanted to believe.

Like the previous year, I worked through all of my ill-gotten booty in just weeks. With only a little left, probably a few thousand, I put Melissa on a plane back to Alabama.

"You're coming back soon, right?" she asked, as we said goodbye.

"Soon as I can. But like I told you, I'm trying to get a little work, first."

"Be careful, Jamie."

Garrett and I decided to take a bus down to Nuevo

Laredo, Mexico, which is a nice place across the Rio Grande River from Laredo, Texas. Apart from being a very busy international trading port, it's a very active drug-smuggling city. We had a chance to look around, but I thought it was time to check in with Jan, and Garrett decided to go on back to Alabama.

"I'll see ya, buddy," I said, as he headed for the bus. "I'll probably catch up with you in a week or two."

"Sounds good. Good luck with your father," he said, as we shook hands.

I didn't see Garrett again—well, not for a long time. He headed east for Alabama, and I headed for the bar.

A few days later I was talking to Melissa on the telephone.

"Hey, baby, how's it going?"

"Jamie!" she said, her voice in a whisper.

"What's the matter?"

"Jamie, they got wanted posters up all over town with your picture on it and they are offering $10,000 for your arrest."

"*Wanted* posters?" I was sick to my stomach. So, our supposed "clean escape" hadn't been very successful; "I guess I better not come back there, then," I said, barely breathing.

After we hung up, I wondered if the feds had seen the posters, and if so, were they now working with the local police to catch me? I wondered how far they would go to get me. My mind started flying in all directions, and by this time I had so many drugs in my system, I wasn't sure where they stopped and I began. And I now didn't seem to have any ability to kick the habit.

After I got a hold of myself for a few minutes, I decided to call Jan.

"Jan," I said, "how you doin'? It's Jamie."

"Yes, Jamie, I recognize your voice."

"How y'all doing?"

"Just fine, thank you."

"Keeping busy?"

"Not too busy. Enjoying the beautiful weather."

It was like pulling teeth. "Well that's nice . . ."

"Yes."

"Listen, I was thinking about coming out to pay y'all a visit."

"You want to come for a visit? That's nice, Son."

"Yeah, it's been a while and all."

"All right. Just let me know when. I will pick you up."

I hung up the phone. All right, I thought, so he said to come over, and he sounded like he would pick me up this time. But something was definitely different. Or was that just me imagining things, paranoid again? Jan had said to come over, but that afternoon I battled with the dilemma—should I go back?

Before I returned to Spain, though, I thought I should meet Billy Joe in Mississippi and see what he knew about what was going on in Alabama regarding the safe theft.

"What's going on with that?" I asked. "Have you heard anything?"

"I don't know, man," he said. "I heard the cops know something, anyway."

"You heard about the wanted posters?"

"Yeah, man," he said, looking awkward.

"They don't say nothin' 'bout you," I said, "or Garrett."

"I been down here the whole time," Billy Joe said. "I wouldn't never roll on you, man, I guess. I don't know."

"It was Garrett, wasn't it?"

He just stood there—he didn't know what to say. Finally he said, "I . . . I guess so, man."

Soon, it was time to fly to Spain. Billy Joe drove me the Intercontinental Airport in Houston. "Be safe, man," he said.

It was a desperate time. Betrayal like that can rip you up inside. With the cocaine banging on your brain, and whatever else you're feeding your body, the paranoia makes you virtually dysfunctional. Aboard the plane, I was convinced someone was watching me from the second seat over. And the flight attendant was keeping an eye on me—or at least, that's what I thought.

When I got to Spain, I had a mild panic attack, remembering my landing in Denmark, when Jan hadn't bothered to let me know about what was going on. Further paranoid thoughts led me to believe maybe he *had*, but my cousins chose to make it look like he didn't keep me informed. In any case, Jan and Leo came to the airport to pick me up, just as promised.

Once we were in the car, he showed his true feelings. "Jamie, you look awful. It is clear to me that you have been indulging way too heavily. What is going on with you, anyway?"

I spelled out the story of the safe, being on wanted posters, and our time in Acapulco, and what I had learned from the U.S. Customs officers.

"Federal officers?" he said, his voice rising a little. "What are you doing talking to federal officers?"

"I don't tell 'em nothing, Jan. Seriously."

"You have been approached by federal officers and you have come here? To see me?" The tone of his voice made me feel like something you get on the bottom of your shoe in a cow pasture. I didn't know what to say.

"I need to work," I said, hoping to appeal to his fatherly instincts. The expression on his face reminded me of something Wendy had told me a long time before: he had no fatherly instincts, he didn't know how to be a father. That seemed too kind to me at the time. He did everything but laugh me out of the car.

"Surely you don't expect to come here with U.S. marshals following you, and begin working for me?"

"I guess I thought we might be able to—"

"Here, turn here, Leo." We pulled into the El Presidente Hotel.

"What are we doing here?" I said, feeling very weak.

"I am very disappointed in you, Jamie. And you do not look good. You look like a drug addict. I cannot take you to the house because I have people there. This is not the happy occasion I imagined. I will get you a suite here for the night."

I sat in a beautiful hotel room that night, staring blankly out the window, not able to appreciate any of the natural beauty or the spectacular city. My heart was so heavy, I couldn't bear to recall my last visit to that country and the lush welcome and comforts I was given. I felt a pounding in my head, and a message that I couldn't quite interpret. Perhaps it was a warning that I should have heeded long ago, but it wasn't coming in clearly. After a while, I gave in to the depression and rejection and fell asleep. The next day, I was taken to the airport and sent home with $5,000 in French francs. I had been disposed of.

As I flew away from the Mediterranean, I considered a brief conversation we'd had in the car on the way to the airport.

"I know how I can get cocaine cheap," I had said. "Can I bring you a few keys to make some quick cash?"

"No," said Jan, as if he were training a Saint Bernard. "I don't mess with amounts that small. Get Trans to help you."

As I mulled this over on the flight, I began to get my bearings, motivated and insulted by the rejection and lack of confidence Jan had shown in me. I was small fry; he didn't rate me.

So, he wants to be a hotshot, I thought. *I'll outsmart that son of a bitch. I'll find myself a good hot business, and he'll wish he'd come in with me at the start.* All this, while I clutched $5,000 tight to my chest—the money he'd just given me. What a twisted world I lived in.

28

AT THE BRAND-NEW George Bush Intercontinental Airport on the northern outskirts of Houston, I exchanged all but a thousand dollars' worth of the French francs my father had given me. A taxi took me to the Greyhound terminal downtown, where I bought a ticket to Laredo for the following morning.

Drifting off to sleep in my hotel room overlooking Interstate 45, I figured I'd eat a good steak dinner when I made it to Nuevo Laredo and maybe have some margaritas before I caught the next bus to Acapulco. From there, I wasn't sure what I'd do, but I was determined to make things happen, no matter what.

We pulled into the San Antonio bus station at noon on Thursday. During the trip, I'd been thinking of the way my father had disregarded me in Spain and how I was supposed to get the keys from Mexico to Europe. I hoped he wasn't expecting me to smuggle them through the airport. *That would be pretty dumb*, I thought, while more passengers climbed aboard the Greyhound.

The last person to step on was a young Mexican wearing big, dark shades and black Dickies clothes. He was a *real* Mexican with Indian blood in him; I could tell by his wide nose and pronounced cheekbones. His glossy jet-black hair was slicked straight back and his arms were ripped with muscles and sleeved in ink. He had a bleeding INRI cross on his left forearm and the other was wrapped around in tattooed barbed wire that was drawn to look like it was ripping into his flesh.

The bus was pretty full but I had my own seat, so I scooted toward the window when I saw him shuffling my way, hunched over a little and rubbing his free hand on his lower back. He gave me a hard stare and said something I couldn't hear, since the volume was so loud on my Walkman.

"What's that, man?" I asked him.

"I said, *Thanks for the seat, Holmes.*"

"Oh . . . you're welcome," I told him, pulling my earphones off.

"What are you listening to?" he asked.

"Some rap . . . The Chronic."

"I like a little of that sometimes," he said. "But I really get into this old time rock-n-roll. Check it out," he told me. He had a Walkman too. I put his headphones on for a second and listened to "Hell's Bells" by AC/DC.

"That's cool," I said, holding out my hand. "I'm Jamie."

"My name is Manuel. But my friends call me Psycho.

Where you headed, Holmes?"

"Acapulco, eventually," I answered. "I'm gonna take this bus to Laredo and then leave from the other side."

"Hey, I live in Laredo," he said. "Today is the first of the month, so I had to come to San Antonio to see my back doctor and fill my scripts," he smiled, flashing his teeth that were kind of pointed. "So . . . are you cool, Holmes? Do you like to kick back and smoke a little mota?" he asked, touching his thumb to his index finger and putting them to his mouth.

"Sometimes I do," I admitted.

"You look like you party a lot," he laughed, digging in his pocket. "Where are you from?"

"Eight Mile, Alabama. I was just in Spain, though. That's where my father lives."

"Oh, for real? You don't really look Spanish."

"I'm not. My father's a Dutchman, from Holland. He just likes it in Spain 'cause the weather's so nice."

"I bet it *is* nice. I'd like to take a vacation there someday."

He showed me a medicine bottle full of Lortabs, something I'd seen a lot of around Aunt Wendy's trailer. He shook out a small white pill with a line through the center that was mixed in with his prescription medicine, and set it on his palm.

"That looks like a Quaalude," I said.

"How did you know that? We're just starting to get these in Laredo."

"This cab driver I met in Acapulco had some of them. They're strong."

"The same as ten M&Ms—ten blue Valiums," he explained. "We call them R2s, or roaches. You want it?"

"I'll take half."

He broke it down the middle with his thumbnail and swallowed his piece. "That's enough for me," he declared. "I ate two whole ones when I left the doctor's office."

"Damn. I'd be passed out."

"You get used to them, believe me. Hey, Holmes—why don't you come by my trailer in Laredo and we can smoke some good mota . . . some Lima-Lima?"

"I never heard of that kind. Sure, I'll come by. I'm not in a big hurry to get to Mexico. How much does that stuff go for around here?" I asked quietly.

"Aw, it's on the house."

"No . . ." I leaned over and lowered my voice. "I mean how much would it cost if I wanted to buy, like—a pound?"

"Oh, a pound? I can get good mota for $250 a pound . . . $150 for some not-so-good stuff."

"Damn," I gasped as the figures raced across my brain. "I could make a *killing* with Billy Joe. Hey, can you get a lot of that stuff?"

"Slow down, man. Let's drink a few Coronas at the trailer, smoke a little mota—get to know each other better. We can talk more later."

I hired a taxi at Laredo's bus station, which wasn't far from the bridges into Mexico. The cabbie drove us north across the city on Interstate 35 and we exited near a shopping mall that had a wall of thirty-foot palm trees planted along the rim of the parking lot. A mile from there, the cab hung a right onto a road marked by a white sign trimmed in flashing lights that read "R.V. Campground."

The entire community of single-wide trailers and many other types of mobile homes were built on a rise, six to ten feet higher than the surrounding middle-class neighborhoods. At the entrance, a circular fountain made up of rust-colored sandstone blocks was encircled by a two-foot-high iron fence painted lavender. On the outer edge of the fountain, within the boundaries of the iron fence, a statue of Jesus in a pastel blue robe watched over the residents of the trailer park. His arms rose at forty-five degrees from beneath his robe.

The statue was set on a pillar of granite a yard high, upon which an inscription had been carved, still visible in the early evening by means of a halogen flood lamp:

I am the light of the world. He who follows Me shall not walk in darkness, but have the light of life.

"The land here, it sure is high," I said.

"Yeah, it makes for a nice view. It's too early now, but after the sun sets, I can see the city lights of Nuevo Laredo from my front steps," Manuel said, pointing to the southwest, toward the Rio Grande.

In Manuel's front yard was an assortment of colorful chickens and an old corroded icebox. He set up two yellow- and orange-checkered lawn chairs between the icebox and the cement steps at the front door of his trailer. "Take a load off, Holmes," he invited. He opened the working fridge to get at his supply of Corona and lime wedges, disturbing a large rooster perched on top.

"These are my *gallos*," he announced as it flapped over my head, startling me. "I have them trained to stay in the yard. And don't worry; they won't peck you or nothing as long as I'm here. They're kind of like my guard birds," he laughed.

"Some big-ass roosters," I said.

"I fight them" Manuel said proudly, patting a two-foot-tall Rhode Island Red on the back. "He's made me lots of money, but he's getting too old to fight anymore. Speaking of money . . ." he trailed off, reaching into the freezer part of his icebox to pull out a two-pound block of weed in a Ziploc bag that he dropped into my lap. "This is the Lima-Lima I was telling you about. You want to roll us a big spliff or what?"

"I could, but I ain't no good at it. I always end up tearing the paper in the middle."

"Here," he said, setting his Corona on the fridge and grabbing the cold package that was making my legs numb. "Just relax, Holmes. I'll take care of that," and he started rolling the biggest joint I'd ever seen outside of a Cheech and Chong movie.

"Yeah, I used to be a big mover," reminisced Manuel, thick streams of smoke seeping from his mouth. "But I'm on that paper now, so I can't mess with nothing."

"Paper?" I asked.

"Yeah—my parole. I don't want to go back to prison."

"Oh, so you don't deal anymore?"

"Nothing big," he answered. "If you started running pounds, it would have to be strictly through Arturo."

"Who's that?"

"This vato loco that lives in the Valley. He's married to my baby sister. He's pretty cool, but if he ever gives you any problems, just come and get me. He knows better than to screw around with my friends."

"All right," I said. "I appreciate that, Manuel."

"Hey, call me Psycho. So, how many pounds were you interested in buying, Holmes?"

"I don't know," I said, trying to figure what I could afford. "You said $250 a pound for this Lima-Lima?"

"For you . . . two hundred."

"All right. Can you get me fifteen—or no—seventeen pounds? Yeah, that'd leave me plenty enough money to travel."

"That much, huh? I'll call Arturo right now if you are serious."

"Oh yeah," I assured him. "I got cash enough for that."

Psycho located his cordless phone and walked across the yard with it; I could hear him speaking in Spanish.

"Seventeen pounds is not a problem, Holmes," he told me after he ended the call. "I'll take you to the Hampton Inn up the road, and he'll deliver it to you in the morning. Is that OK with you, Jamie?"

"Sounds good."

"I would offer to let you stay in my trailer, but my old lady gets off of work in a little while, and she trips out on me sometimes. She thinks I should get a job, but I'm waiting for my back to get better. I'll call you a cab. You should take my number, too. You can call me from the hotel and tell me what room you are in so Art can know where to find you tomorrow."

29

Valley of Death

AT AROUND 8:30 the next morning, someone was beating on the door of my hotel room. I opened it to see a six-foot, three-hundred-pound Mexican with dark skin and a chubby face standing in the hall. He had a thick black mustache, big pork chop sideburns, and a mullet that was spiked on top, which made him seem even taller.

"Is this the gringo?" he asked, looking over his shoulder.

"What's up, Holmes?" asked Psycho, shaking my hand and giving me some dap. "Man, there's been a change of plans. We have to go to the Valley today to pick up the mota. Grab your stuff. You can ride with Arturo," he said, slapping the big Mexican's arm. "Me and my old lady are going to follow you in her car. You see, I don't have my license yet. They took it away when I went to prison."

"You got the money?" Arturo asked me as I put on my T-shirt and blue jeans. "I need to see it to make sure you are for real. I hate wasting my time."

"Yeah, me too," I said, flipping my pillow over to show him my cash.

"What's this?" Arturo asked, grabbing the stack of French francs.

"That's money from France," I said. "But I have plenty enough American dollars to pay for my seventeen pounds."

"That's a lot to get for someone I don't even know," said Arturo. "I always have to be careful when I'm dealing with new people, especially gringos."

"I told you he was cool, *ese*," Psycho said.

"I'll wait for you outside," said Arturo, and he took off down the hall.

"Holmes, why don't you go ahead and give me the money? That way, I can get my cut right now," Psycho told me. "I haven't been working because of my back, and it's time for Arturo to start paying his dues, anyway. This should work out well for the three of us."

"OK, that's cool," I said, wondering what kind of "dues" he meant.

"I'm going to take care of you, Holmes. We will follow you the whole way so I can make sure my brother-in-law does not try anything wi'chu. I can see in your eyes that you are a straight-up kind of person. I will look out for you, Jamie."

"I appreciate that."

"Like I said, Holmes—I don't mess around with a whole lot right now, but Arturo can get you as much as you need. And if he does ever try to cheat you or something, just come to me. I'll straighten him out."

I walked to the parking lot with my bags and spotted Arturo sitting in a gold '91 Buick Riviera with blacked-out windows, thick whitewalls, gold and chrome spoke wheels, and a front fender that was crunched up on the right side.

Psycho and his gorgeous Hispanic wife, Enrica, followed us away from the hotel in a blue Ford Probe. We sped south on Highway 83, which runs parallel with the pale, avocado-green waters of the Rio Grande. An hour into our journey, I took note of the numerous roadside memorials in front of the barbed wire fences on either side of the highway. Every few miles there would be a white wooden cross draped with fresh flowers that had a Spanish name on it and a day of passing.

"A lot of folks die down this way?" I asked Arturo.

"The *borrachos* like to drive fast on this highway because there is never any cops this far in the middle of nowhere. There are more and more of those roadside crosses the closer you get to the Valley." He paused and glanced over at me. "That's why we call it the Valley of Death, Holmes."

"Y'all really call it that?" I asked, starting to wonder if this big Mexican was gonna try to kill me and take my money—even though it was a funny time to start worrying about that.

"I'm only kidding, gringo. Everyone around here knows me as the Joker. See?" he asked, lifting his right sleeve to show off a six-inch tattoo of a playing card—the ace of spades—with a red-eyed grinning skull on it wearing a jester cap.

"Oh, OK . . . nice work."

I became lost in the beauty of the passing countryside after that: sandy plains of dry golden brush dotted by occasional patches of flat-podded cactuses giving way to lush greenery closer to the banks of the Rio Grande.

We exited Highway 83 into McAllen, a border town. Arturo pulled into an Exxon station and went over to Psycho riding shotgun in the Ford Probe to get the money. He walked to the pay phones and called someone while Psycho approached my window. "You're all right now, Holmes," he assured me. "I'm going to take my wife and visit my baby sister while I'm here in McAllen. Just remember . . . as long as you are loyal to my brother, Arturo, I will be loyal to you. Remember that. See you later," he said, shaking my hand. He returned to his and Enrica's car and they drove off.

Arturo jumped in the Riviera. "We have to go up the road to get it. Man, Psycho really likes you, huh?"

"I can get along with most anybody," I said. "He's a good guy."

We stopped at a Church's Chicken further up Tenth Street, across from an HEB supermarket. A maroon Chevy Silverado, with a colorful mural of the Virgin Mary painted onto the hood, entered the lot after us. Another Mexican wearing a cowboy hat, skin-tight Wrangler jeans, and a brass belt buckle with a marijuana leaf on it stepped out of the truck. Arturo received a black trash bag from him and tossed it in the backseat.

"Where we headed now?" I asked, once we were on the road again.

"You tell me."

"I'd like to take a look at this stuff somewhere," I said. "I planned on leaving today. I'd hate to have to waste money on another hotel room."

"We'll go to my place right up the road. Manuel and Lola went to meet my old lady at the supermarket. They should be there a while. Where are you taking this mota to, Holmes?" Arturo asked.

"Alabama, I suppose . . . or Mississippi."

"How do you plan on getting it there?"

"I was gonna stick it in my bag and get on a bus with it."

"On a bus? You got big huevos, huh, gringo?"

"This ain't nothin', man. I carried tons in Spain."

"Tons, huh? Well, good luck. Don't mention my name, that is all I ask."

We hung a right into an alleyway off Nolana Avenue, beyond a Blockbuster Video store, and followed a hedge, turning left after a pair of dumpsters. He parked next to a red Isuzu Amigo under the carport of his townhouse, which was across from an apartment complex. Inside his living room, he moved his kids' toys off the coffee table and emptied the trash bag of weed. It had been compressed into flat, unwrapped bricks—not all exactly the same shape, but pretty close.

"How much does one of these weigh?" I asked him.

"That one is two pounds," he said.

"That's hard to believe," I said, trying to gauge the weight in my hand.

Arturo found a kitchen scale in his broom closet and I

set the brick on it.

"You see . . . two pounds. Rest assured, the mota you get from me will always weigh out. You got eight of these two-pounders and this one-pounder to make the odd number," he explained, after he weighed the smallest brick.

"This is that Lima-Lima, ain't it?" I asked. "Damn sure smells like it."

"Uh-huh. I am going to wrap it for you so you can make it past the border patrol dogs if they stop your bus." He went to the kitchen and returned with an armful of shrink-wrap and a big jar of cayenne pepper. "We have to save a little of this for my old lady. She's cooking menudo for dinner. Give me a hand. This has to be out of here before they get back."

I held the bricks while he wrapped them every which way, dusted the outsides with cayenne, and then wrapped them again.

I grabbed my luggage out of Arturo's Riviera and managed to fit all nine packages into my big black duffel bag. I stuffed some of my shirts around them so it was hard to tell if anything other than clothes was in there.

Arturo drove me to the Greyhound station in McAllen and handed me a slip of paper before he left. "Here, take my pager number," he said. "When you get to where you're going, page me with the number '17.' That way I'll know you made it through all right. And next time we do this, you can Western Union me the money so I can have it waiting for you when you come. And don't worry. I won't rob you, Guerro. I could have done that already today—but I like you, Holmes. I think we could make some money together. You look like a hustler to me."

So I'd gone from a rabbit to a "hustler" in only six weeks. I figured things were finally looking up.

"Thanks, Arturo," I said, shaking his hand.

"Hey, call me Art," he insisted, and drove off.

30

AFTER THREE HOURS of traveling along the border on my first bus ride from hell, we arrived at Laredo. It was just after two in the afternoon, and I had to wait around until after dark to board the connecting bus. I became nervous when it arrived, as I knew we would be passing through the Border Patrol checkpoint on the outskirts of Laredo.

I stared up at my duffel bag in the overhead compartment as we slowed down for the plain black and white signs that read "Federal Agents" and "Canine on Duty." The Greyhound parked under the white metal canopy beside the Border Patrol's green and white Hummers and hydraulic car lifts. The agents climbed aboard in their green jumpers and cowboy hats, passing their hands over everyone's luggage. I tensed up when they got to my duffel bag, and then breathed a sigh of relief after they jumped off and let the bus through.

By the time I changed buses in San Antonio, it was the morning of Saturday, September 3. We passed in and out of thunderstorms going by the Budweiser plant in Houston and driving over the brown bayous of Louisiana.

The sun was starting to set behind us when the bus final-ly arrived at the Union Passenger Terminal near the gilded steeple of Saint John the Baptist Church in downtown New Orleans. Inside the station, I found some pay phones and decided to call Billy Joe.

I left the pay phone number on his pager and waited for him to respond. While I waited, a black man from Nigeria came up to me saying he hadn't eaten in two days, so I give him five bucks, and he went inside the Subway in the station to get a sandwich. It made me feel good to help someone else for a change, even if it was a small gesture, rather than just thinking of myself.

Then the phone rang, and it was Billy Joe.

"Man, I need you to pick me up," I told him. "I'm at the Greyhound bus station in downtown New Orleans."

I spent a few minutes walking around the station, which was mostly empty. I checked the clock on the wall above the Amtrak counter. It was 8:15, only a half hour since I'd spoken to Billy Joe. I wanted some fresh air so I took my stuff outside the black marble walls of the Union Passenger Terminal and sat on the curb. Looking at the sago palms on the lawn, I watched a vagrant harassing some of the Pelican Cab drivers parked in the horseshoe driveway. *There sure are some funny people around here*, I thought.

It seemed like forever before I saw Billy Joe pulling up in that old green Mustang with its T-top missing. I waved Billy Joe over, threw my bags in the backseat, and plopped myself down shotgun on the beanbag seat. He stopped at the end of the horseshoe driveway and I noticed a bunch of wires hanging from the steering column.

"You had to tear it up pretty good, huh?" I asked.

"Yeah," he nodded, turning left out of the station.

"What the hell you do to the windows? Is that spray paint?"

"It's embarrassing riding in this thing, man—with the beanbag chair and the way people would stare at me, wonderin' why I'd have the T-tops off in the rain and everything." Billy Joe paused for a second, looking like he had something he wasn't sure he wanted to say. "Hey, man," he said, "I gotta be straight up with you right now 'cause you've always been straight up with me. Are you missing some money?"

"Yeah, I think I am," I lied. "Why?"

"When I popped off the cover of the steering column, like $3,000 fell in my lap."

"Oh yeah, I stashed that before we went to Mexico," I said. "Where's it at?"

He opened the middle console and showed me the cash. "Man, my mama and her new boyfriend had a pretty bad fight last night," Billy Joe said. "He caught her talking to her old boyfriend, Doug, and told her to pack her stuff and get out. I was wonderin' if I could run with you a while, or if you would loan me some of that money so I can get away from my mama and all that drama in Stone County."

"Is that where you've been staying, in Mississippi, since we did the safe?"

"Uh-huh."

"Have you heard from your boy Garrett lately?"

"Man, Uncle Beavis said they busted Garrett riding through Prichard with a half pound of weed and some white. He rolled on us man, to keep outta jail. As long as I've known him, I can't believe he would do something like that."

"So, he told on us both, huh?"

"As far as I know."

"That's messed up. Guess I'll be lying low for a while. That's all right. I've got a way to make some fast money, so I can set myself up somewhere far away from Mobile. I could use some help, if you're interested. But we could sure use a better car," I said, smelling burning oil.

"I seen a cool-ass car for sale in Gulfport . . . a '66 Lincoln Continental with them gangster whitewalls," said Billy Joe. "It was parked at this twenty-four-hour pawnshop."

"Yeah? We might have to go see about that."

"Hey, and I got weed, man—if you wanna smoke."

"I got a little, too," I smiled, patting my duffel bag in the backseat.

A few days later, after some further planning, we headed to the airport in Mississippi where the pawnshop was located.

"We'll just sneak in and out," said Billy Joe. It was Thursday, September 15, and soon enough we were leaving the Gulfport-Biloxi International Airport having stolen that '66 Lincoln Continental.

"You got that fake driver's license from California, and nobody knows this car anyhow. We need to move this weed, and Mama's boyfriend, Doug, crazy as he is—could probably help us out. He smokes a quarter pound a week himself. Doug used to roll with my daddy and his crew; he knows what he's doing."

"All right," I said. "We'll give him a try. He lives in Semmes, Alabama, you said?"

"Uh-huh."

We took the back roads into Alabama, through Lucedale, following highway 98 to Fire Tower Road opposite a used car lot. "What's this guy do for a living?" I asked Billy Joe as we approached a beige brick duplex with an old beat-up Ford van out front.

"He does sandblasting for MP Painting. MP contracts to the casinos in Mississippi and a lot of these chemical plants around here."

A short woman with straight brown hair and a can of Budweiser in her hand answered the door. I heard a dog barking and then someone yelled, "Who's that at the door, Sheri?"

"It's Billy Joe and his friend."

The living room smelled of dirt, weed, and dog mess from the big boxer they kept inside.

"What, are you moving in?" this guy asked me, with a mid-western accent. He must have assumed I had come to stay for some time, since I was carrying the duffel bag full of weed. He and his friend on the sectional couch both had long hair that went down their backs.

"I'm Doug," said the grayish-brown-haired guy. He wore white coveralls like a painter's, and as he stood, appeared as tall as me, maybe taller. I figured he was about fifty, perhaps older. His friend looked younger than me and his hair was a dirty blonde color; he had an undercut, and when he went to throw an empty beer can away, I saw he stood around five foot seven.

"Y'all bring that grass?" asked Sheri, Billy Joe's mama. "I filled my Lortabs today if you wanna trade me somethin'."

"Wait up, Mama," said Billy Joe. "How come y'all off of work so early, Doug?"

"Got rained out. Can't paint in the rain. So, where's the skunk you bragged about on the phone? What do you have . . . a quarter pound?"

"Naw, we got more than that," I said. "Can we take it to another room?"

"There's an empty bedroom in the back, and some scales. But Kid Brown here is cool as hell if you're worried about him," he said, referring to the young guy. "His grandpa ran Colombian Gold through the Everglades—ain't that right, Kid?"

"Yeah, whatever, whatever . . . don't listen to that dude. You can't trust anyone from Wisconsin," Kid said, and laid back with his hands behind his head.

The empty bedroom had half-naked girls all over the walls; pages torn out from tattoo magazines, it appeared. I emptied my duffel bag on the floor in the corner and turned to Doug, "How much you want?"

"Good golly . . . would you look at all that. I only have enough cash on me for a few ounces, partner. I wasn't expecting to see this kind of weight. How much you charge for a pound?"

"Seven hundred," I said, ready to get things moving faster.

"Hell, I could make a few phone calls. My boy Kid could probably flip some, too. He's always hooking me up with good smoke. Can I bring him in here?"

"Go ahead," I said.

This guy, Kid, got real hyper when he saw that big pile of Mexican skunk. "I ain't seen that much in one place since I left Naples," he said, pacing around.

"These boys are asking $700 a pound for it," said Doug.

"That's not bad for around here," said Kid. "I could do something with that."

"How much you wanna buy?" I asked.

"Dude, I'm just painting now. I did some time in Fort Myers, and I'm just trying to get on my feet again. I could only give you four hundred, but I promise I can get rid of a pound this afternoon and pay you the rest today."

"Well, let's do this . . . you give me what you're gonna give me, Doug—and I'll take your four hundred," I said to Kid, "and leave y'all two pounds. We're gonna ride out to Prichard to try and sling a little more, but we'll catch up with you this afternoon. And if you come through with the rest of our money, we'll front y'all another couple pounds. That cool?"

"Hell yeah."

Billy Joe and I took our weed to my boy Sticks, a guy I knew who ran a car wash off Wilson Avenue between Vigor High and a furniture store. I parked at Greer's Grocery opposite my old high school.

"We need to put this duffel bag in the trunk," I told Billy Joe. "I don't want Sticks and his crew to know all what we got."

With two pounds jammed under my seat, we idled down the road to Sticks's car wash. As I steered in through the six-foot chain-link fence that surrounded the brown metal building, we were met by harsh stares from a group of guys sitting around on old car seats, slamming dominos down on a piece of plywood set across a couple five-gallon buckets. They were sipping on Thunderbird wine and probably wondering who was rolling up in an old Lincoln with windows tinted so dark they couldn't see in. I spotted Sticks, tall and lanky, putting the finishing touches on a pearl-white Jeep Grand Cherokee that had gold Dayton knockoffs with marijuana leaf emblems on the center caps.

I drove up close beside Sticks and rolled down my window.

"Jamie Cobb," he said. "I hadn't seen you in a while. What's up, my dog?"

"I'm trying to get rid of some weed, Sticks."

"Not some of that homegrown you white boys be pushing, huh?"

"Naw, man. This skunk come straight from Mexico."

"Word? I'll take a dime bag from you . . . trade you for a wax job on this nice Lincoln."

"Man, I'll *give* you a dime bag. Don't you know anybody looking for a little more?"

"Chaz," he said, calling over his lighter-skinned friend with a fade who was walking around the lot holding a cell phone to his ear. As he moved closer, I saw he was in his early twenties, sporting brand-new clothes and a shiny gold grill on his front teeth.

"You need some kill?" Sticks asked him. "My boy Jamie from Vigor High says he's got that skunk, straight from Mexico."

"I'd have to sample some first," Chaz said to me, and I noticed the diamond "C" set into one of his gold front teeth.

"Come take a ride," I offered. "We'll make the block and discuss some prices."

"You done with my Jeep?" Chaz asked Sticks.

"Uh-huh."

"Roll with us then, Cousin," Chaz insisted, and they both climbed in the back of my car.

"That's some fire weed," Sticks said after we made a few blocks around Prichard.

"How much for a brick like the one you broke this blunt off of?" Chaz asked.

"Seven hundred," I told him. "Thirteen if you wanted two."

"I got twelve on me," Chaz said.

"That'll work. Just be sure you hook my boy Sticks up with a fat sack."

"Always," he replied, pulling out a stash of ten- and twenty-dollar bills. "I been up all night slinging them cookies," he bragged. "Y'all wouldn't wanna trade an ounce of hard for some more of that ganja?"

"I don't mess with none of that," I nodded. "I'll trade you for that Jeep of yours with the knock-off Daytonas."

"How many pounds for my ride?" Chaz asked.

"I'll give you seven pounds for it today," I offered.

"I'm gonna have to think about that," he answered, as we dropped him off at the car wash. Billy Joe finished counting out all of his newly acquired small bills.

"Give me your number and I'll call you when I need to re-up," Chaz said.

"Write down your pager number, Billy Joe," I said, passing Chaz the bricks.

We swung by Doug's place, where he was smoking with Kid out of a big glass bong in the living room. "Where y'all been?" Doug asked.

"We got rid of them pounds easy," said Kid.

"Your money's right here," said Doug.

"You gonna front us two more like you said?" Kid asked me. "Or, hey—y'all should just come to the party I'm throwing tomorrow. One of my boys is supposed to bring some acid. And with everyone I'm gonna have over, I know I can move the rest of that skunk for you."

"Why don't y'all jus' spend the night, baby?" Sheri asked Billy Joe.

"I got an old mattress I can put in that guest bedroom," said Doug. "And someone could sleep on the couch if they wouldn't mind my dog jumping on them in the middle of the night."

"Actually, since I'm in the area, I think I might visit my girl who lives in Creola," I said.

"I'll stay, then—and we can meet here tomorrow before the party," said Billy Joe.

31

ON THE WAY to Creola, I had to make a stop at a convenience store. I put on my shades and a baseball cap to go inside to buy a bottle of Mountain Dew. On the front double doors I noticed a picture of me, standing in my Aunt Wendy's trailer the night I met my biological father for the first time. "Dammit," I said.

Ten thousand dollars for any information leading to the arrest of this man . . . Jamie Cobb, I read quietly, recognizing the number to Mr. Clyde Johnson's wrecking yard on the wanted poster.

"Where we going?" Melissa asked, when I picked her up.

"Mississippi," I answered. "I don't feel so safe around Mobile with my picture up everywhere."

That night I told Melissa, "I gotta bring you home tomorrow, but I'm rollin' now with this weed. I'll be looking for a place before long—probably in South Texas, on the border. Would you come stay with me if I moved down there?"

"Yeah, Jamie; I could live out there with you."

I dropped her off on Friday morning at one of my old

high schools, Mary G. Montgomery, where her mama met us. "Here's a thousand dollars," I told her, "so you can buy some new clothes, or help your Mama out—or whatever you need to do."

She told me she loved me and we kissed goodbye. "Hurry up and get away from Mobile," she said. "I've been seeing more and more of those wanted posters."

On the way back to Doug's house, I spotted what I swore was Mr. Clyde Johnson's red Silverado coming up Fire Tower Road. There's no way he could have seen in through my tinted windshield, but I slumped down in my seat anyway.

"I got to get away from here," I told Billy Joe. "Ain't it against the law for Johnson to put those wanted posters up offering a reward for my capture? What is this, the Wild West? And how come it's only my face on there? Y'all the ones went in and took it."

"Garrett thinks you're off in Europe, so he must've figured you'd be the best one to roll on."

"Yeah. Hey, I sure hope that Kid fella really can move the rest of our pounds tonight."

At half past noon, I heard Doug's old van pull up in the driveway. He arrived with five of his painter friends all looking to buy quarter- and half-pounds bricks. I sat there quietly, letting Billy Joe deal with Doug and his people, and listening to them complain about Doug's method of putting the compressed bricks in a rice steamer so they would fluff up and be easier to break apart. Apparently, they didn't appreciate having to pay extra for the weight added by the water.

Kid showed up after they were gone, while Doug was getting a shower. He motioned for me to follow him outside. "You still coming to my party?" he asked, scratching paint off from around the edges of his fingernails.

"I planned on it. You still gonna try and get rid of that weed for me?"

"I ain't gonna *try*—it'll be gone after tonight, if that's what you want. I don't mess around with little quarter bags like Doug here. I ain't as wide open as he is, neither."

"Yeah, man . . . I didn't feel comfortable, him bringing in all them people like he done today."

"I'll be straight-up with you, Jamie. I come from a long line of dope slingers. I'll tell you more about that after I show you what I can do tonight. And I have to admit—you're pushing some fresh smoke. For only seven hundred a pound, I raked in more money these last couple days than I made this whole month painting for MP. That's just the only job I've been able to hold onto since they let me out the pen in Fort Myers."

"What was you in there for?" I asked.

"Grand theft auto; something I did when I was sixteen. I served two years and I'm on unsupervised probation now. I moved up this way to be closer to my mom for a while. Hey, when your weed runs out, do you have to go away to get more?"

"I got me a pretty good connection, man. I can always get as much as I want."

"That's awesome. And look, dude, if you wanted to bring

your bags over to my place and chill there until the party, I live in that duplex—the first one down the hill where the white Maxima is parked. You can shower and whatever else if you need. I know Doug ain't much of a neat freak. His place is pretty grimy."

"I appreciate that, Kid. Yeah . . . I've been seeing cockroaches in Doug's bathroom."

"I know," he laughed. "Hey, I'll give you the lowdown on Doug one day. He's kind of on the run . . . but pass by the house and bring your weed, man," he said, and then walked off. Later, I learned from Billy Joe that Doug was hiding out from a murder charge in his home state, Wisconsin. His life revolved around smoking weed, eating Lortabs, and shooting guns. I always felt uneasy in his presence.

And Kid was just eighteen, trying to straighten himself out after a couple of years in jail. Despite this, it took him no time to turn right back into crime.

Doug's blown-out Emerson stereo system was blaring out "That Smell" by Lynyrd Skynyrd when I stepped into his house.

"Hey, Jamie—you feel like shooting some darts?" he asked, with his mid-western accent.

"I'm all right," I said. "I think I'm gonna go grab somethin' to eat. You hungry, Billy Joe?"

"What was Kid telling you out there? He's not trying to cut me out, is he?" Doug asked. "Don't listen to his lies." When he stood up I noticed a Beretta 9-mm tucked down the front of his jeans. "He can't sling that weed like me. You saw me in action today."

I glanced at Billy Joe, who was shaking his head and trying not to laugh.

"It ain't like that, Doug," I said. "We'll still do business."

"Can I get a pound, then, before you leave? Sheri and me are fixing to hit the Creek Club in Eight Mile. I know I could push some there."

"Ain't you coming to Kid's party later?" I asked.

"I'm too old for Kid's parties," he said.

"Let's grab him a pound out of the car," I told Billy Joe.

We walked outside and Billy Joe said, "Doug's speeding his ass off. My mama fed him like five Lortabs, and I think Kid scored him an eight ball. I asked him for a bump, but you know how they are; they don't wanna share nothin' with nobody."

"What's he doing with that gun?" I asked.

"I don't know. He thinks he's some kind of a badass, I guess."

Billy Joe and I ate a box of chicken from Church's and then rode up and down Fire Tower Road smoking a fat one and waiting for Doug to leave.

When his van finally drove off, I pulled into Kid's driveway and grabbed my duffel bag out the trunk of my car.

"Come on in," Kid said. "I'm gonna run those pounds to Dauphin Island and pick up the kegs on the way home if you wanted to ride."

"I don't like riding around more than I have to," I said.

"That's fine. You and Billy Joe help yourselves to some of

that Goldschläger in the freezer. I'll be back in no time."

By the time Kid returned, a lot of people had shown up and I was pretty buzzed. "You look like a soldier on leave sitting there with your duffel bag. Come on, I'll put it somewhere for you," said Kid, as he handed me $400.

At some point that night, he passed me a hit of acid. I started to trip pretty hard sitting on one end of the couch, and I completely zoned out for what must have been a long time. When I came to my senses again, everybody was gone and I was staring at his dog's one white eye.

Kid was sitting next to me, counting money and saying, ". . . Yeah, my grandpa used to run airboats through the Everglades, full of Colombian weed. I was just a little boy but I remember the bags of money him and my dad would bring home. Yeah, that's when Grandpa was Mayor of Naples. He really had Collier County on lockdown in the eighties when my uncle was the sheriff. But then the feds brought Grandpa in for tax evasion—just an excuse to bust up what they had going through the Everglades. My dad and my uncles took the rap and they served a few years for some bogus conspiracy. They gave Grandpa probation and he ended up writing a book about the whole thing before he passed away."

"I bet that's a good book," I said. "My father smuggles boatloads, too—from Morocco to Spain. He doesn't deal less than tons. I worked with him this past winter and made a damn fortune. Blew it all, too . . . like an idiot. But, man—I had a good time out there. Imagine sitting in this mansion on the top of a mountain . . . on a white leather sofa in a living room with marble floors and marble columns, looking out at the Mediterranean Sea while the maid in the kitchen cooks dinner."

"That's wild. I could tell there was something different about you, dude, by the way you carry yourself. These idiots around here, they get their hands on a few pounds and they think they're John Gotti or something. People just don't realize the weight that's being moved out there. I try not to tell too many people about the things my grandpa did. Everyone always thinks I'm lying."

"I hear you."

"Eleven thousand, two hundred," he said, handing me a stack of hundreds, fifties, and twenty-dollar bills. "I sold sixteen pounds of your weed tonight. I made off almost as well as you did, too. If I keep moving as fast as this, you think you could come down on that price?"

"The only way I'd do that was if you'd run to the border and help us carry it."

"So, you're getting it straight from Mexico, huh?"

"That's what I told you. If you fly, I'll let you have it for five hundred a pound. In fact, that would work out good for me. I've been thinking of moving to Texas, and I could use someone like you to take care of things on this end. Billy Joe, he's cool and everything, but he's too young. People don't take him seriously. We're gonna need a few good mules, though. It's risky going back and forth like I've been doing."

"You're the man with the connection, anyway. You shouldn't have to stick your tail out there. I can get your mules—easy," said Kid. "When you going back for more?"

"We can leave this morning, if you're game. I'd like to ride to the airport in New Orleans, just to see how tight their security is. It might be better to pass through there sometimes."

"I'm down," said Kid. He broke out his stash of powder and chopped up a couple more lines for us on the coffee table.

"Fix one for Billy Joe, too," I told him. "He's coming as well, so I'm fixin' to wake him up . . . wherever he's at. Oh yeah, and you're gonna need to wear the baggiest clothes you own so it's not so obvious when we pack the weed on you."

"That's not a problem," he said, tilting his head back and snorting his line way up into his sinuses. "I buy all my clothes like five sizes too big."

32

WE STOPPED IN SLIDELL, Louisiana, to get two-piece neoprene wetsuits at the Walmart there. "I think this'll be a lot better than the way we done it last time," I told Billy Joe, standing in line at the register. "I sure don't feel like riding that bus again."

I wanted to catch some sleep on the flight, but my heart was racing too fast, so I lay still with my eyes closed until we landed in McAllen at nine o'clock on Saturday morning. A taxi took us across a set of railroad tracks and into a motel called the Aloha. I rented a room for us and contacted Art.

"Hey, man, it's Guerro. I need, like, forty-five of them things. I'm in McAllen right now."

"Why didn't you call me ahead of time?" asked Art, sounding like he was just waking up. "I could have had it ready and waiting for you."

"I didn't wanna send that much through the Western Union. Them people looked at me suspicious the last time."

"How are you going to move that much weight? You bring your friend?"

"Yeah . . . and there's another guy I'm bringing," I said. "He's cool."

"What did I tell you, Guerro? I don't like to meet new people, and I don't appreciate you surprising me like this."

"Well, hell . . . do you wanna do business or not, Art?" I asked.

"Where are you at?"

"The Aloha," I answered, and he hung up.

Before long, Art was pounding on the door, as if upset about having to deal with us. When I let him in, he took one look at Kid, cocked back his left arm that resembled a loose stack of pork chops, and slapped him hard. Kid went tumbling over the bed, knocking his head on the air conditioner under the maroon curtains.

Kid popped up with a dark red handprint on his lightly freckled face and his long hair was a mess. "You fat piece of . . ." he started to say as he went after Art, who pulled a snub-nosed .38 out from under his belly and stuck it in Kid's face.

"Sit your punk ass on the bed, gringo," he told Kid, "with your blonde hair and your green eyes."

"Hey, I just came to carry some weed, dude," Kid pleaded with his arms in the air and his eyes bugging out his head.

"You have the money for that extra pound I gave you last time?" Art asked me.

"Yeah, Art . . . you gonna put that thing away or what?"

He sighed and stuck it in his waistband. "Come on," he told me. "Just you."

"Y'all stay here," I said to Billy Joe and Kid, who still had his hands up. I slapped his shoulder on the way out. "Sorry, man. I didn't know he was gonna trip like that."

We drove Art's Riviera toward the airport and passed La Piedad Cemetery. "Give me the money so I can get your pounds from my brother," Art told me.

I passed him $9,000 for my order and he parked in front of an ordinary-looking tan bricked house on a suburban street. A tall shirtless Mexican wearing high-top Converse shoes and a red bandana on his head was barbecuing skirt steak in a front yard full of mesquite trees. His chest and shoulders were covered in prison tattoos of naked Spanish women, fire, and skeletons.

"What's up, ese?" Art asked. "This is the vato who wants the forty-five pounds."

The fella looked over his shoulder at a dark-haired lady standing in the screen door. "Let me take this off the grill, and we'll go around to the backyard," he said.

We followed him to an old Chevrolet Caprice Classic sitting up on cinder blocks with the trunk and hood open. The car was filled with hen nests and big fighting roosters, and when Art's friend went to open the passenger's side door, I noticed the "Brown Pride" tattoos on the back of each of his arms. A white chicken flew out from the floorboards and a healthy buckskin pit bull chained to the frame tried taking off after it. Art's friend kicked him in the ribs and yelled, "Stay away from my gallos, you mutt!" The poor dog yelped and crawled under the car with his tail between his legs.

"Hold these huevos," he said, handing Art a handful of

brown eggs, huevos, that his chickens had just laid on top of one of the trash bags he was reaching for. "Fifty pounds, huh?"

I started to say something, but Art answered for me. "Yeah, with my five. Here's the money," and Art passed me the huevos so he could pull out his wad.

"Get up with me later, Joker," his friend told him. "We go out or something. And hey," he said, looking at me, "that is some fresh mota. We carried it across the river last night on Jet Skis. Here," he said, taking the eggs from my hands. "I bring these in to my old lady."

On the way back to the Aloha, Art asked if I could carry some of the five pounds he'd bought to sell for him full price in Alabama, since I had my compadres with me.

"You know I need to keep paying my dues to my brother-in-law, Psycho," said Art.

"We could do that," I said, "but you would have to do me a favor, too."

"What?"

"I've been thinking of moving down here with my girl. I know you don't like dealing with new people, and if I could be here all the time, I'm the only person you'd ever have to see."

"That's not a bad idea, but I think it might be better for you to live in the country. McAllen is all Mexican Mafia and Border Brothers territory. A high-rolling gringo like you would get robbed and end up in the river."

"Wherever you think, man. If you would keep an eye out for a place that I could rent, I'd appreciate it. Next time I might drive my car here if you can find me something. We're gonna take the stuff back through the airport tomorrow, the way you said."

"Make sure you test your clothes first to see that they don't set off the metal detectors," Art reminded me.

"We'll do that when we buy our tickets this afternoon, and then we'll leave first thing in the morning," I told him, as he idled by a large solitary palm tree accompanied by sporadic clusters of banana trees, in the middle of the motel parking lot.

"Call and let me know you made it all right," Art told me before I stepped out of his car with my trash bags. "And tell your friend sorry I had to slap him."

Me, Kid, and Billy Joe went through the bricks and came across a five-pounder shaped like a big pie with a hole in the middle. "I ain't carrying this one," said Billy Joe. "Why's it shaped like that, anyway?"

"The dude we got it from said they brung it across the Rio Grande on Jet Skis," I explained. "Maybe it's something to do with that. I guess we can saw it up."

"You ain't gotta do all that," said Kid. "I could strap that one to my back."

"You can if you want," I laughed. "That's on you."

At the airport we booked our flight to Gulfport, and then we made sure our clothes would not set off the metal detectors in the morning. Then we bought a hacksaw, picked up a couple pizzas, and smoked ourselves to sleep at the motel.

We woke up at 4:30 a.m. Sunday to start body-packing

under our new wetsuits. A taxi took us to Miller International to catch our 6:30 flight. Kid and I walked in together since we were Caucasian, letting Billy Joe with his dark skin and black hair go ahead of us. This was rather selfish, but we figured he was more likely to get stopped with his dark Mexican looks.

After checking in at the counter, I felt nervous passing the gift shop and restrooms as there was a group of Border Patrol agents standing under a rusted antique plane hanging from the ceiling—it looked like something the Wright Brothers would have tried to fly. Two agents on the other side of the check-in X-ray stopped Billy Joe while Kid and I were still in line waiting to get through the metal detector.

I breathed a sigh of relief when they let Billy Joe go, but tensed up again when I saw the pie-shaped chunk of weed bulging out of the back of Kid's oversized gray-hooded sweatshirt. "Walk tall, man," I whispered to him.

"Do what?"

"You got, like, a big raised circle on your back. Stop slouching over."

"Like this?" he asked, standing at attention.

"Yeah, that's better."

We caught up with Billy Joe sitting at the gate where we were to board our flight. "Why'd them Border Patrol agents stop you?" I asked him quietly.

"They thought I was a Mexican. They let me go as soon as they heard me talk."

Kid and I sat together on the flight, but Billy Joe's ticket had him seated a few rows behind us. "This is ingenious," Kid whispered to me, somewhere high above the sugarcane fields of South Louisiana. "Airport security wouldn't think anyone's stupid enough to try something like what we're doing. They're not even on the lookout for it."

"We ain't made it through yet. Stop talkin' to me."

The only other problem we encountered during the trip was disembarking at Gulfport: the pie-shaped chunk of weed started sliding down Kid's back. "Hold up a second," I told him, as we walked across the runway to the airport. I set my hands on the bottom of the chunk and tried to push it up higher in his wetsuit.

"Why you grabbing his ass?" Billy Joe asked me when he passed by us.

"Hurry up," said Kid. "People are looking at us funny."

"OK, it's good now," I said, having made the adjustment. "Let's go. Just don't walk too fast."

We passed through airport customs no problem, and Kid's girl picked us up. The minute we left the airport parking lot, we pulled the bricks of weed out and threw them on the floorboards of the car, smiling a little about how easily we had brought it through.

"Drive the limit," Kid told his girl. "I'd hate to get stopped right now."

It took us only a few days to sell our forty-five pounds and the extra three pounds we smuggled for Arturo. And for next six months, I put different mules on the plane twice a week, body-packing them with bricks of weed. I organized my crew to pick them up at different airports across the Gulf Coast, until greed took over and Arturo started ripping us off on a fraction of weight for each load.

33

Beginning of March 1996

RUSHING THROUGH LOUIS ARMSTRONG Airport, I glanced at my plane ticket with great effort, trying to discern the information. I was hallucinating so badly, all of the type seemed to have melted together. This was around the second or third of March 1996, but the exact day didn't mean much to me at the time. Sweating buckets, I wore black Ray-Ban shades to hide my pupils, which were heavily dilated from the strong acid I had dropped a couple hours earlier. Kid's newest carrier walked beside me, probably wondering what he had got himself into. The inside of his waistband and insoles of his Nike tennis shoes were lined with cash that would buy the next batch of weed.

I drank several cartons of milk during the turbulent flight that passed through a thunderstorm over South Louisiana. I swore that a Customs agent was sitting up the aisle from me, watching my every move while pretending to read a newspaper. Compulsively, I peered over my shoulder at him every few seconds. I must have looked like a lunatic to the other passengers, especially the guy dressed like an agent whom I kept looking at—he was probably just an accountant or a lawyer.

After landing at McAllen, Kid's carrier had to lead me through the airport by my hand. Sleep deprivation, along with the residual effects of large doses of LSD and cocaine, were working together to do a number on my central nervous system. Waves of disorientation buckled my knees, and I couldn't walk two steps without stumbling around, on the verge of collapsing. My vision momentarily became technicolor fields of swirls and dots. I thought my brain had reached its breaking point and was shutting down on me for good.

The cold morning air outside the terminal helped me through my frightening, drug-induced spell. Pale and shivering, I paged Arturo from a pay phone. His gold Riviera pulled up within moments. I sat shotgun and saw that Melissa and Billy Joe occupied the backseat.

"You are not going to be happy with what I have to tell you, Holmes," Arturo said. "Me and my compadres saw your old lady's car parked at a motel. I listened at the door and it sounded like something was going on, so we busted in . . . found your skinny amigo in bed with your old lady."

Melissa tried to explain that it was all a simple misunderstanding, but my bad trip took an angry turn. The red mist descended and like an idiot I lodged my fist into the windshield in front of me.

"Hey, calm down, *vato loco*," Arturo fussed, eyeing Border

Patrol agents gathered around a green and white Hummer on the other end of the airport parking lot.

"I'm sorry," I said, clenching my teeth and still seeing red.

"Don't you know I'm illegal? You trying to get me deported?"

"I'll buy you a new windshield," I said, coming back to my senses just a little.

"Forget about that," he said, driving us out of the parking lot. "Look at yourself, Holmes. You're letting that white monkey ride your back, hard."

Arturo dropped us all off at the Aloha, where I had left Billy Joe a day earlier, along with a few hundred dollars and another one of my get-around cars, a Chevy Beretta. On a dresser inside Billy Joe's room, Kid's carrier made a neat stack with the money that had been hidden in his clothing.

I aggressively grabbed the cash, threw it down on the bed, and asked Melissa, "Is this all you care about? Is this what you're after?"

I should have been asking myself those questions. She began to cry and Billy Joe stepped in between us. Without even thinking, I backhanded him, sending him crashing into a mirror hanging on the wall.

"Come on, Jamie," he pleaded, nursing the side of his face. "You're like my brother. I would never go behind your back like that."

I went outside to cool off, not knowing who or what to believe anymore. Arturo returned with my order of marijuana bricks in two black trash bags. I rented the room at the Aloha for another night and left the pounds with Melissa and Billy Joe while I drove Kid's carrier across the border to Mexico. Sixteen ounces of weed and the woman of his choice from Boy's Town in Reynosa was what I agreed to pay him for the smuggling he would be undertaking the next morning.

I sat in one of those Mexican brothels, drinking one Corona after another, watching a female performer strut up and down a narrow stage wearing an American flag bathing suit.

What am I even doing here? a voice of reason asked out of the darkness. A voice that had been slowly enveloping what remained of my rational mind. *This isn't what I want, it said. This isn't the life I was meant to live.*

I took out my fake California driver's license and the first passport Jan had bought for me, setting them side by side on the table.

"Jay B. Smith," I read off the fake license.

"James Harold Hendrik van Rijn," I read from the passport.

Who are these people? I wondered.

34

THE NEXT MORNING, I put Kid's carrier and Billy Joe on separate aircraft bound for Gulfport and Mobile. Kid paged me
that afternoon.

"What's up?" I asked him from a pay phone in McAllen.

"Billy Joe got popped," Kid told me. "When I showed up,
airport security had him in handcuffs. I took off before he saw
me and Doug got popped last night at his house. I think he's
rollin' on everyone man."

My crew was dropping like flies, but Kid didn't let any of
that discourage him. A day later, he flew into McAllen with
two carriers, both about Kid's age. With bleached blonde hair,
tattoos, and piercings, one of them reminded me of basketball
player, Dennis Rodman.

I rented a pair of rooms at a Microtel Inn, where Arturo
delivered another batch of pounds for Kid's carriers to fly for
us. Despite Billy Joe's arrest, we were still trying to stick to
our plan and decided it was time to take care of Arturo by
having a talk with his brother-in-law, Psycho.

Being nearly springtime, the days in the Rio Grande Valley were getting longer and warmer, but the nights and early

mornings were still very cold and windy. In some ways, this was beneficial, since our plan was to wait until early the next morning to send the carriers through the airport—they would blend in with commuters bundled up in winter clothing. I didn't trust leaving twenty pounds of product with complete strangers, so I picked Melissa up from the Aloha and asked her to stay in my room at the Microtel to guard the stash.

"I'm sick of this, Jamie," she complained. "I want to go home to Alabama."

"We'll talk about that when I get back," I told her. "I got more important things to deal with right now." She lost her temper and I had to run out of the room to avoid her spiked high-heel shoes she threw at my head.

Later that night, in my Chevy Beretta, Kid and I headed north for Laredo, not leaving until well after midnight. I had a few grams of coke in a sandwich bag that I shared with Kid. Arturo had sold me an entire ounce, but I arose that morning feeling empty and depressed; I hadn't been able to control my pathetic urges. As long as I could hold on to my fix, I wouldn't have to face up to the heap of problems that became dreadfully apparent when my buzz wore off. The white devil was eating away at my soul, and I was a shell of my former self. I no longer possessed the mental strength or discipline required to prevent my addictions ruining my life, or at least that was the lie the drugs led me to believe.

Sitting in the passenger's seat of my Chevy, I drew deep breaths of a dry desert breeze whipping in through my rolled-down window. In the side-view mirror, I saw dim yellow bulbs flashing on and off in the night—probably the weakened flashlights of poverty-stricken immigrants crossing the Rio Grande in pursuit of the American Dream.

"Man, I can't wait to start flying keys to your kinfolk in Amsterdam," Kid told me. "All this nickel and dime business really ain't even worth . . ." he trailed off, as the car's engine sputtered and died. We had been so preoccupied with getting high, we'd neglected to fill up with gas before we left civilization.

"Call your boys at the Microtel," I told Kid.

"I don't have a signal out here," he said.

With coyotes howling around us in the desert wilderness, we remained in the car and tried to figure out what to do next. My mind was racing from the powder cocaine, and the muscles of my body ached from the exhaustion of continually running the roads, chasing after the next stack of dirty drug money. I crossed my arms over my chest, closing my eyes for what seemed like just a minute.

In the darkness, I could hear the eerie sounds of my own erratic breathing and rapid heartbeat, both of which were slowly drowned out by the wailing of sirens.

My weary eyes fluttered open, and I saw the roof of an ambulance. Paramedics were standing over me, cutting my shirt open with scissors and holding an oxygen mask to my face. Waves of pain shot through my concussed brain, and I slipped back into unconsciousness.

I woke up again as hospital workers were wheeling me through a corridor on a stretcher.

"This one's got a nasty bump, but he's in a stable condition," I heard a doctor's voice explaining to someone. "The driver may have fractured a vertebra."

My head was strapped down, but slightly elevated so that I could see Kid being transported just ahead of me.

"What happened?" I asked when the crowd of people around me thinned out. Two Hispanic nurses were wheeling me into a private room.

"You and your friend were hit by a drunk driver," the older nurse explained. "We're going to run some tests on you now to make sure you're OK," she said, loosening the straps from my head and body. The other nurse slipped a hospital gown over my exposed torso and they helped me shift over onto a bed. When one of the nurses went to pull off my right tennis shoe, I remembered that I had a small baggie of coke hidden inside. I jumped to my feet and ran out of the room.

"I need to call my girlfriend to let her know I'm OK," I shouted to the nurses over my shoulder. Jogging toward the nearest exit, I checked to make sure I had my wallet.

Outside in the parking lot, I undid my neck brace and tossed it into some bushes. I approached an old farmer in coveralls getting into a brown Ford pickup truck. He couldn't speak much English, but I passed him a handful of fifty-dollar bills and he figured out that I needed a ride somewhere. The farmer made a couple of turns and we ended up on a service road alongside Interstate 35. I recognized a sign in front of Psycho's campground on a hill, and I asked the farmer to drop me off there.

With the morning sun rising up behind me, I wondered to God when this nightmare would be over. My thought processes were too clouded for me to realize that my own conscious decisions had been the cause of all my hardships.

35

WHATEVER PAIN MEDICATION I'd been given at the hospital in Laredo quickly began to wear off as I gingerly walked through a yard full of chickens. Enrica gave me a crazy look when she answered the front door of their trailer. She yelled out something in Spanish, over her shoulder, and then invited me in.

I took one step into the living room and felt cold steel against the side of my neck. I threw my hands in the air and said, "It's me . . . Jamie! We rode the bus over from San Anton!"

I had lost so much weight Psycho didn't recognize me. When my face finally registered with him, he lowered his loaded 9-mm pistol and led me back into the front yard.

As Psycho gathered country eggs at the break of dawn, I told him how Arturo had been ripping me off with a little weight on each load. "And I remember you told me if I am loyal to you, how you would be loyal to me, and that's why I'm here today."

"I knew Gordo was lying to me!" he fumed, almost crushing the shells in his hands. "He told me he never saw you again after the last time you came here."

Inside his kitchen, Psycho cracked two eggs into his glass of orange juice and then fetched me a couple of his prescription Xanbars. "You look like you hit your head, ese," he told me. I touched the big, fresh knot on my forehead, sending waves of pain through my recently concussed brain.

I listened to Psycho carry on about how Arturo hadn't been paying his dues to their brotherhood, and purple splotches appeared in my vision from the Xanbars. Abruptly, I leaned over and spewed up the only thing of nutritional value I had in my stomach, half a glass of juice, onto the linoleum floor.

"You're bad off, Holmes," Psycho said, passing me a small towel to clean my face. "Go lie down on the couch, get some rest."

I unknowingly kicked off my shoes during my two-hour nap, and my baggie of powder cocaine must have tumbled out. When I woke up, Psycho had it sitting on his kitchen counter while he paced back and forth, speaking angry Spanish into his house phone. He ended the call and noticed that I was awake.

"Here. We found you a cool T-shirt to wear if you want to take off that hospital gown."

"Thanks. Hey, where's my shoes?"

"Under the coffee table. You kicked them off while you were asleep."

"That was Arturo," he told me, grabbing the baggie to

chop himself another line. "He talks big on the phone, but we'll see what Gordo has to say to my face."

Enrica knew a nurse at the hospital down the road, and she was able to arrange Kid's release. Suffering from whiplash, Kid limped out of the building wearing a neck brace, looking spaced out from the pain meds he'd been given. Psycho and Enrica drove us to the police impound yard to see what was left of my Chevy Beretta. The answer to that was, *not much—it* was so crunched up, it didn't make any sense to me how we could still be walking around, especially Kid. The drunk driver had hit the driver's side, pushing the bumper almost to the front seat. Kid wrestled his bag off the rear floorboard and we headed south on Highway 83.

"Here's where we were parked when we got hit," I recalled as we neared a small bridge in the middle of nowhere.

Soon after, Enrica dropped us off beside my Lincoln at the Microtel in McAllen. Our cards weren't working for the rooms that Kid had rented, so we went to the receptionist, who informed us that the occupants had left some hours before checkout time. It looked like Kid's carriers had gone, along with Melissa and our weed.

Enrica, already tired of running the roads with us, went home in her blue Ford Probe to get ready for work. As soon as she was gone, we got in my Lincoln Continental with Psycho, who directed us to one of his brothers in McAllen, where he picked up a fresh bag of coke.

Kid and I were both aching badly, so Psycho chopped us up some more lines while I found Kid a shirt to wear. Darkness fell, and the more Psycho thought about Arturo, the angrier he got. "I'm ready to go take care of Gordo if you are," he told me, brushing his hand over his big flaring nostrils.

Psycho slipped on a pair of black leather gloves in the backseat of my Continental as we drove up Nolana Avenue. He handed me and Kid each a stainless steel buck knife.

"I know you going to help me carve up this turkey," Psycho told me.

"I don't want this," said Kid, passing his knife my way.

"Cut off your lights," Psycho said, as I hung a left by a pair of dumpsters and rolled up to Art's townhouse. "Leave it running, Holmes," he said, opening the suicide door, "in case we have to make a quick getaway."

Amped up on that powder, Psycho hopped out of the car first, cussing in Spanish and waving around a pair of buck knives with brass knuckle handles. Arturo stormed out of his townhouse to the sight of his brother-in-law flattening the last two tires on his Riviera. "Where's my money, Gordo?" Psycho asked him.

Kid pulled his long blonde hair into a ponytail and got in Arturo's face. "That's what you get for being greedy," Kid said boldly, looking up at the crooked dealer who was a head taller than him and at least a hundred pounds heavier.

Arturo shoved Kid aside with one arm and drew a snubnose .38 revolver, aiming it right between my eyes. He was so mad he was shaking. His teeth were clenched, his face had turned deep red, and his index finger twitched against the trigger. I was staring death in the face. In Arturo's bloodshot eyes, I could see that he wanted to kill me for bringing trouble to his front yard where his kids played. Fortunately, they were not around at that moment.

"I'M CALLING THE POLICE!" Arturo's wife screamed, running into the front yard, dialing 911 into a cordless phone, and effectively saving my life. If she had waited another second, I don't doubt that Arturo would have gladly put a bullet in my skull.

"You know I'm illegal!" Arturo yelled, as he rushed passed his wife in a hurry to hide his gun inside, and probably himself.

Psycho and I jumped into the car, and we were a half mile down Nolana Avenue before we realized that Kid wasn't with us. We spotted him out in front of a local restaurant, catching his breath.

We picked him up, and soon after we drove past McAllen's city limits, his beeper went off. I stopped at a service station so he could use a pay phone. Of all people, it was one of his carriers who had sent the page. Kid handed me the pay phone's receiver, and I listened to an arrogant voice.

Your girl don't want you no more, the voice said, so I'm taking her . . . and your dope.

He sounded drunk and couldn't resist the opportunity to rub it in my face.

Back in the car, I informed Psycho, who asked to see Kid's beeper. He recognized the number as being somewhere in Rio Grande City and said that there were only a couple of motels in that area—we wouldn't have any trouble pinpointing where the carriers were hiding.

At the first brown cinder-block motel we came across in Rio Grande City, Psycho knocked on a couple of doors and confirmed that a young Hispanic girl with a white Maltese had been walking around earlier that evening with two fellows. They matched the description of Kid's carriers, and soon Psycho found out which room they were in.

We polished off another few grams of coke to stay awake through the night, waiting until dawn to move in on Melissa and the carriers when they were sleeping. When the first blood-red traces of a South Texas sunrise appeared above the dry desert air on the eastern horizon, we made our move. A few yards away from their door, Kid and I pressed ourselves flat against the cinder-block wall. Psycho knocked politely, sending a small dog inside into a barking fit.

"Maintenance," he announced, looking over at me with a sick smile and glossed-over eyes.

Melissa opened the door with the chain lock still hooked. "No one here called for maintenance," she said sleepily. As soon as I recognized her voice, I gave Psycho the signal to go ahead and kick the door open.

The plan was for me to bring Melissa and the dope to the car while Kid and Psycho took care of the carriers, whatever that meant. Melissa was in shock; she put up no resistance as I led her outside and sat her in my Lincoln. I returned to the room, grabbing two gym bags stuffed with our pounds of weed. As I readied myself to leave, I heard Psycho saying, "You are lucky I don't put you floating in the Rio Grande!"

I turned and saw him stomping one of the carriers with his steel-toed boots. Psycho looked at me with a sinister grin plastered to his face, as he wiped his stainless steel blades and his tattooed arms on a set of white sheets. The beige wall behind the carrier was covered in specks of fresh blood. Kid led the other carrier out to the car, and Psycho followed behind them.

My heart sank when I walked further into the room; I heard a low groaning sound and quiet sobbing. Sensing that pure evil was all around, I crept over to the other side of the bed at the end of the room and found a crimson mess in the corner. The poor guy—the second carrier—was lying in a pool of his own blood. There were deep cuts up and down his arms, which he had used to protect his face and neck from Psycho's unforgiving blades. One of his triceps had been almost completely removed, and it hung from an exposed tendon like a flap of ragged red meat.

He was so out of it, he hardly moved when I used a sock to tie his arm muscle back against the bone. Blood continued to gush from his wounds, and the color was rapidly draining from his face, which was twisted in quiet agony as he slipped in and out of consciousness. I dialed 911 from the room's phone and gave the operator our location. "Someone's having a heart attack!" I yelled, so I could be sure they would hurry. I emptied out my wallet on the floor before running out to the car. Kid was already behind the wheel.

Speeding away from the scene of the crime, I stared down solemnly at my bloodstained hands as Melissa wept quietly in the backseat.

If he dies, it's all my fault, I realized, with much guilt and remorse.

I would learn later that, by the grace of God, Kid's carrier survived the injuries he suffered that morning.

36

AFTER WHAT HAPPENED in the motel room, I didn't intend to spend another day in the Valley of Death. Despite the airports being hot in the wake of Billy Joe getting busted, Kid sent his last carrier to a dealer waiting in the notorious neighborhood of Mobile Terrace, Alabama. We wanted to get rid of the rest of our weed before moving on to anything else, so we decided to drive the remaining pounds to one of Kid's connections in Mississippi.

I planned to let Melissa drive my Lincoln Continental home to Creola, while Kid and I flew back to the border to get our hands on the first few kilos of cocaine that we would smuggle to Western Europe. Looking back on those terrible events, it's hard for me to believe how bad my smuggling addiction had become. Nothing was going to stop me from reaching my misguided goal of becoming a bigger, more successful smuggler than my biological father, Jan van Rijn. Like him, I was nothing more than a puppet being manipulated by the cold, careless hand of greed.

In the commotion of four o'clock traffic on March 7, 1996, and with our cannabis stuffed inside a pet taxi in the backseat of my Lincoln Continental, we made our way through the Border Patrol checkpoint on Highway 77. I drove through the night, swallowing chunks of cocaine and puffing on marijuana cigars that Kid liked to roll. On the other side of the Texas-Louisiana state line, I tensed up when I remembered the number of state troopers I would spot on Interstate 10, especially between Lake Charles and Lafayette. The few times I'd driven across Louisiana hauling weed, I'd followed the back roads, skimming the wetlands along the rural and serene coastal region that I had become vaguely familiar with during my teenage years working in the oil field. But that route took much longer, and greed had me in a big hurry.

At least I wouldn't have to go as far as Alabama, I thought, where Sheriff Jack Tillman's narcotics checkpoint would surely be waiting in Grand Bay. Mobile County liked to throw up unannounced roadblocks to get a good look at the passing traffic—something I'd seen the Guardia Civil do in the smugglers' paradise off the southern coast of Spain. When entering Alabama with pounds of weed on board, I'd simply take the Franklin Creek exit to avoid Sheriff Tillman's checkpoint.

In those years, I wasted precious time and energy trying to remain one step ahead of the law. But no one can sustain it forever, not a small-time street dealer like I had become, or a European kingpin like my biological father. At any level of the game, it's only a matter of time before all that negative energy expended in the name of selfish profit comes back to haunt you, and often in the worst way possible.

Halfway across Louisiana, sometime after midnight, I pulled into a Chevron station at the Henderson/Cecilia exit, 115 eastbound. Melissa walked her Maltese, and Kid phoned his people in Mississippi to let them know we'd be there first thing in the morning. As I pumped gas, a state trooper rolled into the parking lot. He drove past me slowly, eyeing the Texas plates on my Lincoln, and then took off up Grand Point Highway in his souped-up Crown Victoria. My instincts told me to get out of there.

The minute I rejoined the interstate, another state trooper blue-lighted me. My palms began to sweat, my heart rate picked up, and adrenaline rushed through my arteries as I pulled onto the shoulder. This was a far cry from what I'd felt during my first job with Jan. My soul had been tainted with two years of hard drugs and shady deeds. I felt that my time had finally come. The pounds of weed in the backseat were almost in plain sight, and with Kid's record as a felon and my crime in stealing the safe in Alabama, we were both looking at many years of hard time.

Unfortunately, the criminal I had become wasn't ready to wave a white flag of surrender just yet. I waited for the state trooper to step out of his car, and I stomped my accelerator to the floorboard.

Moments later, I had half a dozen marked vehicles in hot pursuit, their red and blue lights blinding me through my side and rearview mirrors. A state trooper passed me with ease, but when he slowed down ahead, I bumped him hard. He moved aside just as I got on the Atchafalaya spillway bridge, a nineteen-mile elevated portion of the interstate.

Traffic was virtually nonexistent in the early morning, so I opted to ride on the centerline at well over a hundred miles per hour. The convoy of police vehicles maintained a steady distance behind, making me wonder why they didn't attempt to overtake me. The answer soon came: we sped up to a pair of eighteen-wheelers, riding side by side and slowing down with every second. The authorities must have contacted the truck drivers on their CB radios, asking them to cut me off.

I swung my Lincoln onto the narrow shoulder and jetted past the moving roadblock. Kid was in the process of swallowing the rest of our coke, and he almost choked to death when his side of the car scraped against the guard railing, producing an explosion of sparks and a sickening racket of steel grinding against concrete. With my free hand, I used the empty Ziploc bag to store my wallet and my address book filled with drug contacts in McAllen, which were as good as money to me. Several thousand dollars were hidden in the trunk of the car, but it didn't seem like I would be getting another chance to stop on my own terms.

A few miles beyond the end of the spillway, West Baton Rouge Parish Sheriff's deputies had parked their cars lengthwise across the interstate. It became a game of chicken, and I didn't slow down one bit. At the last moment, they pulled their cars out of my path, setting up behind their opened doors with shotguns and assault rifles.

"Get on the floorboard!" I yelled at Melissa. "Keep your head down!"

She screamed as the rounds rattled in my rear tire wells. With great effort, I steered what was left of my Lincoln onto the off ramp leading to the small town of Grosse Tête.

"Stay put," I told Melissa. "You ain't done nothin' wrong."

Kid grabbed the Pet Taxi full of weed, and we jumped from the moving vehicle that was slowly rolling on its rims toward a shallow ditch. The clatter of the smoking engine died away, replaced by the pounding of my shoes on damp grass, my panicked huffs of breath, and the wailing of sirens converging on the scene.

I scaled a tall hurricane fence, landing beside a steel cage that housed an old Bengal tiger, a truck stop's gimmick for drawing customers from the interstate. With his neck still in a brace, Kid struggled to get over the obstacle.

"Leave it behind!" I yelled, and he dropped the Pet Taxi so he could make it over the top. I found a patch of woods for us to crouch down in, though it was only two minutes before a German shepherd ran toward us. We went our separate ways, with the dog deciding to pursue Kid.

I was pulling myself up on the other side of the cold Grosse Tête Bayou when an officer's voice commanded me to "Freeze!" With both of my shoes lost in the muddy bayou, I peeled up my drenched shirt to reveal that I didn't have any weapons on me.

"I ain't got a gun!" I yelled in the direction of the beam from the officer's Maglite. Waiting for a bullet to strike the back of one of my legs, I took off on a dead sprint toward a distant tree line of live oaks draped with Spanish moss. I ran zigzag through marshy woods, hoping that the creeks I splashed across would throw off the canines that I could hear some distance behind.

Briars scratched my face and arms. I dodged cypress trees and tumbled over water-soaked logs. My aching feet went numb as I moved east, following the lights of the Interstate. When a police helicopter flew above, I buried myself into a patch of mud, face up so I could breathe with my nose and mouth sticking out. In time, the chopper's searchlight disappeared into the night. The droning sound of its rotors faded into an eerie and lonely silence.

37

JUST BEFORE DAYBREAK on March 8, 1996, I stumbled upon the parking lot of a motel in the town of Lobdell, on the outskirts of Baton Rouge. I found a faucet on the side of the building where I quickly rinsed off as much of the cold mud as I could from my face and body. Returning to the parking lot, I wrapped my dripping wet shirt around my elbow and busted in the driver's side window of an eighteen-wheeler. In the sleeping quarters, I found a set of dry clothes.

I walked awkwardly through an I-10 underpass wearing a straw hat, oversized coveralls, and tennis shoes that were two sizes too big for me. Taking the liberty to use the restroom of a Waffle House, I saw in the mirror that I was trembling uncontrollably. My sickly, pallid face was a mess of welts and scratches from the onslaught of briar patches during my flight through the woods. I couldn't help but think back to the warning Coach Riley had given me in high school, that if I didn't straighten up I would look at my reflection one day and not be proud of what I saw. I was also struck with the memory of peering into the mirror in Aunt Rudy's bathroom the first time I got high. And here I was a decade later, twenty-four years old and still running from my problems.

From the Waffle House, I called a taxi to take me to a bus station across the Mississippi River, near downtown Baton Rouge. To get a ticket to Pascagoula, I sold the J. H. van Rijn chain I'd bought in Gibraltar to a teenager loading suitcases into the storage compartment of a Greyhound.

There was a wall-mounted television in the lobby where I sat waiting for my bus. A local morning news program started reporting the high-speed chase I had just been involved in. A couple of folks glared at me in my unusual clothing; self-consciously, I pulled the straw hat down over my scratched-up face.

During the ride to Mississippi, choppers skimmed the roof of the bus, as I remembered they had near Jan's house in Spain. Or perhaps there weren't any choppers at all? Maybe years of paranoia, substance abuse, and living on the run had overloaded my mind. I wondered if I was slipping into insanity.

I called my brother, Junior, from the bus terminal in Pascagoula. Luckily for me, it was a slow Friday, and he didn't mind leaving the cabinet shop early. For many years, I suffered a lapse in my memory with regard to Junior picking me up late that morning—only recently have I been able to recall the journey and arriving at his new house on Ching Dairy Road in Mobile.

There was a sense of tranquility at Junior's. He had successfully carried on the stable family environment of Mama and Daddy's house when we were growing up. His wife cooked me a plate of grits and fried eggs. Before I could finish the meal, however, we became paranoid when a worker from the local telephone company climbed a pole in the neighbor's yard. We feared it might have been an undercover FBI agent looking for me.

Junior agreed to drive me to Aunt Kay's home, a manufactured house on stilts in the middle of a cow pasture, down a red dirt road called Outlaw. I could see uneasiness in my aunt's eyes when she answered her front door, but she let me in just the same. She found a better pair of shoes for me to wear, while one of my cousins copied my phone numbers onto a fresh sheet of paper. The Ziploc bag had done little to protect my wallet and address book during my twelve-mile run through the Louisiana swamp. My hands were shaking badly from the ordeal, and my mind was so disoriented that I couldn't hold a pen steadily enough to write the numbers myself.

The Prichard police had already visited Aunt Kay's house, looking for me after I stole the safe from the owner of the wrecking yard, and understandably, she didn't want to be charged for harboring a fugitive. On the ride over from Junior's house, I saw Daddy tending to J&J Grocery. I crept through the woods that fringed my aunt's property and made my way to Lott Road, where I ran across into my parents' front yard.

On sight of me, their dachshund hurled himself against his side of the chain-link fence in the backyard. My appearance had changed so dramatically that the little dog wanted to tear me to pieces.

"Jamie!" Mama exclaimed, when she answered the door. "Everybody's looking for you. Get your butt in here."

Mama had kept some of my high school clothes, which I changed into after a hot shower. I went into the kitchen where Mama had made me a grilled cheese sandwich and poured me a glass of milk.

"What am I supposed to do, Mama?" I said. "I've got no place left to run. This all feels like some kind of a bad dream that I can't wake up from.

I'm scared," I admitted.

"Jamie, you just went too far," Mama said as tears welled up in her hazel eyes. "You know I love you, but I can't help you anymore. You can't be here when your Daddy gets home."

"Mama . . . if they catch me, they gonna probably give me a life sentence."

"Well, then you need to get out the country. Call your father in Europe and tell him to take you back over there with him. I'm sure he's the one who put you in all this mess to begin with."

"It ain't all him, Mama," I said. "I've done this to myself."

"You need to stop making excuses for him. Me and your daddy, we both knew what was gonna happen when that man showed up two years ago to take you away from us. Even your Paw Paw said that you would never be the same."

"Jan is mad at me . . . because of the safe I had stolen I don't think he'll be willing to help me anymore."

Mama just started to cry outright then. "I can't help you either," she said. "You need to get on your way. You don't want your Daddy to catch you here. He's some kind of upset with you right now."

I put my hands over my face and just started to cry, deep sorrowful crying. My emaciated body fell back against the refrigerator and I slid down the door, leaving a trail in the clutter of decorative magnets on my way down.

38

April 1, 1996

I SPENT THE REST of March 1996 looking over my shoulder and suffering panic attacks every time I saw anything that looked like a cop car or a police uniform. I thought about shaving my head to change my appearance, but I realized that would make me stand out even more. So I dyed it light blonde instead and hid out with one of Doug's regular customers, LSD, whom I also knew through Melissa. They had dated before and it was with this old head that I retreated off Hayfield Road in Theodore, Alabama.

It wasn't meant to be, I guess. I was only at LSD's a week before along came April Fool's Day—the day when things were to change irreversibly.

I had agreed to a lucrative deal with a Mexican guy in Mission; he'd been sending pounds of weed to me at LSD's via the U.S. Mail. I was doing well, and planned on having enough to skip the country by the summer.

As far as I knew, from information gleaned from LSD,

Kid had been caught and was incarcerated in a Louisiana jail, but Melissa's mama had bonded her out just a few days after the chase. Fortunately, it seemed Melissa would be released on probation. Kid, on the other hand, was a repeat offender. His bond was set at a quarter of a million and he was facing hard time.

At LSD's, I smoked some gummy Mexican weed, waiting on a pot of Chef Boyardee *x's* and *o's* to heat up on the stove. I wondered if LSD was going to arrive before the mailman showed up with the eight and a half pounds I was waiting for. My Mexican hook up had sent the package "Priority", so I knew it would be arriving any minute.

Soon enough, someone knocked on the front door of the old trailer and I had no choice but to answer it myself. I quickly sprayed some air freshener around before opening the door to greet the gray-haired mailman standing on the steps with a cardboard box under his arm. "You Jay Bobby Smith?" he asked.

"Yes, Sir. And I see that you have my speakers I've been waiting on from Texas."

"Uh-huh," he said, with a curious expression, or maybe I was paranoid from that weed. "Here you go."

"Thanks."

I brought the parcel inside and ripped the box open, fishing out my pounds. I immediately noticed something unusual: a black device strapped to the vacuum-packed block of weed I held in my hands. It was small, like a pager, with a red light blinking.

"Why would my hook up send this to me?" I asked myself.

I heard gravel crunching in the driveway. I peeked through the dirty blinds to see a white van pulling in, followed closely by a line of unmarked cars. I panicked and sprinted out the back door, over a barbed-wire fence and into a cow pasture.

Searching for cover, I crossed Hayfield Road, jumped a ditch, and headed into some pine woods. Over my shoulder, I saw two undercover officers hot on my trail. I came across a creek while the smaller, faster officer, a white fellow, caught me by the back of my button-down shirt.

I threw an elbow and ripped the shirt off, scattering buttons, and giving the officers a glimpse at my "Laugh now, Cry later" undershirt displaying two theater masks.

I made it halfway across the murky creek before the bigger of the two officers, a black fellow, landed a hard right on the side of my face that put me out.

I came to, lying face down on the red creek bank while they secured my wrists and ankles with plastic ties. They carried me across Hayfield Road like a slain deer with blood dripping from my nose onto the blacktop road.

I saw the guy who'd delivered the package. With a badge hanging around his neck like the other undercover officers, clearly this was no mailman.

They tossed me into the back of the van, and I lay flat in the dark for some minutes, the undercover mailman opened the doors and read me my rights. In the background I saw them snapping pictures of the officer's nose I had busted earlier with my elbow.

"Are you Jay Bobby Smith?" he asked.

"Yes, Sir . . . but I don't have any kind of identification at the moment. Lost it all in the swamp in Louisiana about a month ago, Sir. I can give you my old address in Texas."

"Are you willing to claim sole responsibility for what we intercepted in the mail this morning?"

"Yes, Sir. That is all mine."

"Do you have anything else to state at this time?"

"Naw . . . but could y'all please put me in some regular cuffs?"

"The city police, they'll cut those ties off when they get here."

They shut the doors again.

The Mobile police were escorting me into one of their cruisers when I spotted LSD's purple Ford Ranger slowing down on Hayfield Road and then speeding up, LSD no doubt having seen what was going on.

We headed to the Mobile Metro Jail. While I was sitting in the male holding tank, I rubbed my fingertips forcefully against the beige cinder-block wall until they became raw and started to bleed. Remembering the time my adopted parents took me to Charter Hospital for being depressed about my adoption, I knew my fingerprints were on file, and I didn't want them to link me with the events in Louisiana.

A laser scanned my prints and my blood got all over their new machine. "They beat you up pretty good, huh, boy?" asked the guard, who wore latex gloves. "You won't run again, will you?"

They snapped my mug shot and I weighed in at a measly 135 pounds.

The guard took me to a shower room, strip-searched me, and gave me an orange jumpsuit with matching slippers and a bedroll. I was escorted to Cellblock 1005, where I slept for the next couple days until they brought me to an interrogation room to be questioned by the undercover mailman, who turned out to be a U.S. postal inspector.

The officer whose nose I broke was there too; he wanted to press third degree assault charges against me, that is, until he saw how swollen my face remained from his partner punching my lights out.

The postal inspector told me that after I stood before a magistrate to hear the initial charge against me—receiving and sending drugs through the U.S. Mail—there was a possibility I could be released on a signed bond.

"What does that mean . . . a signed bond?" I asked.

"Well, Mr. Smith, it means that you could have someone come down and, basically, sign you out after your court date tomorrow."

The following day, I found that this was indeed the case; however, I would need $7,500 against the $75,000 bail. I called Jan, thinking he might wire it, but Leo was at his place, said *no, a*nd that Jan was in Africa. I called LSD next, but his girl said he'd just left for Texas. They picked him up a couple of days later with twenty-five pounds of marijuana in the car. Things were definitely coming down in Alabama. I had even seen Doug earlier at the Metro Jail, standing at the phone. He looked OK, but I knew they'd caught him with a load of supplies in his house, and he might be facing some serious time. He also had that elusive murder charge from back in Wisconsin to contend with.

I returned to my new wedge 405, a more permanent cell where I met my cellmate, John. I was starting to feel a little better about things, especially with the possibility of the signed bond.

"Well," John said to me, "did you know that character, what's his name, Doug something?"

I said, "Yeah, I sure did. I guess they're catching up with all of us now, huh?"

"It doesn't look too bad for him, I guess."

"What do you mean?" I asked.

"Well, I watched him on the phone, and right after that guy hung up, along comes a couple a Federal marshals. They took off with him. I heard they call Doug something, ATW."

"ATW. What's that?"

"It's All The Way, means you're getting out."

"That's kinda strange, ain't it?"

"I've been in twice before you know, and I seen it all. That guy got put in the van down there, Federal marshals' van. And he got driven right off the premises. He's going home. He snitched somebody out."

I just shook my head in disgust at first, and then a cold chill ran through me. It was me! He'd turned me in, told the feds about my activities with Kid. I might as well have told them myself. I guess John could see something in my expression—he just shook his head.

After a while, we spoke more, and it turned out that John had been picked up on a bogus charge. "I let my cousin use my car to go hunting," he said. "And he goes and leaves his gun in the car. I'm an ex con. I can't have weapons. Somehow they found it."

"Oh, man," was all I could say. Here was a guy who hadn't done anything and he was being charged for the third time. And I hadn't been charged for the majority of what I'd been up to . . . yet. That night was a rough one.

The next morning, a deputy sheriff took me to the state courthouse at Government Plaza in downtown Mobile. The deputy was a thin black man, kind of like Barney Fife.

"You've got squinty eyes, fellow," he said. "I bet you smoke a lot of marijuana."

I couldn't deny that, but I wasn't sure if the squinty eyes had come first or the marijuana.

When I got inside the courtroom and my case came up, the prosecutor introduced me with six different aliases—some of which I'd never heard of. And that's when I knew they had me. All of my fears about old Doug were realized in that moment. I was charged with third degree burglary of Mr. Johnson's safe and first degree for the theft of a Bronco that Billy Joe had stolen just for the heck of it. That was it for a start, but I knew there was more to come.

I was returned to my cell feeling much less optimistic than I had the previous day. John could see I was not doing so well, and I think he felt like talking anyway.

"How do you stay so upbeat, John?" I asked. "You might be in here for life."

He shook his head and looked at me with calm eyes, impressive under the circumstances. "My mama told me all I have to do is read these here verses in Psalm 71 seven times every day until my day in court, to prove my faith to the Lord. And I know that He will set me free after that, because I *am* actually innocent this time."

Our conversation reminded me of the time I had returned from Florida with Jay, and the day after when I had spoken with my father, Jan, on the phone for the first time. Maybe the reason I got caught up in this was, to some extent, due to his influence; this would not justify my actions, but perhaps the blame didn't rest entirely with me. That night, I slept a little better.

A few days later, I was summoned to the interrogation room once more, this time to speak to another guy in the sheriff's department, a detective. He was a flashy kind of guy, wore snakeskin boots and lots of overt gold jewelry. It seemed a little out of place. He said that I'd be better off pleading guilty, since there were several written statements against me.

"Would you like to make a motion of discovery?" he asked.

"I don't know. What's that?"

"It means you get to see what we got on you."

"OK."

That's when I read Garrett's big story; according to his

account, there was no another person involved. Somehow I managed to commit the crimes alone.

While I was reading, the detective couldn't resist talking. "Boy, you're an original, I'll give you that."

I kept reading, so he carried on the conversation with himself.

"I never seen a thief with such a wealth of aliases, who likes to come and go, in and out the country, as much as you do."

I suspected the comment implied that they had further charges waiting.

"You should just go ahead and plead guilty, boy," he said. "Forget the third degree burglary—you got so many burglaries under your belt. I'll tell you what, why don't you come on along, take a ride with me? You can point out the houses that you hit, and I'll be able to close up some cases."

It's funny, I knew what he was talking about, and I even knew who it was that had committed all those crimes. It was actually the son of a Prichard Police Department captain. It was common knowledge, since he would take his stolen booty and make trades with Chaz for crack cocaine. But I didn't say anything.

"Sir, I'm afraid you have me confused with someone else," I said. "I don't want to turn anybody in, but the person you're looking for is not me."

"OK," he said, as if I'd told him a lie, "you'll be seeing the Feds next."

I waited out in the hall, and who should be out there

but Chaz himself. It made me remember having seen Doug, and it set off some internal alarms. But my fears were unwarranted.

"Hey man," I said.

"Hey," he replied, shaking his head.

"What's going on, man?" I said. He didn't look good.

He stared at me straight in the eye and said, "They got a brotha messed up for two keys of crack. They tryin' to give a brotha forty years. A brotha ain't going down like that. You gon' see me in the sky tonight. Watch the news, man. You gon' see me in the sky."

I was mulling that over when our reunion grew—Kid arrived to join us. It would have been funny had it not been so horrible. He'd overheard some of what Chaz had said, and with no time to stand around, he passed me and said, "Don't give 'em nothing, man. They already got what they need on us, and man, sometimes, you just gotta go to prison." He nodded, "It's just me and you."

He wasn't far wrong; we'd be charged as co-conspirators.

Soon after, I was called into the room that Kid had just left. Inside was a table full of officials, six, maybe seven of them. Most of them belonged to U.S. Customs or the Drug Enforcement Agency. I was told to sit at the far end of the table.

A U.S. Customs agent started the questioning. "Mr. Cobb, we'll be charging you with conspiracy to distribute five thousand pounds of marijuana. What do you have to say about that?"

"Well, Sir, what I have to say is that there's a lot of mistaken identity going on today."

"OK, so we got a smart ass. Well, listen smart ass, you're going to give us someone. We don't want you. We want your daddy. Interpol knows you're tied in with your father. How about we take a look at some movies?"

He switched on a monitor with some surveillance footage of Jan on his boat with someone that looked like Popeye McLean and another guy they named Gary Hunter. Then he turned it off.

"Now look. Here's what you do. You help us set this guy up with a hundred keys of cocaine. Do you understand?"

"Sir, all I know of my father is that he owns a clothing business."

"So you're gonna play the smart ass, huh?" he said.

"Sir, could I return to my cell?" I asked. Considering the way he was regarding me, how disappointed he was that I wouldn't play ball, and the effect of coming down off some serious drugs, I somehow deduced that they were planning to kill me.

"Fine. Get him outta here."

The next day, I was taken to the federal courthouse, where it was announced that, since Jan was a "major drug lord," I had probably conspired with him to smuggle two tons of cocaine with a street value of $150 million. I thought about proclaiming mistaken identity again, but I figured they'd probably heard enough of that, so I just denied it. Later, I learned that the "big job," that Jan told me they had abandoned, did go ahead.

I was assigned an attorney, and the prosecutor read the charges against me: sending and receiving marijuana through the U.S. Mail and conspiracy to possess with intent to distribute marijuana of the quantity of 245 kilograms.

"The defendant James H. Cobb will be held without bond," the magistrate announced, "because he is believed to be a flight risk. Next case."

It wasn't a big surprise to me, but it hit me hard. I was coming out of my withdrawal from the stuff, and reality was starting to settle in. It's not a feeling any human being can desire, to be held against his or her will. But it's made even worse by thinking, reflecting, seeing, and hearing what you've done repeatedly—thoughts, accusations, and images made not only by the authorities but also by the voice inside your head. There's no escaping the onslaught, and it's amazing how much can catch up with a person.

And yet, the upside is that you are not alone. There are people who deal with the same demons—maybe not the same crimes, but the same feelings of guilt and regret.

I was fortunate to get to know my roommate, John, during the next few months. I could have had a monster for a roommate, or somebody who didn't think he'd done anything wrong or somebody who decided the system was out to get him. John, however, accepted he had done wrong in the past, but he also accepted that in this instance, he himself had been wronged. Despite this, he was patient and confident that he would be vindicated, that justice would prevail.

"I just place my trust in the Lord," he would say, "like the Bible says, and no harm will come to me. Even if it does, I know I walk with the Lord. He loves me, and He loves you, too, Jamie."

It was hard to hear that at first, not just awkward and embarrassing, but painful too. I'd been given an opportunity long ago to avoid the mess I'd got myself into—avoid embarrassing my family, my friends. If I had turned to the Lord with the sorrow in my heart back then, I wouldn't have found myself in such a dire situation, and that was the harrowing thing. I had not. I'd gone right ahead, diving in and grabbing the easy money; trying to impress my biological father, who I had come to realize bore little compassion or love for me, harboring only a desire for me to aid him in his quest to make his millions. But even when I was no longer able to make the easy money, I continued to make drug money, any way I could.

Worst of all, I remembered the ugly, nightmarish scene in the Texas motel room with Kid and Psycho. How had I ended up doing business with such demented, underhand criminals? Had Arturo been killed? Maybe he too ended up dead like the English fellow in Spain, whose house was burnt to the ground even though he had not actually shorted Popeye McLean. And where would my sorry tail have ended if I hadn't been taken in by the U.S. Customs people?

John planted some healthy seeds of growth, spiritual growth, in my mind during those few months through the summer and into the fall.

After I'd been charged, and realized I wouldn't be getting

out on bail, I called Mama.

"Looks like I'm in here a while," I said.

"I know it, Jamie. I just been waitin' on your call."

"Been goin' around, huh?"

"Yes."

"I'm sorry for embarrassing you and Daddy."

"Do you need anything, Jamie?"

"No, Mama. You have done enough for me already."

But you know what mamas are like, and mine was the best. She sent me money, which was kept for prisoners in an account for use with a form of ATM card. With this, I was able to buy some personal items, notepaper, and stamps to post letters. When buying a stick of deodorant is the highpoint of your day, you know you're experiencing a change of perspective.

After a while, she came to visit me, the only one who did, despite the resistance she would no doubt have received from other family members. This was a big gesture for me, a lifeline, and remains as important to me now as it always will. I believe that kind of faith shown to somebody who has lost their way is one of the brightest lights to guide them on their way back home. My parents were never that religious, but the faith Mama inspired in me led me see the value of leading a good life in a way I'd never fully understood.

October was soon upon us, and I noticed a pretty female marshal putting shackles on a stocky black man with a Jheri curl. "Detective Smiley?" I asked. Amos Smiley worked for the Prichard PD and I'd always see him around my daddy's store when I was growing up. "What are you doing here?"

"Where do I know you from?" he asked.

"My daddy is Ray Cobb; runs J&J Grocery on Lott Road."

"Oh, yeah—now I remember you. They finally caught up with you, I see."

"Yeah," I said, as we climbed into cargo van with government plates.

"The snitches put me in here," Smiley told me. "This district court we're going to today has a 99 percent conviction rate, and I'm facing 240 years," he almost laughed. "They caught me buying condos in Miami with a million dollars. They got me on all kinds of charges; money-laundering, racketeering, extortion . . ."

"Dang, man," I said, thinking that I didn't have it so bad. I looked through the black steel grate over the windows of the van at a park where lawyers and court workers were enjoying a breezy autumn day, sipping coffee and feeding scraps of their deli sandwiches to a flock of eager pigeons. I heard church bells nearby, chiming out the twelve o'clock hour, while one of the other felons started complaining that some of the guys he had dealt with on the outside were even snitching on their grandmothers in exchange for lighter sentences.

That day, I was sentenced in federal court to sixty-three months. The judge looked at me and asked if I had anything to say, and I requested the opportunity to give my mama a hug goodbye. He denied me that privilege.

The following day, I appeared at state court to be sentenced for the state crimes for which I'd been charged. There, for the first time since Acapulco, I saw Garrett. He sat with Mr. Johnson, whose safe we'd stolen. The judge asked me repeatedly if I had worked with anyone on these crimes, and since I'd already pleaded guilty, I said, "No, your honor. I acted alone."

I'm guessing that statement threw old Garrett. My intention was to get the whole thing concluded, and ready for sentencing. By that point, I was ready to do my time.

The judge held a different view and felt that, since I had taken responsibility, deserved a lesser sentence: two years hard labor, with eight years' probation. If I failed to uphold the terms of probation, I would return to serve the eight additional years. He ordered the two years of hard time to run concurrently with my sixty-three months of federal time, and since the federal time took precedence, I would never serve any state time.

After the sentencing, I informed John of the technicality. "That's good news, huh, John?" I said.

"Oh yeah! You gonna just serve federal, you won't be seeing the inside of no Alabama state pen—that's the way to go, boy."

The following day, John had good news of his own. "They're letting me go," he said. "They realized I was not guilty of violating my parole, and they are sending me home."

I was happy for him, and happy to see what can happen when you have faith. He may not have realized it, but he made me a believer, not just with his good fortune, but with the faith he had for all those months—faith that he *would* have good fortune, one way or another.

After I said goodbye to John, it was my time to leave for federal prison. There was, however, a mix-up in the state system. Years later, I learned that such mix-ups are common in cases where prisoners refuse to inform on, or "rat out," other folks. This was Alabama in 1996.

As the other federal prisoners were being transferred to their facility, I alone was taken to a state transport.

"I'm supposed to be going to a federal prison," I told the guard.

"I don't know nothing about that," he said. "I'm just doing my job."

The decision had been made. Before I made it to the state facility, I was to spend some time in a holding facility called Kilby Correctional, where I and a few other inmates were allocated the task of digging a hole the size of a dump truck in the heavy red Alabama clay . . . and then refilling the same hole at the end of the week.

But I couldn't continue to have such a "great time," and there was nothing as soul wrenching and black as the next stop on my journey out of the darkness, on Thanksgiving 1996.

Volume 3

REFORMED

39

ONE OF THE THINGS that stands out in my mind about state prison is the ubiquity of tattoos. When I first entered Cellblock 6, nicknamed the Thunder Dome, I was caught off guard by the tattoos that many of the inmates displayed on their abdomens, words and accompanying artwork delivering sayings such as *THUG LIFE* and *ONLY GOD CAN JUDGE ME*. They were everywhere and worn by just about everyone within the predominantly black population of Draper. The rap star Tupac Shakur had just been murdered that September, and his messages were something that many of the inmates clung to somewhere between the free world and life in Draper. Of all the things I'd done, I guess putting a tattoo on my body was one I had managed to avoid. The sight was quite overwhelming.

Going in, everyone that rode in the van from Kilby on the first day was assigned to sleep in Cellblock 6, the Thunder Dome. I was scared to death when I heard the black dudes pressed against the bars at the front of the cellblock, yelling out about the new white boy. I maintained a blank look on my face and remained silent, remembering something John told me once about never showing your fear to anyone.

They'd given me a sheet of paper in the laundry room with my bed number on it. Walking through the cellblock, I saw one inmate jamming out Tupac on a speaker box he'd rigged up using a set of headphones and the core of a toilet paper roll with holes drilled into it. Other inmates on the second level peered down over the railings, some of them winking at me and making obscene gestures.

Bed 47 was in the back corner of the Thunder Dome by the bathrooms. From the leaky pipes in the wall, I had a big puddle of water on the floor beneath the half-inch sheet of iron upon which I laid my mattress. I tried not to make too much noise while fixing my bed and storing my toiletries in one of the steel drawers welded to the bottom bunk.

My brown-skinned bunkmate wore wire-rimmed glasses and was on his knees on the top bunk, hugging his Bible and praying. As I secured my drawer with the combination lock I'd been issued, I heard that he'd finished his prayers, so I stood up and introduced myself.

"I am Jamie Cobb. Good to meet you."

"My name is Clarence Cunningham," he said in return, "but everyone here likes to call me Preacher Man. I had been praying for you since before you arrived. I saw the empty bunk and knew there'd be somebody new showing up. Where are you from?"

"Eight Mile."

"I'm from Pineapple. And I don't mean to come on too strong with you, Jamie—but I just had something on my heart that God wanted me to ask you. I've got a prayer circle in here that I would like for you to be a part of. We pray every morning and say Grace every day before we go to the chow hall. In all actuality, it's only me now that does these things, but I know God is gonna make my circle big one day because, as He said, 'Ask and you shall receive.' So . . . can I count on you to start praying with me, Jamie?"

"Let me think about it, Preacher Man."

"Don't think too long. The devil will stay after your soul in here."

I stretched my legs, and after the fluorescent lights went out, a lot of commotion continued in the cellblock.

I lay on my bunk wide awake, wearing all my clothes and even my boots, hearing strange sounds over the running showers. There were sick things going on in that place throughout the night, and I was afraid to let myself fall asleep.

By Sunday night, I was settled in well enough to doze off for at least a few hours before a ripped, bald-headed black guard in a blue jumper and combat boots went around banging his billy club on every bunk. He carried himself as if he'd served in the military.

"Chow time! Five minutes!" he shouted.

We lined up in a stark corridor, waiting to shave and brush our teeth. The barred rollout windows had no screens, and through them I could see it was still dark outside. Ahead of me, Preacher Man turned around to say, "We're going on the farm today, Jamie. The best thing for you to do is wear at least three pairs of socks to keep the shackles from rubbing your ankles raw. And be sure that you shave thoroughly. If the guards detect any stubble when they pass your ID over your face and neck, you'll not only miss breakfast, but you'll spend the day either in the Mexican jail or handcuffed to the hitching post outside."

I took Preacher Man's advice and then followed the herd to breakfast.

Passing through the metal detector into the chow hall, I was issued a spoon, which I would use to shovel the cold grits and fake eggs into my mouth as quickly as I could, washing it all down with a cup of powdered milk. We had fifteen minutes to eat and get ourselves out to the blacktop by the guard shack.

They were shackling us up five together when it came to my turn.

"Man, I don't want to be chained up to no cracker!" said the black guy next to me.

It wasn't unusual to be referred to in slang, and I didn't take offense, but I could have done without any attention being drawn to me. I didn't say anything, and didn't have to, as Preacher Man came to my aid. He nodded faintly, head down, humbly toward the corrections officer, saying, "Boss, I'll go on that chain in his place. For my God does not see color, only the souls of men."

The CO went ahead and put me with Preacher Man instead. I guess he could see that I wasn't looking for trouble, and Preacher Man was a peacemaker.

But he was a lot more than that. Preacher Man's dream was to see the entire cellblock praying together before chow time. He said this was something that God had placed in his heart to do, and having been sentenced to twenty-five years for armed robbery, he had plenty of time to accomplish his task.

We shuffled across to the old wagon to get our tools and Preacher Man pointed out the furniture plant and vehicle garage where many inmates were assigned to work after their mandatory six months on the farm. A tall Spanish fellow behind me, G. Fuengirola, didn't seem the talkative type, but two other white men on the tail end of our chain were having a quiet argument. One of them, R. Chancellors, a thickset, blue-eyed fellow with a real strong country accent, was fussing at a much younger inmate with pale skin and dark features. "I done warned you about that borrowing in here, Brent," Chancellors scowled at the younger guy, taking the last few pulls on a hand-rolled cigarette. "Big Brown's gonna turn your ass out if you don't pay him back for every stogie you bum off of him. And you know how his interest works— every week your debt triples."

"Aw, he's cool, Chancellors. I sweep up hair in his barbershop in the afternoons. That's how I pay him back. Anyway, my family's gonna send me money before long."

"Stop lyin' to yo self, boy. You ain't got no family. You killed them all. Ain't no one mailed you a dime since you been here."

During that first day, I cleared fence lines and knocked down bushes, with a bag lunch consisting of a peanut butter sandwich, an apple, and a few cups of water to keep me going till three o'clock when we headed back to the prison.

After my shower, sitting on my bunk, I rubbed my fingers over the blisters on my hands, remembering what my Paw Paw Mizell once told me while I was washing and waxing his truck. "A hard day's work never hurt nobody, Jamie," he'd said. "Hard work will calm your nerves and strengthen your body. Ain't nothin' wrong with that."

Just before chow time, a guard passed around with a mailbag; I gave him my AIS number, 189914, so he handed me a letter that had come from Daddy.

Included in the envelope was a receipt for twenty-five dollars my friend John had sent to them on my behalf. Our ATM cards could be used in the prison with balances of up to twenty-five dollars to buy snacks and art supplies from the commissary. Daddy had made me a homemade Thanksgiving card and I had the feeling maybe he'd had a few Miller Lites before he typed it up. It read:

Jamie, this is your Daddy. Playing with the computer. Thinking about you a lot tonight. This is Thanksgiving. I am cooking turkeys, something you never liked. But you are not here to get the chicken I always smoke for you. Hope you have learned a lesson and you will be a better person when you get out. You hurt me very bad. Hope I can forgive you one day. But I will never forget what you done to me. Happy Thanksgiving. LOVE, YOUR DADDY, JESSIE RAY COBB.

I served my six months of farm time and, based on my good conduct, was placed on Draper's Substance Abuse Program. I started attending Catholic church services with my Mexican friend, Fuengirola, and also Protestant church services with folks I'd come to know during the farm labor days, including Randall Chandlers and Preacher Man. I never understood the difference in the denominations, just that they all served the same body, that of Jesus Christ. And that's all that mattered to me. I guess you could say that Preacher Man's influence was powerful and starting to take effect on me. Daddy probably would have liked Preacher Man.

The Substance Abuse Program was a turnaround for me, or maybe I should say, it completed the turnaround. I had known it was time to change when I saw Mama back in Eight Mile in January when I was on the run. As well as Mama, so many other people along my path had provided encouraging messages, such as John in Metro, and Preacher Man in Draper.

But Miss Harrison, my SAP counselor, had a message I could understand with a clarity above all others. It was an instruction: Always put your faith in something greater than yourself. It's one thing to stop doing wrong, and try to be responsible, mature, all of those good things. But without any actionable kind of guidance, it's hard to get a footing. I guess she must have known that. She was teaching a substance abuse class, but she had her own way of making that message stick. She made us all learn the Serenity Prayer:

God, grant me the serenity
to accept the things I cannot change;
courage to change the things I can;
and wisdom to know the difference.
Living one day at a time;
Enjoying one moment at a time;
Accepting hardships as the pathway to peace;
Taking, as He did, this sinful world
as it is, not as I would have it;
Trusting that He will make all things right
if I surrender to His Will;
That I may be reasonably happy in this life
and supremely happy with Him
Forever in the next.
Amen.
—*Reinhold Niebuhr*

That prayer made a lot of sense to me, gave me something to live by, and I expect it worked for many people. Miss Harrison would sit us in a circle of chairs and have us talk openly about our feelings. She advised that if we took our negative energy and channeled it toward something positive, we could accomplish anything. I genuinely saw the light of God in this woman.

An older black lady, her gracious spirit fostered immediate trust in her. We didn't see a lot of that spirit in Draper, and I believe some of those fellows had never been around that kind of wisdom in their entire lives.

She recommended we start each day with a positive thought in our mind and hold that thought throughout the course of our day. It wasn't easy to do at Draper, but it was something I worked toward. And attending class every day reinforced the idea.

I believe that the substance abuse program is one of the best programs that a prison can offer its inmates. It's something that anyone can benefit from, if they only apply themselves.

The discipline of the farm labor had instilled in me the value of hard work, a notion that wasn't new to me, but one that had diminished somewhat over the preceding years. My Paw Paw Mizell had always urged me to realize that hard work makes you appreciate all the little joys in life, like Chicken Sunday and having the privilege to go to the prison chapel for the different services. The chapel was our only retreat that was air-conditioned, a small mercy perhaps, but one that I came to fully appreciate.

The night before graduating from the program, I had a dream in the middle of the night. I woke in the upstairs half of Cellblock 5 to witness a familiar sight: the other inmates with white sheets pulled over their heads. This was to keep the mosquitoes off, something we had to do even while enduring the heat of the summer, since none of the old roll-out windows in Draper's cellblocks had screens. Within my dream, God put this thought in my head: *I do have power over sin, through Christ.*

I got up and wrote the message down in a maroon Bible

given to me in the Metro Jail. It was timely that the message had been delivered to me at that moment; soon I would graduate from the substance abuse program. I felt like Ms. Harrison's work would not go to waste, that I would be carrying it a little further.

The message in that dream remained with me always. In time, it made me understand what He died for on the cross, for our salvation. There I was, running around Europe with hundreds of thousands of dollars in my pocket, living high and wild, a life that never once gave me the inner feeling of satisfaction and contentment I had yearned so much for since I was thirteen. And yet, ironically, coming through some of the ugliest times in my life—or anybody's life for that matter—may be where you figure out how to feel at peace again, how to appreciate the fundamental values of real importance. Having been through it, and come out the other side, I guess that's when I got the message.

By writing apology letters, I'd asked for forgiveness from the people that I had hurt, and I found it in my own heart to forgive those who had hurt me. It was long overdue, but a heavy burden had been lifted from my shoulders.

In what was a heartwarming event, I graduated from SAP the next day. My sentence had long to run, but it was wonderful to sit with Mama and eat what they call "free world" food. And the commissioner of the Department of Corrections came to give a speech about how, when we were released from prison, we should change the people, places, and things that we had grown accustomed to, prior to our incarceration.

He said that by achieving this, we could remain free men and be productive citizens in society. That sounded like the correct thing to do, but I wondered how difficult this challenge would be. For years I'd been hanging around with druggies, the only people I knew. And would my family wish to help me in this goal, and if so, how?

Soon, I got to bunk in what they called the Recovery Dorm, a nicer place to spend the time. I was made an orderly for our cellblock, and here I met an important person.

When I was sentenced, I was informed that I would serve my state time concurrently with my federal time, the time would be served in a federal prison, and I would never see the inside of a state penitentiary. Well, we see how that turned out. Nevertheless, while working as an orderly, I met a Panamanian guy, Luis, who knew something about getting prison "mix-ups" corrected.

"Hey man, I know somebody who can get you straightened out," he said. "I got a friend who knows about all this stuff. He's helping me with something else. I'll ask him for you."

I didn't hold out a lot of hope at that point, but I said, "Thanks a lot. Anything you can do."

"What you workin' on?" he asked, looking at the drawing I was making. I'd returned to my interest in drawing and had started to develop my ability.

"It's a card to my daddy in Eight Mile. He's having a major aneurysm surgery today on his aorta. He's only got a fifty-fifty chance of living."

"Oh, man. I hope he makes it out all right. That picture there looks damn good. Can I read the inside?"

"Sure," I said, and handed it to him.

This was what I'd written in my best handwriting:

Any man can be a father. But it takes a special man to be a dad.

"Ain't that the truth."

Not long afterwards, Luis came to speak with me at my bunk.

"I got some papers for you, dog," he said. "My homey who bake the bread in the kitchen know all about that law," he said, handing me a stack of paperwork.

"What is this?" I asked, a little guarded against having my hopes raised in vain.

"I told him how the courts screwed up your sentence. He said all you do is fill out these papers, file them to the court-house, and they will let you out early."

"Aw, for real? Well, thanks, man," I said. "What do I owe you?"

"It's all good, dog. Just draw me a picture for my wife in Panama."

Soon after, I spotted a guard going around with a bag of mail he'd saved for the inmates who went to church or had to work late. I received another card from my daddy that night. It was homemade again, but this one had a little bird on the front over the words *Life is what you make it.*

On the inside it read:

Jamie, I want you to know that I miss you very much. Wish you were here to eat Thanksgiving dinner. Take care.

Love, your Daddy

The following day, I received a call from my mama. "I got some news, Jamie," she said. "Your brother Donny's wife come by the store this week. It seems they busted Donny and your biological father in Scotland with three tons of drugs."

"What?"

"A Customs officer was killed during the raid and they're facing a lot of time. Donny had asked for your address and I give it to his wife, if that's all right."

"I don't have anything against Donny," I said. "He's a good guy."

"I kind of feel sorry for him, having to be locked up in a foreign country because of that mess y'all's father got y'all into."

"Like I said, Mama—I made my own decisions."

"Well, what kind of father would do that to his own son?"

I didn't have an answer for that.

The day I was moved from state prison to federal prison, I remember walking by Cellblock 2, seeing my friend Randall Chandlers sitting on his bunk, depressed. At the time, I was on my way to meet the U.S. marshals who were finalizing my paperwork to take me to federal prison. I went and sat beside him and let him know I was headed to federal prison. He assured me that the food was going to be better. His dad was in the federal system, on death row. He was the first man in the United States to receive kingpin status for marijuana, and he was given the death penalty. While in the Recovery Dorm, I had remembered seeing *60 Minutes* and CNN specials on Randall's daddy. Randall was like a celebrity around Draper. He used to tell me, walking the track, that the only reason he was in prison was because of his daddy's name. Randall was in there for shooting a man in half with a shotgun. It was in Randall's own front yard in Piedmont, Alabama. The guy was coming after him with a buck knife, and he was just defending himself.

He started telling me how hard it had been for his mom to make a living out there in the foothills of Piedmont, more or less in the middle of nowhere. I told him the good news of my own adopted daddy surviving his aneurysm surgery, after I prayed for him every night. Randall wanted me to pray with him for his daddy to get taken off of death row, which I did. I found out later that during Bill Clinton's last year in office, he pardoned Randall's daddy on death row.

After this conversation, I was called to the front gates to be released to the Federal Marshals.

40

IN MARCH OF 1998, I was transferred by U.S. marshals from Draper to the Montgomery, Alabama, city jail. I was put into a cell with some outlaw bikers, also waiting to be transferred to the federal system. By then, the idea of mixing with outlaw bikers didn't faze me, and it wasn't a rough week like it had been entering Draper. A week later, I was transferred to Atlanta USP. Here, I was processed into the federal system, and what they call "classified," which means they go through your records to see what you've been doing up to that point, and what you should be doing while you're in their system.

I was issued another orange jumpsuit and a pair of blue cotton slip-on shoes. Sitting in a holding tank with the other transfers, I started talking to a bald-headed Texan of Irish descent named Patrick Ford.

While shooting the breeze with him for a few minutes, I ascertained that he was well educated, but short-tempered.

He had two years left to serve for pistol-whipping a Border Patrol agent in Brownsville. The agent had tried to arrest him for public intoxication.

An ebony-skinned English guy across from us was talking, very politely, to a lumberjack-looking fellow who I noticed had an Alabama accent. He seemed more than a little on the slow side, but very friendly. He was around his mid-thirties, hairy as all hell, with a full brown and silver beard. "You know I love you, Big Country," the English fellow was saying, "but I couldn't take another day in that little cell with those stinking feet of yours."

"I'm sorry," Big Country responded, real slow and sad, staring at the floor. "They just sweat a lot. I tried to wash my socks out every day so the smell don't get so bad."

"Yes . . . you washed them in the sink where I brushed my teeth and then hung them over my bunk."

"I'm sorry."

After a week in Atlanta, I was flown to Fort Polk, Louisiana, then taken by bus to Oakdale Federal Correctional Institution (FCI).

As they processed me in, they concluded that I had been assessed as requiring entry onto a GED (General Educational Development) program. It had been years since I attended school, and I wondered how I'd get through the GED, but there was no option. It was also decided that I complete another drug treatment program, though only forty hours long this time. I was assigned to what they called Evangeline Unit II.

There were many skinheads at the prison, all of them refusing to be put into a cell with a non-Caucasian. With this in mind, the guards thought it would be fun to see how I reacted when assigned to a gay black inmate by the name of Foxy, who was very sick and infected with HIV. He was throwing up everywhere in an upstairs cell, and I didn't care what they did with me, so long as I didn't stay there.

When I complained, I was told that they'd need time to reassign me to the Special Housing Unit for a week. I was happy and relieved to hear that—until I found that the SHU was just a fancy name for the Hole, or solitary confinement.

On the first day of my release from SHU, I met Joseph Bonanno, son of the Sicilian-born American mafioso Joe Bonanno, Sr., who wrote the book *A Man of Honor*. Joseph went by the nickname of "Chile."

"I'm just getting out the Hole. Are you the fella I'm supposed to meet with?" I said.

"That's me. And I don't blame you for doing what you did. I couldn't live with a milksop like Foxy either. You just got caught up in the game that goes on in here between the skinheads and the black guards. It's good that you stood up for yourself."

He extended his hand. "Name's Chile."

"Jamie. Pleased to meet you, Sir. Are you gonna hook me up with a cellie?"

"Sure. But first—can I see your PSI?" (presentencing investigation).

"Yeah, it's right here in my bag."

"Walk to my cell with me," Chile said, standing up. "I'll show you mine, too."

Chile's cell was what you'd call "well appointed" for something you'd find in a prison. His glossy floor was adorned with a gray throw rug, which was really a wool blanket with a fringe sewn around the edges. He had a full bookcase that sat beside the toilet, and the four walls were freshly painted. The air smelled of garlic and olive oil, and I could hear soft classical music coming from a big set of Sony headphones hanging on his bunk.

"Nice cell, Chile."

"Thanks," he said, opening a drawer on his desk.

We exchanged PSIs and he passed me a folding chair with tennis balls stuck on the bottoms of the legs. I flipped through his report and read that Chile's father was one of the youngest New York mob bosses ever—he even ran for governor of the state in 1963.

"Well, you're no snitch," Chile said, after a few minutes. "five hundred forty pounds conspiracy, that's a good bit."

"Damn, you stole a million dollars," I replied. "Extortion, racketeering . . ."

"Yeah," said Chile, "I've done it all. Your father is Dutch, but you were raised in Alabama. That's interesting. Van Rijn . . . that name rings a bell."

He returned my PSI and pulled a stack of newspaper articles from his desk. "Here's some of what I was doing in New York. Stay put. I'll go to the guards' office now and set you up somewhere."

I studied the clippings for a minute; most of them were from the *New York Times*, centered on John Gotti and the Gambino crime family.

When Chile returned a few minutes later, he said, "Your new cell is 411, upstairs. Your cellie's name is Patrick Ford. It was a black fella that was supposed to bunk with him, but he thought this Patrick was a skinhead and said he'd rather go to the SHU. How you like that?"

I chuckled. Patrick had simply lost his hair. He'd never been a skinhead. "Shoot, I know him," I said. "I met him back in Atlanta, at transfer. He ain't no skinhead." I was glad to be bunking with Patrick.

As we talked, I learned that Chile had spent most of his life between Manhattan, New Jersey, and Arizona. He was an orderly at Oakdale and more or less ran the Evangeline Unit, amongst other duties, overseeing bets on football games. The guards seemed to like him, and thus he was rewarded with many privileges.

I settled in well at Oakdale and never got into any trouble, kept my nose clean. Every country in the world seemed to be represented in Oakdale since it was a holding prison for deportees, except for the Cubans, as they had rioted there in the eighties, setting the prison on fire, raping the guards and sending them down the stairs in flaming laundry carts.

I learned much about the world from the different people I met at the facility. Many were involved in organized crime across the globe. The Russian mafia was on the rise during that period, and we had our share of Russian gangsters at

Oakdale. Also French and Mexican criminals, and mobsters of many other nationalities.

And many were like me, people who'd simply become mixed up in doing the wrong things. I was able to strike a rapport with these inmates, since I had seen my share of the world with my biological father, Jan, and was adept at picking up different languages.

Three or four months later, I met the tutor from Oakdale's GED program, Richard Barnett. He stood about six feet four inches tall, had thick brown hair, and a strong southern accent. Born and raised near the North Louisiana city of Monroe, he had moved to Lafayette after high school to study petroleum engineering at the University of Southwestern Louisiana. Barnett became a big player in the international oil business and a pillar of his community there in Lafayette. I didn't have a clear idea of what he'd been jailed for, and didn't feel comfortable broaching the subject with him, but Richard Barnett would become instrumental in transforming my approach to education.

"Nice to meet you, Jamie," he said. "How's it going for you here?"

"Going good," I said. "And I appreciate that they want me to get my GED, but I have to tell you, it's not going to be an easy thing."

"Good things usually aren't," he said.

Barnett taught my GED class. One day, I fell asleep in the back of the classroom. I had persevered and tried to concentrate in these classes for a while, but I had trouble keeping up and no longer bothered paying attention. My reading level was low and I couldn't even dissect a basic fraction. Like an old unwanted friend, my feelings of helplessness returned to haunt me.

I knew I'd bettered myself in Ms. Harrison's class, but at the GED class, I knew I was way behind; I felt I had little hope of figuring out what they were talking about, let alone actually gaining my GED.

Nevertheless, I must have lurched forward a bit in my slumber, as Barnett hollered at me.

"Cobb! This ain't nap time!"

I snapped to. It was not only embarrassing but nerve-racking too. You never knew when you'd get thrown back in the Hole.

He called me to the front of the class and asked me if I wanted to become another statistic. "Here's one for you," he said. "Try 90 percent. Yes, that's right. Ninety percent of all inmates who don't get their GED end up right back here in prison once they get out. Is that what you want?"

"No, Sir."

"Then what are you doing sleeping in the back there? You expect to learn the material in your sleep?"

"Mr. Barnett, I've struggled with a learning disability my whole life—"

"Don't!" he said, and stuck up his hand as if to stop traffic. "I don't want to hear about learning disabilities. Everybody has some weakness in the learning department. Let me tell you something, Cobb: if you want to, you can do this. You just put your mind to it. Pay attention in class. You do that, and you can accomplish anything."

I thought of all the tortured hours in elementary and middle school; it was hard to imagine that I could come up to par.

"Here's the thing. I don't want you to be afraid to ask for help. I don't care if you feel stupid. Nobody here's Einstein. If they were, they wouldn't be here, would they? And you ask me for help as many times as you need to in order to get it right. Do you understand?"

I nodded. That was a new one on me, a new approach that took me by surprise. In my past experience, special education teachers tended to hide behind stacks of books on their desks, hoping nobody would ask for anything. "Yes, Sir," I said.

"Listen up, you all," he addressed the class. "My goal here is to see that as many of you as humanly possible graduate this course, test for your GED, and take it home with you. There's others of you in here who aren't putting anything into this work, not just Cobb. I want to see some real effort. I don't want anybody back in here."

Barnett had been a pillar of his community in the free world, but he'd given in to one seriously bad temptation that led him into trouble. Teaching us, getting us through the course to earn a piece of paper that we could do something with, was his way of giving back, a recompense for what he had done.

Soon after my sleeping incident in the classroom, I was sitting in the TV room of the Evangeline Unit, when a big

Mexican bandito and a black guy from New Orleans who had converted to Islam (he was inside for conspiracy to sell cocaine for the New Orleans Police Department) got into a scuffle. It was ironic, since at the time, I happened to be watching the *60 Minutes* special in which Mobile, Alabama, was being portrayed to be the "snitch capital" of the United States, and how the county boasted a 99 percent conviction rate.

In the middle of the report, the Mexican got up and turned the channel to a WWF wrestling show. The black guy calmly got up from his seat and went to his cell. He returned wearing a well-pressed long-sleeve shirt. Nothing much wrong with that, but my cellie pointed out a bit of rope around his wrist.

"OK, Jamie," Patrick said, "be ready to run. Something's about to go down here and you don't wanna get caught in the middle."

Sure enough, the Muslim guy walked over to the TV and turned the channel back to *60 Minutes*.

That didn't go down well with the bandito. He jumped up in protest, and as soon as he did, the Muslim pulled out a shank that was attached to the rope we'd seen, and he ripped the Mexican's stomach open, spilling his guts out. It was a dizzying experience I will never forget—the sight of that man's insides bursting out right in front of us. And for basically no reason. That's what anger does to you: it festers inside, creating its own little hell, and in some folks, it takes over to such an extent that they think little of ripping out somebody's guts for changing the TV channel.

Not surprisingly, I stayed away from the TV room after

that incident and also determined that I needed to read more, something Mr. Barnett had advised I should do. I began reading everyday works: novels, history books, and newspapers. It was a start.

On October 11, 1998, I received a visit from a relative, Sarah, whom I'd always known as my cousin. She lived in Lafayette, Louisiana. It can be awkward visiting someone in jail, and I guess she wanted some company, so she brought along a friend of hers from church, named Lynn.

When Sarah excused herself to go to the restroom, I had a chance to talk with Lynn for a moment.

"I'm working on getting my GED," I said. "I never actually made it through high school. Part of what we're doing is writing what they call essays. It kind gets you prepared I guess, for writing longer papers, or something."

"Oh yeah, essays, I remember those!" Lynn said, laughing a little.

"Hey, what do you think about writing back and forth, you and me, like pen pals or something?"

She thought about it for a while and then said, "Sure. That'd be different."

When I first met Lynn, I'd been nervous, but even having spoken for over a half hour, I still had a hard time looking at those beautiful green eyes of hers. She was sure something to see, and I got a funny feeling inside every time I looked at her. That had never happened to me before.

That same year, the week before Christmas, I sat at the desk in my cell, and wrote this letter:

Dear Lynn,

I hope this finds you in good spirits. I was very happy to receive the picture of you in your last letter. Sorry it's taken me so long to write you back, but we have been on lockdown for a week. The Mexican Mafia put the Black Hand on someone in here who they found out was a snitch, which means they killed him. I was in the hobby/craft shop when it happened, using pastels to put the final touches on a portrait of you.

It was an awful sight when they snuck up on that man with scissors from the leather shop and put it through that poor fellow's neck. I hope and pray I never have to witness nothing like that ever again.

Enough about all that. I was thrilled to hear you got into that nursing school in Eunice. I know you will do just fine. Take it one day at a time and watch for them special signs that God sends you, like the doves in the tree you seen the first day we met.

Well, that's about it for now. I can hear the guard's key in the door. It must be mail call.

Your friend and pen pal,
Jamie

"Jamie Cobb," I heard, after the meal slot in the door fell open.

"Yes, Sir . . . 06274-003," I said, reciting the federal register number off my ID. I stuffed the letter to Lynn in a cardboard tube along with her portrait as two incoming letters fell into the slot.

"Mr. Smith," I said, recognizing my counselor—a distinguished-looking older black man with round bifocals—through the narrow window. "Would you send off this artwork for me?"

"Sure, Cobb. I hope you haven't sealed it up. I have to inspect it first."

He unrolled the sheet of sketch paper and his eyes lit up behind his thick lenses. "Wow . . . this is pretty good, Cobb."

"Thank you, Sir."

"You know, I have something in my office that maybe you could draw up for me, if you wouldn't mind. I'll let you see it after mail call."

I got three letters that day. The first letter was from my father, Jan, locked up in a Scottish prison. It read:

Shotts—14 December 1998

Dear Jamie,

I received your letter from November 20. I hope that you receive this letter doing well. Here, not much has happened lately. We are waiting again on another hearing. Our appeal has still not gone through and could take again a few more months. All they do is continue to put it off and hope we give up. Well, I have news for them. We will never give in to this unjust system here. We will see what happens, soon I hope.

So you are going to learn French from your working out friend in Oakdale. I try to speak it sometime, but not very well. It is too hard for me, I think. What I really need to learn better is Spanish because I will go back to Spain to live, as I like it there very much. Good food is everywhere. I don't believe that French is best, Jamie, but Italian. And I do not mean pizza and spaghetti, but the real Italian food that I know you remember. Mamma mia, that's good.

Was glad to hear that little Kyle is doing well. In the picture you sent, he shares many features with us both. Also I don't think it is wise to use your birth name in America for the moment, until all of these trials are done with. Cobb is better for now. Trust me on this.

I am working on an exposition of thirty of my paintings. I made the frames for them as well and they will sell probably for about $50 at an auction, maybe, in a Glasgow college of art. The money will go to a good cause.

All is good with the four of us, except that Leo will maybe have to go for heart surgery soon. There is much stress in waiting for these appeals, and this place can get to you sometimes. Last summer we saw the sun for maybe a day or two. Give me Spain any day.

Let me hear from you again soon. Let me know if you get into the treatment course to take a year off your sentence. Donny has written to you as well, if you did not read his first.

Love and Greetings,
Your Dad, Jan van Rijn

Donny's letter was brief and read:
Merry Christmas, Jamie.

I got your last letter and of course, Little Brother, I'd be more than happy to help you with that, if that's something God put on your heart, keeping other kids from making the choices we've made.

Not much is going on in our case at the moment. Some-time next year we'll get another hearing, but they seem to be dragging this out as long as possible. A few of the London newspapers have really blown this thing out of proportion. Maybe next letter I'll send some of the articles I've seen.

It made me proud to hear you were working on your GED. I'm glad to hear that your eyes are wide open to the world. I've always thought you were smart, only you needed direction, and now that you have your goals and dreams laid out, I know that absolutely nothing can stop you.

Yes, when we finally both get out, we will spend lots of time getting to (re) know each other and become as close as brothers should be.

> *My Love Always,*
> *Your Brother, Donny van Rijn*

I recognized the address on the other envelope—from my biological mother. It wasn't much: an unflattering picture of her dressed like a witch, sitting in a wingback chair and holding two .45 revolvers aimed at the camera.

On the back she had written, "*I'm not this bad. Making costumes now in New Orleans for the girls at Big Daddy's on Bourbon. Job at the mission didn't pan out. Keeping my head straight. Will write more later. Love, your mother, Wendy.*"

I heard keys turning in the mail slot and saw my counselor standing at the door again. He dropped something into the slot. I unrolled the paper to see a picture of a black Jesus.

"You think you could draw this for me, Cobb?"

I was taken aback momentarily, but then I said, "Of course. I could certainly do that for you, Sir."

"I was thinking it would look good maybe as an 18 × 24," he said. "I can get you some good paper, if you need. By the way, I just put you on the waiting list for the intense drug treatment program in FCI Marianna. You probably won't be transferred there until the summer, but you do get a year off your time if you complete the program."

"Yes, Sir. Thank you, Sir."

In 1999, my Mama made the trip out to Oakdale and paid me a visit with my nephew, Dusty, and my son, Kyle. Dusty was a lot like me. He could draw fairly well, but he struggled with a learning disability and anger issues. He had spent his younger years watching his father beat up on his mom, my adopted sister, until he was six or seven years old. It was then that my mama and daddy took over the raising of Dusty and his two sisters as their own, like they had done for me.

I told Dusty how I had recently learned fractions from Mr. Barnett.

"Oh, fractions," he said, sighing.

"They givin' you a hard time?" I asked.

"I don't understand any of it," he said. I could tell he'd rather not talk about it, but I got a piece of paper and a pencil and showed him a few examples. "Look, Dusty, you see this circle?"

"Uh-huh."

"Suppose I draw this line through it. See that?"

"Uh-huh."

"What'd I do?"

"You cut it in half."

"What did you say?"

"You cut it in—oh!" And he laughed a little.

"Yep, that's half. And *then*," I said, drawing a line through the middle of both of the halves, "I draw another line. How many pieces are there of that poor old circle I've started cutting up?"

He smiled. "Four."

"Right. So guess what each one of those pieces is called."

"What?"

"A *fourth*!" I said.

A big smile crept across his face. "Fourths!" he said. "I get it, if there's four, it's fourths."

"How about if there's six?" I asked.

"Sixths?"

"Yep!"

"How about ten?" Mama asked him.

"Tenths!"

It was gratifying to see the triumph on his face. But Dusty was actively clinging on to the pain he knew as a very young child; he didn't know how to let it go, I guess. It was important to me that he knew, early on, that no matter what, his Maw Maw and Paw Paw loved him dearly.

"There's nothing in this world they wouldn't do to help make you happy and a good and successful person," I told him. "Not too many people can say they have that kind of folks."

Mama and I had become pretty close by this time. In fact, we were more or less confidants, like best friends.

"You know, Jamie," she said to me one day, "when your father found out that you were responsible for his safe being stolen, that man . . ." her voiced cracked a little, "that man broke down and cried."

Hearing that made me want to cry. I had been taken in by two of the best folks in the world, full of love, full of willingness to teach and discipline a tough kid with learning disabilities and a drug-addicted mother. And what had I done in return? Had I known how deeply I would hurt them, I may never have made those choices.

But there's nobody out there to tell you and, often, little experience to draw on when you're young. You think you're a "grown-up" and you're making all your own choices—until money is low and you can't get by. Then, through pride, anger, desperation, or many other factors, you turn to those who have never let you down—your family—and you take what you can get. It's a classic case.

In a strange irony, my pain in knowing the trauma I had caused them made me realize how much I truly loved my parents.

"Oh, don't you worry none, Jamie," Mama said, when she saw the expression on my face. "He's long since forgiven you. And Jamie, he's so proud of you, all that progress you made, and working at getting your GED and all."

That was a relief to hear, but I knew in my heart that he

had already forgiven me, and I sensed they were both proud of me. I tried not to do too much talking, though. After all, Mama was doing so much for everyone, and it was a listening heart that she truly needed. That wonderful woman carried a heavy load on her shoulders. It made her feel good to have someone to talk to who could practice listening. All she and Daddy ever wanted was for the kids she had raised—and that was quite a few more than she'd actually had—to succeed in their lives.

Now I was trying to do my part.

By the year 2000, I had completed the required 40-hour drug treatment program, during which I learned the precise effects of drugs abuse on the brain, including the hideous physiological damage caused on brain cells. At this time, I also studied hard for my GED test, scheduled for the spring of 2000.

Soon after the test, I was transferred to the Oklahoma City federal prison, which was used as a transfer center. Coincidentally, my GED teacher, Richard Barnett, was sent there at the same time, and it was over a game of chess with him that I learned I had passed the GED exam.

It's hard to explain how a kid with a learning disability feels when he or she accomplishes something that involves academia. These days, folks refer to learning disabilities under a new term, "learning differences". I believe that's a more accurate description, since most kids with learning differences tend to excel when they listen to audio material or watch a video rather than read it from a book. During my school education, however, while such opportunities did exist, they unfortunately weren't offered at any of my schools. So, passing that test, and gaining a qualification with the equivalence of a high school graduate via my own reading and writing skills, gave me a strong sense of personal accomplishment. I had built a certain level of self-esteem simply by studying for it, but when I learned that I had passed, I felt a completely new kind of personal high.

I took the letter telling of this good news and forwarded it to my adopted parents.

Apart from this valuable sense of achievement, I realized that I now held the credentials to enable me to apply for the kind of work I ultimately aspired to prior to becoming involved in this whole mess back in '94.

I thought of the dedicated and determined Ms. Harrison, back at Draper, who had taken the time and trouble to haul us substance abusers out of the mess we'd got ourselves into. Around that time, I started thinking that perhaps I too could reach people with experiences similar to my own—people who had taken the wrong path and might be able to relate. Maybe that day I received a little message from God, a message that took root over time.

Barnett was waiting to be transferred to a lower-security prison in Fort Worth, Texas, and I would soon be transferred to Marianna, Florida, another FCI, where I would undergo an intense, year-long drug treatment program. If I could get through that successfully, my sentence would be reduced by a year.

That day, Barnett advised that I should consider nunc pro tunc, a remedy for prisoners who had a legitimate complaint against the procedures carried out by the Department of Corrections. It applied to that "mix-up," the technicality that had sent me to state prison rather than federal. My time in state should have run concurrently with my federal time. In fact, I should not have gone to Draper, the state facility, at all. The mix-up that occurred resulted in me starting my federal time at zero, even though I had already served 18 months in the state facility. I gave the idea some thought, but although I was a newly graduated GED student, I didn't possess the legal knowledge to take action at this point.

Around early June 2000, I arrived at Marianna FCI, Florida, and was placed in a special housing unit due to prison overcrowding and a lack of beds. I was in the company of a fellow named Booger Boudreaux, an outlaw biker from Eunice, Louisiana, who was confined to solitary (in effect, the special housing unit), after a tool was found to be missing from the welding shop.

I had met Booger previously in the Montgomery city jail on my way to Atlanta USP (you do a lot of transferring within the federal system). He asked me some questions about my case, and after hearing the details, he said that it sounded like the experience of his former cellie.

In a remarkable coincidence, his former cellie turned out to be Kid Brown, my old partner in crime. I was amazed that we'd ended up in the same facility—at least for a while. After a few days in the SHU, they found me a cell in the Apache

Unit of the prison.

I was reunited with Kid outside the chow hall, hanging out with his friend, Heavy D, who was in the process of smuggling tomatoes and bell peppers back to his unit. Heavy was in prison for being caught in Mississippi with fifteen hundred pounds of marijuana in the back of a watermelon truck.

"Hey! Jamie!" Kid said, greeting me like an old friend.

I'd been through a lot of changes, and I didn't know where Kid's head was; I was cautious, and felt like he might be bad news for me. Things were going well enough for me, but I'd had no chance to test my new accomplishments against the old temptations. Being in his company seemed like a threat to my new direction.

He asked me to come over to the gym on the next recreation call, so I headed over despite my reservations. And there was old Kid thrashing his long blonde hair around, singing the Creed song "What If?" with a band of Mexican rockers. After he finished singing, we sat on the bleachers and I told him how I'd got my GED. He said he'd got his, too.

That immediately made me feel better and I figured we'd been on the same track, at least as far as education was concerned. I told him about the nunc pro tunc provision that Richard Barnett mentioned, and how Booger told me he'd been through the same thing. I suggested he should also see about getting credited for his state time.

"Come on," he said, "let's walk around the track a time or two."

"Sure," I said. I thought it would be a good opportunity

to talk about what I'd been through with the drug education and other programs.

But then he pulled out a pin joint.

He began telling me about the connections he'd made while in Marianna, and how he was set up to make some good money when he was released.

"No thanks, Kid," I said, looking at the joint. "I don't know, I think I've had enough of the messed up lifestyle I was leading. I don't know if you get this or not, but I really don't want to become a statistic, going in and out of jail my whole life, like my biological father."

Kid put the joint back and I had the feeling he was either listening to me or wishing he hadn't invited me to go on the walk. We had a way to go before we got back, so I continued. "I'm just set on learning as much as I can so that I can do positive things with my son when I get out. The last thing I want to do is bring him into the same mess Jan brought me into."

We walked for a while in silence, and then he said, "Man, I think you're right. I got a set of twins to raise. I was thinking I could learn a trade in here that I could use on the outside."

That made me feel better. I wondered what my year in the intensive drug program would be like, and I presumed it could only help. I was also pleased that Kid had was thinking of changing his life for himself, and for the sake of his children.

Over the course of the next four months, I got visits from Mama, and Lynn, and received letters from my biological father and my half-brother. I was fighting to become a better person and put the whole drug mess behind me, while Jan, my "father," appeared to be doing everything he could to maintain the life to which he'd become accustomed to prior to being jailed. Despite my knowledge of his criminal activities, he didn't admit the truth. Of course, our letters were vetted before being handed to inmates, and sometimes before they left the prison from which they were sent, and this no doubt had a bearing on what he felt he was able to write. And yet I sensed there were no feelings of contrition in his words or any hints at an apology for how I'd become embroiled in his elicit dealings.

On the other hand, it warmed my heart to learn that Donny genuinely wanted to change. In the past, he'd slavishly followed whatever underhanded tasks Jan had assigned, a cynical move by the only father figure Donny had ever had. I used to resent Donny because he'd always known his true father, but I'd come to realize that this knowledge was no privilege. I had been brought up by a fine man, a man with a strong sense of moral duty, whereas Donny had known a fellow who appeared to have little regard for right and wrong or any sense of love and responsibility for his family.

To compound problems, Donny's relationship with his wife was falling apart—a result of his incarceration in Scotland, while she remained alone in Alabama. He perhaps believed that if he straightened himself out, things might still work out for them.

But no matter how you look at our lives and the predicaments we found ourselves in, we had made our own decisions to lead us to this point, and we had our own decisions to make in the future.

One day, I received an important letter from my Paw Paw Mizell, encouraging me to live up to my potential after my release.

> *Dear Jamie,*
>
> *I am not too good at writing and you might not be able to read this, but try hard anyhow. So glad to know you're getting out soon. I hope you can prove to everybody you can make something of your life. I heard about your friend in Louisiana. She sounds like a real sweet person. She might be the right one for you, but you will have to work with her, like anybody, and keep an open mind.*
>
> *I was glad to hear about you getting your education because you need high school learning to dig a ditch this day and time. I am also glad that you found the Lord. If you had been living for Him all the time you would have never ended up where you are now.*
>
> *I seen a picture Janet showed me of you with your friends in Oakdale prison. You sure have grown up into someone who will make us all proud, a changed man and not the scared little boy that went in there so many years ago. You had a good home and Janet and Jessie Ray would have done anything for you, but the grass was greener over the hill until you got there to see that the grass had died. That is the way it goes. Nobody will love you like your family.*
>
> *So much for all that. Hurry home and show everybody you are a reformed man and can go on with your life. Five*

years is enough to give away. Life is too short. I love you lots and waiting for you to give that truck one more good cleaning and polishing like you used to do. I'll pray for you every night until I see you at your daddy's store. And don't worry. I won't ruin the surprise.

Love, Paw Paw Mizell

I told him that I would be free one year earlier, once I completed my drug program in Marianna. At that point, however, I didn't realize what was about to happen to my sentence. Due to the papers I'd filed, the government was working on my behalf, and I received a letter from the Federal Department of Corrections stating that I would be released in 90 days.

I didn't think that was any time to fool around, so that night, I agreed to go to church with Kid and Heavy D. Later, Heavy D and Big Country came knocking on my cell door. Country had trimmed his beard to a respectable degree and slicked his hair straight back.

"Jamie, you gon' have to attend church with us tonight," said Heavy D. "I gotta go repent for all them vegetables I been taking from the kitchen. And plus they gonna let me sing a little solo. We gotta get on our way, man. I can't miss my chance in the spotlight."

Heavy asked if I would go to church with his mom in Mississippi when I got out, and even drew a map to the church. He just wanted me to go and sit beside her, let her know that he was doing fine and loved her. I told him I'd try my best to do that for him.

Kid told me how he had secured a place in a plumbing program and had been writing to his cousin back in Naples, Florida, who was a Christian and serving as a witness to him.

"You know, Jamie, that guy's all right. I think he knows the one way to go. At least for me. When I get outta here, I'm gonna get my plumber's license in Naples, and take good care of my twins."

"I know what you mean," I said. "I got some plans like that of my own."

At the service, Heavy D got up and stood beside a lady playing an organ. He led us in "Amazing Grace," singing with a deep, smooth voice like Elvis, making us feel that this was what music was all about.

Those last ninety days went by swiftly. But it's amazing how some people stick to their ways—even on the day of my release, some Colombians were trying to persuade me to hook up with some of their criminal associates on the outside. A news program came on the TV around that time, reporting on how plans were being made to build thirty-three new federal prisons to accommodate the growing inmate population. I was determined to never be part of that population again.

41

MY NEW FRIEND, LYNN, picked me up at Marianna when I was processed ATW at last—All The Way out. It was great to see her, and had the feeling that we could talk and laugh without worrying about what time it was or how long we had before visiting time was up.

Driving out, I was ready to get out of the visitors' parking lot without delay. I couldn't let go of a nightmare scenario whereby the prison officials might actually change their minds!

"I have to get gas," Lynn said. "We've got a long drive ahead of us."

"Oh, let me get out and have a look around," I said. It was overwhelming to see how the cars had changed, and even the gas pumps, during my time inside. And I was nervous, simply pumping gas; everything seemed unreal. I had yearned to be on the outside for so long that I now felt that I was in a dream. Fortunately, though, this was a dream with a good ending, not the nightmare I had lived through with my bio-logical father.

Lynn and I stopped at the Oyster House on the Mobile Causeway. I ate the best meal of my life, sitting with her, enjoying the food, and taking our time to discuss whatever we wished. I had an urge to store food in my pockets for lat-er, feelings I guessed would diminish with time, and part of the survival instincts that kick in when you're in dangerous situations, like jail.

After the meal, Lynn and I headed off to J&J Grocery, where I knew Mama was working. When we arrived at Eight Mile, I pointed out my grandfather's old Chevy Silverado in the blacktop parking lot of the store.

My Paw Paw was by the register, wearing a "Would'a, Could'a, Should'a" cap and standing over two wooden buck-ets, one filled with yellow squash from his garden in Chick-asaw, the other brimming with okra. Mama was in the back.

"Here I am, Mama. I done bust myself outta prison."

"They let him out early. Don't mess with your mother like that, Jamie," Paw Paw said.

"Hey, Paw Paw. Where's Daddy?"

"At his camp with Banks and Shanks," Mama replied. "He didn't even tell me he was going. He just up and left. Since his surgery, all that man ever wants to do now is go fishin' every day."

"It's good for his blood pressure, Mama."

We caught up on a lot of hugs, me, Mama and Paw Paw, and new ones for Lynn, whom I introduced to everyone.

"You think you can behave yourself now, Jamie?" Mama asked.

"Yes, Ma'am . . . I'll be good. I learned my lesson."

"OK, then. I believe in you, Jamie. I know your mind is right now. Don't let anyone change that. Remember what you learned in that SAP program—people, places, and things."

Mama closed the store early and arranged for a special homecoming dinner at her baby sister's house. Driving up Outlaw Road with Lynn, Mama's gray Astro van bringing up the rear, there were maple trees I had never noticed before, bright ruby splashes against the fading blue sky. They swayed gently in the wind that carried a loose flock of birds south for the winter.

So much had changed. More houses had been built along the stretch of red dirt between my Aunt Kay's place and the store since I'd last visited. The pear trees in her front yard had grown a lot in five years; their leaves were just beginning to turn a beautiful deep yellow color.

Sitting with Lynn and my family around me, I realized that the nightmare was finally over. Ultimately, it was the gift of my family upbringing from my earliest days that gave me the strength to strive for the right goals, and to achieve them. Life will be a struggle every day, as it is for all of us, but I knew that the nightmare had come to an end and it was time to move on.

EPILOGUE

THE ONLY TRUE PEACE I made with Aunt Wendy before she passed was when I presented her with a copy of my manuscript. I sat down beside her, we held hands, and prayed together that God would open her heart to my story. That was 2007, and the first time in my life that I witnessed a calm peace in her eyes as she listened to me. It's what I try to remember about her today. She called me the next day to say that she'd stayed up all night reading my book, and to tell me she was sorry for her life choices. Unbeknown to me at that time, she wrote down *her* life story in a letter—a way to help me understand why she made those choices.

A few months later, she passed away after her heart stopped in her sleep, and I finally read the letter. At that moment, I came to understand the pain in her life, and how my father broke her heart after leaving. With her life in turmoil, she did what she thought was best for me at the time: gave me up for adoption to her sister, Janet Cobb. Of course, in my youth, I didn't understand the reason behind this traumatic decision.

The process of writing a book has taught me much about my family and myself. It's been an incredible learning process, and I feel I am better person for going through it. I thank the Lord for giving me the strength and perseverance to make it through the many challenges involved.

> *Dear Lord, I can hardly believe I've made it this far. But if you hadn't been watching over me, I wouldn't have survived the life I lead.*
>
> *—Wendy Mizell*

Dear Jamie,

I'm 54 now. It's hard to think back to when I ran away from home at 14. I was just determined to do as I pleased. First, I hitchhiked to New York City and got put in jail for vagrancy. I told the judge, "Someone stole my suitcase and purse," and also that my name was Hope Robertson. Wouldn't you know he believed me, bought me two outfits and a one-way ticket to New Orleans. So I had to make it work.

This was around 1964–'65. Across from the airport was a go-go bar . . . girls in cages . . . fringe benefit customers. Not bragging, but I did look good with long tanned legs, the figure any 18-year-old would die for, and long—very long—blue black hair. So I walked in there and got a job. This man who seemed to be in charge said he was going to let me work for his brother at the Jazz Corner. He promised that I would be protected from pimps and hustlers. I only knew this nice little Italian man as Carlos Marcello.

There was this other Italian, Joe _____, who liked me and wanted me for himself. I thought he was a longshoreman foreman. But you have to understand, I was just a child. It never crossed my mind that Joe was involved with the Mob . . . racketeering. All I know was he took very good care of me . . . protected, spoiled me. I had no idea people considered me a Mafia Mistress. Believe me, it shocked me when I did find out.

For company, Joe let me have two roommates. They were twins, Jeanette & Antoinette from Chicago. See, Italians never leave their wives but they make sure their mistresses are happy. Joe is dead now, but he taught me to survive without being a whore. I was a dancer in those years, well-respected mostly because everyone was scared of Joe. I never did drugs then, but a couple of years later when I learned he was actually a Mafia gangster who would eventually be convicted of racketeering, I met Sarah's daddy and moved to Franklin, Louisiana. I was the first go-go dancer in that town, at the Matador Club. Martin told me I made him a rich man, and he was a good boss. Sarah was only six months old. Martin kept promising me he was going to leave the wife that I didn't know he had when I first met him. Finally, I realized he wasn't going to keep his word.

Three hundred women in that town took up a petition to have me leave Franklin. But the sheriff wouldn't accept it because there were no men's signatures on it. So I met Tyler, a respected businessman and the boss of _____ Brothers Construction. He loved me but knew I didn't love him back. He said he could make me love him and if I married him, no one would say anything about me. I wanted a good home for Sarah, so I tried. I never wanted for anything with Tyler. But you can't make yourself love someone. I liked and respected him and he would always be my friend. But I was restless.

Kay came to live with me and Tyler. I was determined to dance again and to please me, he agreed I could, as long as it was not in Franklin. So I went to work at a place outside Morgan City called The Torch. Tyler carried me to work and picked me up. But one night, a Dutch tugboat captain docked across the road. We had glass in front you could see out of, but not into. That's where I first seen Jan van Rijn. I even remember how he was dressed, in gray slacks and a black silk shirt. I fell in love with him at first sight. The next day, he moved me to New Orleans with Sarah, to a beautiful apartment. Then we went to pick Donny up from a babysitter. I loved him at first sight, too. I just wanted to be a good mother to him, a good wife to Jan, and to have another child . . . you.

I was 7 months pregnant before I found out Jan was a criminal. My heart truly broke, but I still loved him. I visited him in jail, prison, and seen him deported from this country, promising all the time that he would send for us. I believed that lie for a long time. When I realized it wasn't going to happen, that's when I started giving up on happiness and got involved in drugs and crime. The more dangerous, the more it interested me. It seemed to make me forget my pain. Drugs, concerts—the hippie life—was all I did.

I was too afraid to think of everlasting love or happiness. I started running my own bars in New Orleans and Morgan

City, real clip joints . . . B Drinking, making men spend their money. It was my revenge for not having a good husband and a happy home with my children during any of this time. I always loved my children, but I wasn't a mother a child could look up to, or even respect. I don't even remember the times I tried to take my life. But God knew it was not my time. I think He was protecting me and making sure I learned from my mistakes.

I hope this letter clears things up for you, Jamie. I didn't want to give you up in the first place, but looking back from today, maybe it was for the best.

Love Always,

Your Mother Wendy Mizell

Me, Daddy, and my brother Junior in front of my school

Where we did the first and second jobs in Spain

Mama, Me, and Kyle at Draper State Prison

Kyle and Me in Oakdale FCI Prison

The day I was arrested

*Drawing of me at my Daddy's fishing camp around the age
I found out I was adopted*

Drawing of Jan and me around the first time I met him

Drawing of Sneek in the Netherlands

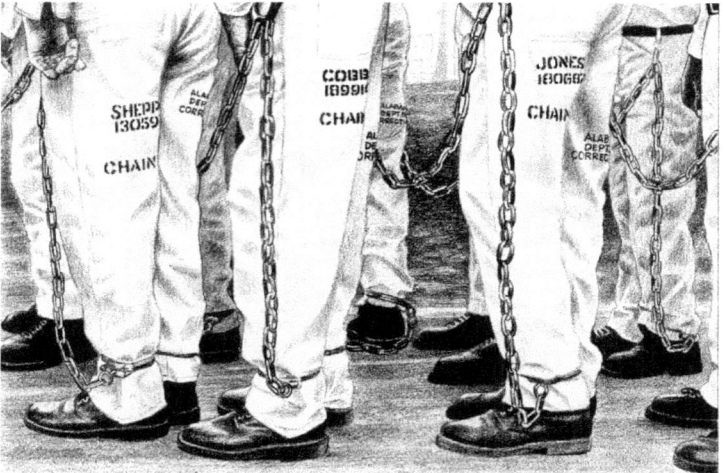

Drawing of me catching the chain to Alabama State Prison

Drawing of Mama and Daddy after Prison

About the Authors

J. H. Cobb

JAMES COBB is an American writer, motivational speaker, and author of the memoir *No One Knows the Son*, released under the pen name J. H. Cobb.

Born James H.H. van Rijs in New Orleans, Louisiana, October 1st, 1971, Cobb was soon adopted by his aunt and uncle from Eight Mile, Alabama. His biological father, Jan van Rijs, was an international drug smuggler from Holland, while his biological mother, Wendy Mizell, was an exotic dancer who, at the time, worked for Carlos Marcello, also known as The Godfather and "The Little Man", boss of a New Orleans crime family.

After becoming involved with his biological father's drug smuggling business, Cobb served five years in prison on charges of drug conspiracy. Once released, he worked as a butcher for Albertsons, where he first conceived the idea of writing a novel after telling his life story to a young English student in 2001.

Although Cobb was diagnosed with a learning disability at the age of seven, he finished writing his book in 2006. Two years later, while promoting the novel *No One Knows the Son,* Cobb met New York Editor Stacy Creamer, who encouraged him to turn the novel into a memoir.

The years that followed saw the death of Cobb's birth mother, divorce from his wife, and many other tragedies. Nonetheless, the author persevered and, while working for Cajun Constructions, he met his co-author, Stephen Cirfus. With the help of editors from England, New York, and Louisiana State University, the two authors were successful in publishing the memoir *No One Knows the Son.*

Today, James Cobb tours schools, colleges, organizations, and prisons, while mentoring at-risk youth and ex-offenders who wish to put their past behind them and start a new life.

Stephen Cirfus

STEPHEN CIRFUS WAS BORN on Lajes Air Base located off the coast of Portugal. Since the age of seven, he called Belle Chasse, Louisiana, his home where his wife and four children spend most of their time enjoying the outdoors. Stephen studied Occupational Safety and Health at Columbia Southern University and now works in construction as a Safety Professional.